CW01467917

The Obesity Secret

Revealing the Code to Weight Loss

To Janet,
many Thanks for coming down!

from James

First Published in Paperback in 2024

Mention of specific companies, organizations, or authorities in this book does not imply endorsement by the author or publisher, nor does mention of specific companies, organisations, or authorities imply that they endorse this book, it's author, or the publisher. Internet addresses and links were accurate at the time it went to press.

Copyright 2024 'The Obesity Secret'

James Michael Smith is hereby identified as the author of this work in accordance with section 77 of the copyright, Designs and Patents Act 1988

All rights reserved,

No part of this publication may be reproduced, stored in a retrieval system, or transmitted, in any form, or by any means, without the prior permission in writing of the publisher, nor be otherwise circulated in any form of binding or cover other than that in which it is published and without a similar condition including this condition being imposed on the subsequent purchaser.

The contents of this book are intended as advice and guidance, should you be aware of an allergies or pre existing conditions seek proper advice based on your situation. Provided for exercise is information only, t o ensure safe and effective use in all exercise guidance, seek out an accredited trainer as required. I cannot be held responsible for any injury or potential injury of any kind following the exercise advice as I cannot be there to ensure guidelines are properly followed, the situation of an individual reader is unique to their environment. As a personal trainer this needs to be assessed on an individual one to one basis. Also the author strongly recommends that you consult with your physician before beginning any exercise program.

ISBN: 9798870193700

MUM & DAD

Contents

Foreword

Our planet has been increasing with obesity and its health-related issues over the last several decades, I have seen what's going on in different cultures which got me inspired with the topic over ten years ago. If we can see what's going on in the world, and to see ourselves in that context then we look at what our influences are and how we can change ourselves, I want to put my knowledge and experience forward so we can do this in the best way possible. Doing what we are designed to do, no fads, no magic just cold hard facts and everything we need to know in losing the weight and keeping it off and of course what the Obesity Secret is.

I wanted to write a book with the main aim for the reader to get through it from the start to finish. Not to be just another weight loss book where one chapter is read and then cast aside. I want to inform, entertain, and educate the reader in what they really need to know. This is an ideal addition to a weight loss plan for any person looking to lose weight. The minimum, you will have a lot of practical information from my years of experience to help you in your quest of losing weight. At best in following all the guidance you will have an ideal plan to get you where you want to be.

Working with so many people overweight and meetings on the subject I had with people, instead of being contacted for help or advice I wanted to get it all into a book that can offer more detailed practical guidance to those seeking help.

Introduction

Across our planet, we see ongoing world events, changing environments, war, famine and a phenomenon of the modern world, obesity.

'A century ago, obesity was rare. Now people all over the world are gaining weight'[1]. In 1890, a man named Chaucey Morlan worked at a sideshow circus. People paid to see him, as it was a rarity to see someone obese, 'Chaucey was referred to as 'the human freight car', people came from all around (and paid money) to see him'[2]. Things have changed to what we see in the western world now, what's happened in the last one hundred years. We are gaining more weight as a population, is it one of convenience, living a fast paced and want it now life ?

UNIVERSAL PILLS Nº3.

Have we changed as a population? Has our makeup altered to make so many of us gain weight into the obese categories? We will look at the what's, why's and how's of what is going on and what we can do about it. I bring my experience working with so many people to meet their goals. I would advise reading the book all the way through then scan through a second time, take in all the relevant information needed to work through and put into action. I am focused with creating a better quality of life for us considering the health implications associated with being obese and the need to lose weight.

Get reading and get your plan !

From then into the early 1900's, World Wars One and then Two happened, a terrible time and on recovery populations stabilised and grew, along with new mass food production methods. Leading to more products being cheaper and tastier to the consumer. Fast forward to now, the taste of doughnuts, chips, wine, chocolate, beer, gorgeous fast food or if it's for a sit down with burger and chips & then the ice cream dessert. That waft of cooking grease hits you in the face as you pass yet another fast-food joint on the high street while you are just out walking. I do tend to have a bit of fast food and beer at the weekends, bacon, waffles, the odd burger, fries, curry. My mum has asked me several times over the years 'why am I not fat' well, I have never been on a diet in my life but then I have never needed to, I will have more healthier times and more unhealthy spats. Always regretting the hangover after a night out saying, 'never again' and then I may do it again, as a lot of us do.

So why am I not fat, I'm 44 (at the point of writing) and pretty much eat and drink what I like. Well, we are going to look at this and find out why. I'm going to try to make it light-hearted as my first aim is for you to get through the entire thing. Hopefully not a struggle as some might be, getting through the first chapter of a paperback & cast it aside to be used as a block propping up the wobbly fridge. A friend did this with a fitness book he had bought, he didn't get to the end nor the end of the first chapter, written by a well-known fitness guru. I have asked around friends, clients and family, and many people have good intentions when they buy such books but don't seem to finish them, and I don't finish them either but for different reasons.

I've bought loads of books from charity shops, all big names, revolutionary diets and so on; I flick through after the first couple of chapters really so I can get the gist. Many I have questions for where an answer isn't present, this really got me thinking. I thought ok, let's have a crack at it. I'm not a storyteller; I'm like the rest of us. I figured this is what I know, and I will give it a go. If it is not up to my entertainment aspirations, and mentioning I do like a beer then send me a complaint message I'll take it on the chin. Not all trainers are gurus who live like Shaolin Monks and abstain from all temptations, and that's not always sustainable nor balanced in our modern-day environment, but we can learn and do the right thing to help ourselves when it comes to our weight. Being in the fitness industry for near on twenty years, I think I can help. My job is to get the right info to my clients, and as you go through, I hope you are engaged enough to go from start to finish. You are my client now, and we will discover what you need to know to fully understand how to manage your weight. So that's it; there will be some stats, a voyage of discovery into obesity and how our bodies work, planning, all the things we need to know in being active. With some of my traveling photos thrown in and a few interesting stories from that.

We will go through strategies how you can change your own environment to become a weight loss hub, and tailor an ideal exercise plan suited to you. We will look at a lot of relevant information, after looking at fast food, a bit of ourselves in habits and eating patterns, and go through some of the big weight loss diets out there. Then an ideal diet approach with examples in a food guide of what to do, and what we really need in this 'modern day diet'. Into a part on how our bodies work and then goal setting. I also want you to understand how we can get the excess fat off our bodies, looking at an ideal lifestyle and some of the experiences I have had with clients which can help with perspective. I reiterate, my advice is to read through everything, then go again and take relevant notes. Going through the tasks there to help you to start your weight loss plan.

My aim is to make this read interesting with meat on the bones and not just a weight loss book with all the facts and stats, but with experience / insight from me to make it a bit more interesting for you, I hope. Unlike the endless meetings I had to endure in boring corporate jobs before I got into fitness. In those places, I struggled to keep my eyes open from the sheer droning on of stats, bar charts, graphs and resulting boredom. The times I was sure some kind of horse tranquilizer gas had been put into the air con & the only way to stay awake was sheer determination, forcing my eyes wide open causing flared nostrils. I hope you enjoy this, and it gives you some fresh insight into what's going on in the world regarding obesity and perspective on what you need to know for weight loss, it can be ideal as an additional read next to attending a slimming club or meeting with likeminded friends. At the very least I want you to finish and walk away with a lot more awareness of what you can do straight away, knowing that you can achieve your weight loss goals.

How can I Help?

My background is working in colleges teaching exercise, fitness and all the aspects involved including nutrition. While I worked in the first college fitness facility in my free time, I studied to become an accredited personal trainer. After five years I moved into teaching students the exercise courses, by this time the 2008 credit crunch was hitting the country and affected funding to education across the board.

Soon enough I left and then decided, now just over ten years ago, I wanted to work more one to one with people in all aspects of self-improvement and in particular weight loss. I invested in two courses which were specifically aimed at obesity and diabetes. I studied a G.P. referral course which allowed me to work with specific groups of people with different conditions, which is really where it started.

I have worked with many people all shapes and sizes and some big names in showbiz, music, and media over the years. In my twenties, I used to work at themed nights for bigger girls, it was great events in central London, and met a lot of people who are good friends to this day. Much of their experiences we would discuss and gave me the view that I wanted to study and work with people in the situation of wanting to understand about losing weight and how to keep it off. I have really wanted to write down what I know, my experiences and what questions in this area of weight management that need to be answered.

Whenever I would teach about weight management it would really interest me, so I went with it and learned more about the subject area. My goal is to have a facility or many facilities which can really help people to learn and discover how to live and lose the weight they desire. A facility in ideal locations where there's no temptations and only focus on self-improvement. In my home country, England and other nations, the United States, Thailand. Other initiatives are part of the plan which will come to fruition in time.

I think the reason for wanting to help people and self-improve comes from a background of being very competitive in sports as a teenager, my goal then was to become a professional rugby player. I tried to do too much all the time, train, gameday, job and social life with a complete lack of resting. It resulted in developing a chronic fatigue syndrome from nearly two years. I went back into education at the time completed a business degree and my path went into a different direction. For the last ten years since I had visited South-East Asia, seeing different populations and how obesity is affecting different people, I have wanted to write a book on obesity and weight management. it started when I was in Chiang Mai after completing those specific courses I had mentioned. It took years of working with people and developing my knowledge / skills to really get going with it, until now. I have worked in a lot of industries before finding the work that's right for me, that's working with people to help them help themselves.

A Few Clients in London, Film, TV and Local

My good friend Lewis MacLeod, never have I laughed so much when training someone in the gym. The comedy voice impressions he does are spot on, my favourite is his version of Christopher Walken. Imagine spotting someone on a bench press and they suddenly do a rendition of Alan Carr chatty man straining to get the last few reps out, I was in tears. Lewis has had some fantastic roles in his career, a character voice in Star

Wars, the voice of Postman Pat and more recently now in 2023 as soon as a Just Eat advertisement comes on, I always cheer, 'wahey, it's Lewis'. He voiced a lot of the Spitting Image characters in their latest series along with parts in comedy TV shows.

I have trained a Hollywood director, John Irvine in preparation for the film 'Goose Green' which right now is still in development. In central London, we would train at an exclusive gym in Knightsbridge a signature club part of an exclusive UK chain. Going through the session then coffees in the café area after. He would tell me about some of the cast members he had in his films, Arnold Schwarzenegger in John's film Raw Deal back in the 80's and talking about Stallone and Jean-Claude Van Damme. These were film icons of mine when I was growing up in the 1980's and '90's. Sitting there in the restaurant area of the health club holding a coffee, with it suspended mid-air & my jaw to the floor listening to this. Then his film Hamburger Hill based on the hill 937 as it was known in the Vietnam War.

Ian Shaw a renowned Jazz-musician, a regular in Ronnie Scott's of Soho, we worked a couple of sessions just before lockdown and another charismatic and interesting person. Other such examples from music and media include Matt Goss from the iconic 80's band Bros, I was going to train, but at the time he just went into the Strictly come dancing TV show and the training regime for that really is a full-time effort. People I also train in my local area, are great too, one friend Alan at 76 we have built up in each session for quite some time now is regularly running up long flights of steps in our local area on the coast. People are amazed at Alan's age, and when I drive past the long high steps opposite the local train station I always say, 'that's where me & Alan train', another local friend Helen, in her early 60's is doing well, with regular fat burning sessions and exercises on the planned routes averaging around 3.5kilometers distance per session. They both look so much younger, thanks to the regular exercise and good healthy diets. What is nice, being clients but many are also good friends. Everyone has different viewpoints and that all so interesting and these people really have a purpose which radiates when you are there helping and discussing how you can help make a difference, what it does for your motivation and perspective is something else, talk about focus and positivity. I found a change in perspective at that time that 'I can do this'; originally, I was nervous before seeing John, the director as I thought I was kidding myself, yet it went well. You will find as you move forward in a positive way that you can do this, and things will start to happen, doors will open, and you will become a better version of yourself, and it could be in many more ways than what we are setting out to achieve.

Part of my South-East Asia adventure was visiting Cambodia's Angkor Wat with the surrounding temples. Clues were showing themselves as I recollect the experience on the impact of obesity compared to the western world. In the likes of Cambodia, as we will see in the coming section.

The Bayon temple of Cambodia, believed the face is a representation of Avalokitesvara, the bodhisattva of compassion. As we look around the world at obesity and its emergence and impacts, I hope to reveal to you what is going on. We mention Cambodia in part of the world tour which could harbour some secrets into the prevalence of obesity.

A Fat Finding World Mission

The obesity ranking scale is based on the information of the world population review in 2023 of 'Most obese Countries in the World, 2016 measured by percentage of obese adults'[3], at the time of writing. They are classified by BMI or Body Mass Index, which is a general population scale used to classify weight to height to see if it's a healthy weight range for you, you may have heard of it. I use it when assessing someone who I term is of the general population, isn't a keen sportsman or fitness training.

The BMI calculation divides an adult's weight in kilograms by their height in metres squared. For example, A BMI of 25 means 25kg/m2. BMI ranges 18.5 25 30 Underweight Normal Overweight Obese	The BMI rankings explained, again I use this for general population health. **Not for specific sports people or people in certain fitness routines which can skewer the results Body mass were more so looking at fat weight.** Below 18.5 · underweight range Between 18.5 – 24.9 · healthy weight Between 25 and 29.9 · overweight range 30 or over · the obese range

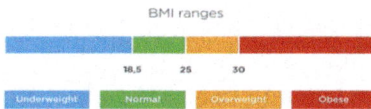

I have used the NHS Body Mass Index classifications[4] to show exactly what we are looking at, the chart is from Tanita, the manufacturer of the body measurement kit I use and via the WHO.[5] Bodybuilders and certain sportspeople with muscle could be classed as overweight or obese but it's their muscle weight which can distort the result. I train regularly with a healthy bodyfat but am classified as overweight, I hope you get the idea but as I say BMI is what is used as a general population measurement. I'm writing this in England, on the South-East coast and our national obesity numbers are increasing year on year. My NHS studies, specifically in obesity and diabetes, started back in 2009 where in 2010, 'tackling Obesities: Future choices estimates that about 28% of women and 33% of men in the UK are now obese'[6], fast forward to now and:

'26% of adults in England were obese, a higher proportion of men than women were either overweight or obese, 69% compared with 59%[7] it furthers with 'obesity prevalence was lowest among adults living in the least deprived areas (20%) and the highest in the most deprived areas' (34%)[8]

That's staggering at almost a third of all adults here in England are at least obese, putting that into numbers per population, the last count made by the UK government[9] being 59.6 million in England and Wales, so in obese numbers were looking at around 15,496,000 obese adults. As I add this piece in, the medical waiting lists for routine procedures is huge in-light of the after-effects of the covid pandemic. We see that in England nearly a third of the population are obese, so what nations have the highest and lowest obesity rates in the world, let's have a look at the top five adult obese nations and then five least obese, there are a few special mentions too so we can consider what's going on further in different places. I have included some of my travelling snaps when I was in South-East Asia as a couple of the countries are in the category of least obese and friends have also offered travelling pictures for some of the other nations included. We then look at two superpowers which includes the United States and China. Now let's have a look with popcorn at the ready.... provided it's air-popped and lightly seasoned not the movie stuff, (getting into the good habits right away); I am joking by the way. We are now heading off to Paradise in the middle of the Pacific Ocean.

The World's Most Obese Nations

The Most Obese Nation on Earth

A small island tucked away in the South Pacific Ocean, following the coast of Australia around Cairns. At that point, veering off in a north easterly direction out over the Coral Sea for just under 3000km to a little island in the South Pacific Ocean is our first destination, and it's called Nauru. It's suggested to be one of the least visited countries in the world. Ranked as the most obese nation per adult population on earth, with a population under 10,000' it is dwarfed by most capital cities around the world and '61% of adults being overweight or obese'[10].

'A raised, fossilised coral atoll, Nauru is one of three great phosphate rock islands in the Pacific Ocean the other two being Banana (Ocean Island) in Kiribati and Makatea in French Polynesia. Nauru has a total land area of 21 square kilometres'[11], so a relatively tiny place.

The locals diet (and now I am going to sound like a tour guide, but hey as I write this part with the covid lockdowns going on for well over a year now I need to visualise a sunny holiday destination) Is all natural wholefoods, a google search shows Nauru has Coconut fish, broiled fish, fruit bat soup, Taro a starchy root vegetable similar to a potato, Pandan a local plant with the leaves crushed, all-natural and grown or locally harvested. A large portion of the population in Nauru are from mainland China and it is said by travellers that there are around 140 Chinese restaurants[12] in the place. Backed up by a food blogger who visited the country stated 'Nauru food is basically Chinese food'[13] and found it hard to find any of the local traditional cuisine I mentioned. It also has the 'highest rates of type 2 diabetes in the world, with more than 40% of the population affected. That's not far off every other person. With the huge rates of diabetes comes out-of-control incidences of heart disease and kidney disease'[14]. Looking at the decline in the nation's health into what it is today, years ago Nauru was making a lot of money from the phosphate mining & trade links with the west, their diet was a traditional one of what we had initially discussed, all the healthy stuff. This made me wonder why there is such a health issue, however after '68 the country gained independence[15] and becoming rich through the phosphate mining, many of the inhabitants didn't need to work. With this resulted in less physical activity and exercise, as everyone had more money in their pockets, the western food started to get imported into the nation and everyone started to eat far more processed stuff. They have a cultural phenomenon, that being overweight is seen as a status symbol, one of prosperity and affluence. 'Nauruan's see obesity as a sign of wealth, an indication that you don't need to work physically to get by. In a society that, until recently, relied heavily on the physical labour of the inhabitants, a sedentary lifestyle is something admirable, something to which one should aspire'[16]

In recent times Nauru's Gross domestic product (the total value of goods produced, and services provided in a country in one year) ranking is extremely low in comparison to other nations. The unemployment rate is around 90%, [1] which really is far too high for any nation. The total population in our most obese are small which could impact the rankings. Naurus total population is dwarfed by many nation's capital city numbers alone.

The Second Most Obese Nation on Earth

The Cook Islands coming in at number two with a national adult obesity rate of 55.9%[17],is a paradise and pretty much untouched by the west, or from anyone, for that matter. No building is taller than the tallest coconut tree[18] and 'you cannot buy a house in the Cook Islands at all. Property in the Cook Islands are handed down through generations, from parents to their children, so everyone that lives on Rarotonga owns a piece of property. Because of this you'll notice if you ever managed to visit the place, that there are no homeless people'[19]. Wow, that is good isn't it I mean everyone has their place preferably getting some sunshine and a cool breeze off the ocean.

Paradise, a beach in the Cook Islands, I could really do with heading there right now, how about you. Maybe one day, sitting on the beach in the sunshine and a cocktail in hand. I always say when on holiday do relax.

'The 15 volcanic islands and coral atolls of the Cook Islands ae scattered over 770,000 square miles of the South Pacific, between American Samoa to the west and French Polynesia to the East'[20]. Two people I trained some time ago headed all over that region and said out of it all French Polynesia is really something else, so if you get to travel around that way head there, Rarotonga is small and the islands, 'so the Island isn't very big covering a land mass of around 93 square miles. It contains a population of around 17,047'[21] The Cook Islands had a major crisis in the 1990's according to the Asian development bank[22] in the mid 90's it was hit by a recession. Partly from less tourism, a financial crisis by growing wage bills, welfare system and external borrowing. In recent times, the last ten years it was 'considered the most prosperous country in the island region[23] so people became more affluent with a bit of cash in their pockets, they are still ranked second in obesity. Then hit by lack of travel during the pandemic, 'Cook Islands suffered the largest contraction in 2021' then 'After these large declines economic recovery will begin'[24] Looking at the cuisine as with Nauru, their traditional food is fresh seafood, a nice bit of octopus & clams, pig, lamb and fresh fruit, all healthy again. As with Nauru why are they in the number two spot for the world's most obese?

They also import a great deal due to location and are pretty much sedentary like Nauru adding to this healthcare isn't on their doorstep. To further, 'they have no airports or seaports and must rely heavily upon cargo ships for transports due to lack of land. Furthering with 'these islands are so isolated they must import nearly all their supplies'[25] As with Nauru the traditional diets are being replaced with more takeaway options by the locals, and stated 'The traditional diet, like Tupou's, has been replaced by imported, often calorie rich and nutrient poor processed foods and sugary drinks'[26].

The Third Most Obese Nation on Earth

In at number three is another of the Pacific islands. The next destination is 4,872 miles from the Cook Islands. Still in the same region but the distance between these islands is phenomenal, remote in the Pacific Ocean now we are headed to Palau. Palau's adult obesity rate is 55.3%[27]

'A country in the western Pacific Ocean. It consists of some 340 coral and volcanic islands perched on the Kyushu-Palau Ridge'[28]. A population of 18,055 as of 2022[29], which is similar to our number one and two places, again a small population with the concentration of obese people being so high. Palau also has its own take on the burgers and various fast food but isn't of the original scourge of the west's chain restaurants or is it. There are 340 islands and 16 states that make up Palau[30]. The inhabitants are from a background of different races the main being the Palauan's, Japanese, interestingly did occupy the country during WW2.

'Palau food is wonderfully varied and draws heavily on influences from the United States, Japan and the Philippines, Indonesia and Malaysia'[31] There appears to be a lot more traditional options in restaurants in Palau, and the 'local's main industries are in tourism, farming, fishing, building and garment making'[32]. They appear to be involved in active industries to work in.

It is also suggested that Palau has a 'policy of eat what you grow economy. It produces and exports food grown in Palau'[33] It could mean that their diets may not be exactly like Nauru and the Cook Islands, yet here they are in as the third most obese nation. The World Health Organisation highlight the fact that 'Palau has shifted from mostly subsistence living and reliance on locally produced crops and fish to a more western lifestyle of sedentary occupation and more reliance on imported foods'[34] so in fact they are more reliant on imports as with the other nations we have so far looked at.

With all these Paradise Islands, it can be always the same. When you're not there and want to visit it's amazing but living there 24/7 it's likely to be a different outlook. Rocking up to the main islands and island-hopping sounds like and ideal trip of adventure to me. With 340 to choose from, what an adventure !

The Fourth Most Obese Nation on Earth

In at number four is the Marshall Islands, it's in the same region as the three we've already looked at. 'The Marshalls are composed of more than 1,200 islands and islets in two parallel chains of coral atolls'[35]. At 750,000 square miles of Ocean but around 70 square miles of land, so again with similar features of these nations of the region in limited land mass yet surrounded by plenty of ocean. Furthermore 'coconut and pandanus palms and breadfruit trees are the principal vegetation. Soils are generally sandy and low in fertility'[36], sounds like yet another paradise to me. As with the Cook Islands, no one from outside can purchase land or houses here, it's handed down through generations as we've already seen, but 'After their populations were removed to other Atolls, Bikini and Enewetak served as an official testing ground for U.S. nuclear bombs (1946-58). The tests stopped in 1958 and the clean -up efforts began in the late 1960's[37].

A NUCLEAR TEST OF A HYDROGEN BOMB AT BIKINI ATOLL[38]

A ring shaped reef surrounding a 25 mile by 15 mile oval lagoon. Many nuclear tests were conducted at this location.

Bikini Atoll : Nuclear testing A devastating nuclear explosion then, the after effects have been felt so many years later from such testing, devastating cancer rates went up. Much of the area is still contaminated with radioactive material. Today we now also look at the issue of obesity in the region. A paradise torn from the past......

The Marshall island's traditional food also healthy wholefoods, same as the rest but as with our other examples they now also import a lot of their foods. One of the reasons in the Marshall Islands is from that soil contamination from the past nuclear weapons testing, so crops cannot be grown along with a high population density and so as with Nauru and the others their traditional diet has been switched to 'ultra processed imported foods rich in fats and sugars'[39], termed nutrient transmission. Poverty is seen as a major issue with 30% of the population in the islands main two cities living below the basic-needs poverty line. 'Poor and unhealthy shanty towns are sadly commonplace'[40]. A similar trait with Nauru and appears in the Marshall Island region. The people have talents which represent their environment, they are skilled navigators at sea which makes sense to be an isolated Island to get to the next then you need to sail. The main source of income for the locals top three is in agriculture, fishing and tourism. This seems to go against what we have seen in the damage caused by those historical bomb tests however this could be part of the export trade as major exports for the islands are 'copra cake, coconut oil, handicrafts and fish'[41]. One main source of income for the nation is from the United States in 'US assistance and lease payments for the use of Kwajalein Atoll as a US military base'[42].

The Fifth Most Obese Nation on Earth

Our final entry in this section is again in the South Pacific, Tuvalu. 'The small island nation of Tuvalu has the lowest GDP in the world. The poor economic standing of Tuvalu is mostly due to lack of industries and natural resources within its territories. Tuvalu is also one of the smallest countries in the world (26 Km2)'[43] I would then assume the high obesity rate goes against what this describes with poverty, but here we are. 'It is home to just around 11,500 people'[44]. 'Consisting of nine Atolls, Funafuti, Nanumea, Nanumaga, Niutao, Vaitupu, Nukufetau, Nui, Nukulaelae and Niulakit [45]Tuvalu is an archipelago in the Pacific about 3700km away from the Australian mainland. The dwarf state has a total area of only ten square miles and nearly 15 miles of coastland', and 'is considered one of the least developed countries in the world'[46].

'Tuvaluans are Polynesian and their language, Tuvaluan is closely related to Samoan'[47]. 'Despite its small size and remote location, Tuvalu has a developing economy that relies on a mix of traditional subsistence farming, fishing and international Aid'.[48] So as we can see the nation really is struggling and it is also suggested that the nation has issues with the surrounding waters rising. With a nation having scarce resources in some ways yet an issue with obesity must have influencing factors.

A mixture of paradise with poverty in these island nations. I would love to see the landscape, with all the lush tropical plantlife and volcanic rock under the tropical sun. As with anything out of the ordinary, here our British weather really needs to be sunnier. With long winters and cold spells, the sun shining always helps.

Well, 'Nobody goes hungry, it's a country that's very small, very close knit. Tuvaluans spend just under $2 on food per day. Ironically, so many in Tuvalu are overweight. The population eats about one fourth of the recommended intake of fruits and vegetables per day, when it comes to food scarcity, it all comes down to what's easily accessible. Tuvalu imports rice and sugary foods and they are cheap to buy while vegetables are hard to grow and fish are getting scarce'[49], 'Tuvalu has shown limited progress towards achieving the diet-related non-communicable disease (NCD) targets[50]. All linked to what we have again seen habit of these most obese nations, all with similar characteristics. Also 'the Asian Development Bank (ADB) reported a 2.5% under-5 mortality rate, and that only 6.3% of the population had safely managed sanitation services in 2015'[51]. That is shocking, so less than 10% of the population has access to adequate sanitation, yet it's in the top 5 nation for obesity.

Summary

Restricted land size of these nations with limited facilities due to the remoteness added with the infertile land due to the past nuclear testing as one reason for restricted home-grown crops. There isn't much mention of sporting events with these nations, we can generally look around the world and know of countries and what kind of sporting activities they are renowned for yet in this region that doesn't appear to be so. They do appear to have mostly followed a pattern of nutrient shift from their traditional foods to the more processed, more sugar and fat with less good nutritional choice. Through several reasons being that lack of resources to grow, convenience and taste preference change. Could it also be due to lack of money meaning cheaper choices, possibly but the Cook Islands appear to be doing comparatively better yet are the second most obese. They have tended to shift 'nutrient transmission' to the more processed more unhealthy stuff, too. Culturally we see examples that bigger is seen as better, the bigger waistline suggesting you are more prosperous and likely to be a big discouragement to take part in any form of physical activity for health & self-improvement. Imagine sitting in the sunshine and the bigger you are the better it is seen as, like some kind of Roman Prefect. Look at the influences in the west of the body beautiful in music and media. If that positivity was to just be bigger far less people would be exercising with no intrinsic incentive, no reason as a big proportion of those training, are not doing it necessarily for health but the look it gives them. They do appear to all be similar obesogenic environments, areas that encourage people to gain weight, the restricted size of these nations and involving a lot of islands could encourage less activity such as simply walking to get about. Coupled with the unemployment figures, possibly feeling there's less prosperous futures and the types of work available people are generally leading a lifestyle which is more sedentary. Limitations in that home grown produce for the reasons seen are all leading to wide reaching health issues. We can see there are many factors causing these nations to be the most obese in the world and it's quite clear what is going on from all the influencing angles on these small populations. Could it also be the numbers, these countries are so small, yet the percentages are so high. They may have such high percentages, but the total populations are a small fraction of bigger countries. Well, we go with the percentages and regardless of size and population numbers these do have the highest adult obesity percentages. Could there be further influences which we haven't looked at such as genetic makeup of the indigenous people? If so, it doesn't counter the health problems these groups are facing, it shows that being in the obese bracket means more chance of the metabolic syndrome of health issues including diabetes, heart problems and associated conditions.

It appears they all have similar characteristics in environment type, food preferences, a mix in lack of opportunities and their view culturally of obesity. Let's hope these factors can change for the benefit of the populations in future, as our world becomes ever closer via media and the internet there must be new ways for people to get skills to provide a good livelihood for themselves.

The Worlds Least Obese Nations

Shout Out to South Korea and Japan

Before we head into the five least obese nations in the world, I want to give a shout out to two very much westernised nations who have very low obesity scores. South Korea in at 9th and Japan ranked 7th from least obese. They are well developed nations yet uniquely with extremely low obesity rates. Unlike Ethiopia which is in between Japan and South Korea coming in at 8th least obese sadly 'one of the worlds least developed countries'[52] which as could be assumed would be a big factor in such low obesity levels.

South Korea

'One of the world's largest economies and is currently at rank 10. If this is calculated per inhabitant, taking purchasing power parity into account, then South Korea ranks 30th in the list of the richest countries'[53]. In terms of prosperity & affluence it is right up there, unemployment rates are at record low levels 'the unemployment rate was 2.6% in February versus 2.9% in January'[54] As for the size of the population, 'South Korea has a population of 51.77 million'[55].

All the western style chain fast food places are in South Korea, 'include McDonald's, KFC, and Burger King. If burgers are not exactly your cup of tea, Pizza Hut, Papa Johns, and Domino's Pizza and so do Taco Bell and Subway. It furthers, 'with the exception of the pizza franchises, all the aforementioned restaurants are quite cheap, and you can get a decent menu for around KRW 10,000'[56].

There is lots of them, they are quite cheap and South Koreans are known for liking their alcoholic drinks 'South Korea has an unmatched love for the bottle – specifically hard liquor – than any other country in the world'[57] which we could question as there are so many places where drinks are part of a social setting.

Interestingly 'South Korea requires all male citizens to serve in the military for two years'[58]. That could make an impact on the male population, learning discipline with rationing and being in active duty which involves disciplined exercise. Their traditional diet is more of the healthy stuff, 'fruit, soy, steamed vegetables, rice, fish and fermented foods such as kimchi, a cabbage-based dish thought to be the centrepiece of the Korean diet[59]'.

'Every culture in the world has its dining etiquette that embodies the values, traditions, and civility of its people, further with 'For Koreans, having good table manners brings harmony to everyone sharing the meal'[60]

,some characteristics do seem to compliment the idea of weight management, if they are meant to or not. Characteristics include, don't hoard, traditional dishes are shared, balance flavours meaning with the soup stew, rice, meat, and vegetables meaning have some of everything. Eat calmly and chew thoroughly, not wolfing down big portions but savour it and enjoy. Finish with grace and suggesting no leftovers which may be conflicting as other sources suggest politeness is to leave a little to show there was enough, these points are of traditional South Koreans. Taekwondo is Koreas national sport, very energetic to say the least, from sources across the web, also football, basketball, golf, baseball, volleyball, and badminton would suggest such an active nation. As is with Japanese food culture, Koreans believe that food should be harmonious. The strong belief in yin, yang, and the five elements (wood, fire, soil, metal, and water) influence the taste and presentation of food. The five elements are represented by five colours (blue, red, yellow, white, and black) and five tastes (salty, sweet, bitter, sour, and spicy)[61].

'Hansik (한식) or traditional Korean cuisine is a healthy and well-balanced meal made of fresh and natural ingredients[1]'. Furthering with the same insight that South Koreans see food as medicine 'food and medicine are grown from the same root," thus "there is no better medicine than food'[1] And for Koreans, food is not just for physical healing but also mental and emotional well-being. This makes sense as to the good selections they are likely to make to be so far down the obesity rankings. As I find, good food is good for us, but it makes me feel good to. When I have fast food I can feel funny, sluggish.

It could be considered South Korea is linked with Japan's culture in their view & approach to food, hence they are both so low down in the charts, for such prosperous nations. South Koreans also love spices to flavour their foods, including onion, garlic and ginger. These are healthy, good for the body and away from the sugar and fat preferences in the most obese nations. These oriental cultures go back far in history and have done well to remain a big part of the population's traditions in the present time.

Japan

In at a rating of just 7th from the least obese in the World with 4.3% of adults nationwide and a population of 125.7 million[62]. That is the lowest score for such a westernised & advanced nation, so what is it about Japan that makes it do so well.

'Rice is the staple grain of Japanese cooking and is included in most meals. Short – grained, sticky japonica rice (cultivated in Japan) is the most widely consumed'[63]

We need to see what's going on in Japan with their food, 'The traditional Japanese diet consists of minimally processed, seasonal foods served in a variety of small dishes. This style of eating emphasises dishes, natural flavours rather than masking them with sauces or seasonings. The diet is rich in steamed rice, noodles, fish, tofu, natto, seaweed and fresh, cooked, or pickled fruits and vegetables but low in sugar and fats. It may also contain some eggs, dairy, or meat, although these typically make up a small part of the diet.'[64] Sounds very healthy and nutritional, yet 'It contrasts with some modern Japanese cuisine, which has a strong Western and Chinese influences and includes larger amounts of animal protein and processed foods'[65] Yet this doesn't take away the fact that also 'their diet is traditionally high in soy and fish this may also play a significant role in reduced risk of cardiovascular disease'[66]. Japan does have many of the westernised fast-food chains, which more people are using now due to accessibility. We can ascertain they haven't got a foothold yet due to Japan's healthy population regarding obesity levels. Surprisingly Japan's most popular fast-food outlet is MacDonalds and 'Japan is in the third place with 2,900 restaurants'[67] that's of the most outlets in countries around the world!

Japan's scenery of temples, shrines and gardens is well known, it is suggested the Okinawan diet of Japan is one of the healthiest in the world. This says a lot about the low levels of obesity in the nation. The traditions, life longevity and culture. An area which would need more research, as our focus is weight loss.

Steeped in such strong traditional roots, Japan's love of sports and Saki are well known in the land of the Orient, including baseball, combat sports, and sumo Wrestling steeped in Japanese culture to name a few.

Traditional customs in Japan are seen as a fundamental part of their society. *'The Geisha (Geiko) are professional entertainers who attend guests during meals, banquets and other occasions'*. Above a bean curd cake, containing Tofu as the main ingredient.

Unemployment rate 2021: 2.8%	
Services	72.4%
Industrial	24.2%
Agriculture	3.4%

With a low unemployment rate, Japan doesn't appear to be mainly physically active in its workers, yet this doesn't impact on Japan's obesity levels. Japan has a strong economy being one of the worlds major economies, and the low unemployment rate . It has a high standard of living and as we can see from the nature of the jobs, services could be percieved to be more sedentary in nature. Unlike manufacturing possibly Industrial and agricultural. The nature of work may appear to not influence its obesity levels. The coutry is situated at the East Coast of Asia, 'it consists of a great string of islands in a northeast-southwest arc that stretches for approximatley 1,500 miles (2,400 km) through the western North Pacific Ocean. Nearly the entire land area is taken up by the countrys four main islands'[68]. Far bigger than what we had seen with the most obese nations, in terms of Island size.

The Metabo Law

In Japan, which is quite unique, from 2008 a law was introduced to combat the scourge of obesity. 'The Japanese policy, called 'Metabo law' is, in theory, simple – stay below a government-mandated waistline or face the consequences. It is policed through an annual mandatory check-up of the waist measurements of 40-75 age group, that's over 56 million waistlines, or about 44 percent of the entire population'[69]. What's the targets of this law, well 'the waist limit in Japan is set at 33.5 inches (85 cm) for men and 35.4 inches (90 cm) for women over 40 years old'[70]. Some suggest it infringes the right of the population but if it is helping prevent obesity related illness then I think it's a great idea. The individual doesn't necessarily get harshly penalised but big business is held to account for their employee's welfare and so for the individual to help manage their waistlines. Japan is said to have a 'mass-transit-centred urban design which encourages Japanese to walk a lot'[71] being quite the opposite of an obesogenic environment relying on driving & looking for the nearest space to the shops with minimal walking. On the flip side Japan as does South Koreans love a drink, it's part of the culture and it's legal to drink alcohol on the street, park, beach and even on the train. They have vending machines for alcohol too, in Japan 'Alcohol isn't regarded as a drug, nor alcoholism considered a problem by most of society – leading it to be abused by many'[72]. The nations level of alcoholism being still relatively low on the world stage by the way, but along with their being all the fast-food chains it shows Japan's obesity levels are in great shape.

The Fifth Least Obese Nation on Earth

India comes it at 5th least obese nation with a percentage of obese adults at 3.9%[73]. On first perceptions I assume India is here due to their impoverished society, and sadly yes 'Two-thirds of people in India live in poverty: 68.8% of the Indian population lives on less than $2 a day'[74]. We can say this is a big factor for the low obesity with two thirds of the people in India live in poverty. It is also 'the second most populous country after China with around 1.2 billion people and seventh largest country in the world'[75]. From this we can assume that is the biggest factor for any impoverished nation, a very low obesity ranking but for all the wrong reasons. There are mega slums in India with inadequate infrastructure and illness is rife. So as far as the traditional diet, exercise etc we can leave it there with India as really it needs major development to get the citizens into a better situation for them to develop. The disparage between rich and poor really is quite startling as in accordance with a report that:

'The richest 1% own 40.5% of India's wealth' [76]

A friend headed out to India, Hyderabad the image is the Charminar, meaning 4 pillars. A mosque in the historic city some years ago. He enjoyed the experience but was unwell. As were from different nations our immune systems can work in different ways, food related, I saw that in Thailand.

Busy roads, lots of traffic. The levels of poverty within India we see are huge, irrigation is vastly inadequate as he experienced frequent floodings in the area. A visit to a restaurant is a privilege for many and not necessarily a regular occurrence. MacDonalds has a presence in India 'add 200-plus McDonald's outlets in the next 3 – 5 years, to the existing 316 stores in 44 cities77'.

The restaurant located in central Hyderabad named Tabla, we see wholefoods. Rice, chicken, seafood and vegetables. Traditions of eating in food selection with a relative low income for many, food selections can come from necessity that treat based.

The Fourth Least Obese Nation on Earth

'On the Indochinese mainland of Southeast Asia, Cambodia is largely a land of plains and rivers. It's 181,035 square kilometres'78 in size approximately half the size of France. Cambodia's obesity rate comes in at 3.9% the same as India yet at a population of 16.9 million79 as opposed to India's 1.4 billion. At joint 5th & 4th position between India and Cambodia. I travelled to Cambodia ten years ago, one thing I did notice was the lack of obese population. Spending a few days in the Capital Phnom Penh then travelling by road to Siam Reap the country appears quite poor. Due to this the local's diet is quite simple and healthy, therefore obesity will not be an issue through necessity. The tourist areas had many different restaurants and Cafes, I did not see any western fast-food outlets there. In neither the capital Phnom Phen, nor at my second destination Siam Reap. As I saw the population is young, reflecting the genocide in the country dating back to the 1970's, a very sad time for the people and the country. Cambodia's main foods traditional and good wholefoods including 'Fish amok, (steamed coconut fish in banana leaves) Salmor Machu trey (sweet and sour soup with fish) Char kroeung Sach ko (stir fried lemongrass beef) Two ko (Cambodian sausage) Nom Banh Chok (Khmer noodles) and a sixth example being Bai Sach Chrouk (grilled pork and broken rice)'[80] They do tend to eat their local food, having the land and affordability for home grown 'Food imports (% of merchandise imports) in Cambodia was reported at 5.57% in 2021 according to the world bank'[81] I travelled through the nation's capital, stopping off at a real nice place on the main street running adjacent to the Mekong river.

At my second destination in Cambodia after a six-hour journey by minibus, I sat with the Remorque (as they are known in Cambodia) or cab driver eating a meal near pub street in Siam Reap, a popular tourist destination with many restaurants and music, I wanted to know about the local area. I didn't see any of the western chain restaurants on my travels out there, which was a positive. I got us a meal each of rice and a Cambodian chicken red curry, and a beer each Angkor, Cambodia's national beer. He told me about the local area and about his family. He worked long hours to earn a liveable daily wage. Food portions are quite small but tasty, the bill for two meals and two drinks came to $5.50 that was 10 years ago, I showed my driver the bill and said you would not be able to get two pints of beer in England, my local pub for that. He didn't believe me as the exchange rate was so good in Cambodia. Possibly a factor why there isn't all the usual fast-food chains out there. Maybe they don't get the custom and certainly the locals won't be able to afford them. On my second day in Cambodia's capital, I was sightseeing today. I found the oldest guy with the most run-down bike, I gave him a dollar for the ride.

The food was very healthy and quite exotic. In this area of Siam Reap I went for the meat platter, chicken, Snake, Crocodile, Frogs legs. Quite tasty and the local area very clean, all local cuisine and as with the region all healthy stuff. Mostly all local independents places to eat and drink. No sign of a western fast-food place in this area and kept in a spotless condition.

He cheered like he had just won the lottery and I was glad it made his day ,he was a great guide for where I was headed. What I did see out there was many Cambodians were very traditional, their eating habits. Anything imported won't be cheap and in the region a lot of the food is grown or cultivated locally. They're likely to be healthier eating wholefoods and keeping to a healthy BMI. Cambodia was a gem, the people were so nice and accommodating also very petite and slim, that went for both men and women. This was a feature I witnessed throughout South-East Asia. As with my time in Thailand, the local cuisine in Cambodia was traditional & healthy. I wanted to try what the local foods were, as with most places I visited out there.

I did see people work very long hours out here, my driver would be working all day provided he was getting the fayres from morning to night. As I sat eating and a few drinks late into the evening the locals, children would be out selling wristbands and books in the local area. I got the impression more that life is hard out there for many, working long hours for relatively low wages. Cambodia is a poor country, 'poverty is still rife in the country with almost 13% of the population living below the poverty line'[82]. This is a likely factor in our five least obese nations, along with a huge problem in the country of Cambodia's water and sanitation crisis as 'Out of its population of 1.6 million people, 12 million people (72% of the population) lack access to reliable, safely managed source of water, and 3.8 million people (23%) lack access to improved sanitation solutions'[83]. Another consideration in their low obesity ranking.

A local Khmer curry in a perfect little place in Phnom Penh on the Mekong River, it couldn't get much better than that with perfect weather and a perfect day. A meal of noodles, vegetables, and a Khmer curry. The heat was a little less than Thailand but had its own amazing unique flavour. The food & beer was so cheap, 75 cents for a pint of Angkor beer during happy hour. I would recommend visiting Phnom Phen.

Angkor Wat, it is considered the largest religious structure in the world measured on a site the size of 402 acres and referred to being of such high stature in the Khmer Empire of Cambodia. Dating back to the 12th Century, the design and architecture when I was inside was breathtaking. Travel by roads are something else, like a racetrack and glad I got back from the Odyssey all in one piece. An amazing experience.

The Third Least Obese Nation on Earth

In at number three, an island that is positioned to the North-West of Australia and to the south of Indonesia, Timor-Leste comes in at 3.8% of obese adults[84]. 'The country is 15.007 square kilometres, Southeast Asia's youngest and least visited nation'[85], Timor-Leste has some of the most significant marine resources in the world. 'Recording an average of 253 unique reef species across 10 dive sites'[86] 'Currently, Timor-Leste is one of the world's poorest nations with an economy that relies heavily on energy resources in the Timor Sea., with a population around 1.4 million'[87] and one of the youngest countries of the world, having only gained full independence in 2002. 'Timor-Leste enjoyed just nine days of freedom before the encroaching Indonesian military launched a devastating invasion from the west in December 1975. Timor-Leste wouldn't see independence again until 2002, after years of occupation and guerrilla warfare'[88].

'Approximately 70% live in small settlements in rural areas. The population relies heavily on the country's natural resources (oil, agricultural land, marine resources, and forests) for its livelihood[89], so being active jobs and not in the office all day. More than 40% of the population live below the poverty line and therefore get by with whatever means they can, yet the natural environment is breathtaking from this image[90].

Another paradise, yet a large portion of the population seem to live in poverty which for anyone in the world is a shame. Surely things can be made right to alleviate such disparity across the globe with a security of base needs that people can rely on. With such unique marine life could encourage tourism.

The countries traditional diet is yet again rice being a main staple. Sweet potatoes, maize, Cassava which are mainly produced for local consumption[91] Taro added with beans, cabbage, spinach and onions. Here we see wholefoods again, natural, not processed nor fast food. There are restaurants with different national foods, also Burger King fast food restaurants are there. Pretty much in the fast- food infancy but looks like it could expand over time, we may see changes in the population in the future but for now Timor-Leste remains in the lowest ranks of obesity. If much of the nation's locals work on farms and the low income means they are less likely to purchase from restaurants or fast- food outlets, even from the limited range in the country.

The Second Least Obese Nation on Earth

The second least obese nation, Bangladesh adult obesity rates are at 3.6%[92]. With a land mass of 148,460 square kilometres[93] Bangladesh is mostly flat alluvial plain & hilly in the southeast. A lot of the land is used predominantly for agriculture at 70% est. and a population of around 167 million[94] Bangladesh has like so many of these nation examples traditionally has nutritious dishes, with many flavours and spices added. 'Bangladesh is the fourth largest producer of rice in the world and so rice is the staple of the Bangladeshi diet, accompanying most meals, especially curries. meal'[95]. The nation 'is the world's 8th most populous country as well as one of the world's most densely populated'[96] 'Bangladesh has the largest textile industry in the world. The industry remains the strongest root of the economy and the leading source of export earnings, accounting for about 80% of the total export. Bangladesh is the second-largest textile exporter behind China'[97] Also big in agriculture, so quite an active population and the majority less likely behind a desk. The nation has many issues it does need to work out and develop, with the child mortality rates lack of education and life expectancy. 'The majority of the population earn their income from agriculture. Bangladesh's primary crops include rice, jute, tea, tobacco, wheat, tomato, and pulses. Because the country has fertile soil, rice can be grown and harvested three times a year. In 2000, it produced 35.8 million metric tons of rice, effectively making it the country's principal crop'[98] The poverty ranking of Bangladesh is in the top half of world rankings, so it is very much in a development stage, as is Cambodia and with a bright future. This could be an influential factor in the nation's obesity rankings too. Conflicting research to the active assumptions suggests the adult population is quite inactive and this needs to change for health reasons. However, the number one big chain being Macdonald's is not setup in Bangladesh.

Out of all nations here, Bangladesh comes in at the fourth highest impoverished nation. There appears to be KFC and Pizza hut in Bangladesh, but not yet MacDonalds. They must have their reasons, and it is linked to high real estate costs, building standards and cold storage of their products. It's likely to change soon.

Famous for its 'colourful festivals, flavourful cuisine with strong spices, and incredible nature, including the largest mangrove forest in the world'[99].

The Least Obese Nation on Earth

At an adult obesity rate of 2.1% of a 98 million population Vietnam has the world's lowest adult obesity rate[100]. Starbucks, Subway, Burger King, and KFC all have a presence there with McDonald's opening its first outlet in Vietnam's Ho Chi Minh city[101] However, it didn't work out, Vietnam has its own style of fast food 'essentially locals in Vietnam were not getting access to McDonald's food at a faster pace compared to other establishments'[102]. Burger king's success is no better as the locals turned to other options. You can grab a local Pho or sandwich quicker anywhere, below are facts of Vietnam[103];

Fast food in Vietnam :

- **Fast food service is not as fast as the Vietnam food service.**
- **Local food is more competitive than fast food.**
- **Fast food company has a higher price in comparison with local food.**
- **Vietnamese prefer healthy food to fast food.**
- **Vietnamese come to restaurants to eat and talk**

Examples of the local foods include Chicken Pho, broken rice, steamed rice rolls with pork, fried spring rolls and Beef Pho[104], all traditional and healthy. The Vietnamese are an active population, '44% of Vietnamese respondents stated that they either exercised a lot, very often, moderately, or fairly-often. In the same survey, 89% of respondents considered themselves very healthy or healthy'[105]. It's furthered in the research suggesting the Vietnamese enjoy football and badminton, walking, cycling, and running, favouring public parks where exercise is free.

Vietnam has a low unemployment rate at 2.05% so relatively low in comparison to many other nations[106], along with the 'main industries being electronics, food processing, construction and mining they are not a sedentary nation[107]. Furthermore, regarding employment in Vietnam 'In 2021, almost 14.3 million people worked in the agriculture, forestry, and fishing sector in Vietnam, making this sector the largest employer among all industries'[108]demonstrating further examples of an active labour force. Part of my South-East Asia trip was a visit to Vietnam's capital Hanoi and onto Ha Long Bay. In all honesty I didn't see any local obese people, more that everyone was slender and quite a small population, I regularly felt quite tall walking around the nation's capital at 5'11.

A picture taken in Hanoi during the daytime, the hotel I stayed at was in a side street to the left, the locals would sit on small plastic chairs. I was near the main back packer's hostel and that was full of westerners partying a lot. I flew to Hanoi from Laos, other took an overnight bus which broke down. Taking over 24 hours to get there.

While in Hanoi, I did see a KFC and had lunch there just to go to a western fast-food place in South-East Asia. It does seem for the last several years there has been an increase in these chains entering the country. I enjoyed visiting the local restaurants and bars in Hanoi and the backpackers hostel a busy travellers social paradise. The following day as I walked around a lot of the locals were sat outside the local hospital, I saw patients in the open back yard area with umbrellas I can't say what was going on but seemed the place was very busy with patients. From what I was told then, Vietnam had a desire to increase links back with the west. Post war there were no chain restaurants for years, so the people were not exposed to such options and having time making their own established traditional fast-food outlets which flourish today.

A side street in Hanoi by night, all the locals sitting on small plastic chairs drinking lemon tea eating sunflower seeds. The leaves on the ground are visible and in the morning piles of shells are dotted around the area. I found it quite astonishing, much of the street food is preferred by the locals and it shows.

The food was amazing at a recommended local restaurant, the owner made me very welcome. As with Cambodia, the portions were relatively small but was enough. We sat after the meal and chatted for a while he offered some rice wine and had photos with the staff. They were great people, a boat trip the next day also saw lunch as healthy fish with rice and vegetables. As within the region such as with Thailand and Cambodia the local traditional food is very healthy and appears the population are not willing to let go of those traditions, so here we have Vietnam with the lowest adult obesity rate in the world.

A great evening at a local restaurant in Hanoi, I asked for their recommendation on what to eat (the best way) it was nice local food and Saki with the staff after ! Seeing the culture and how the people are the least obese makes sense as they prefer all the traditional healthy foods. I was seen as quite tall out there, quite a petite nation unlike back home in the UK.

As I only had four days in Hanoi, I wanted to see a pagoda, I had spoken to the people working at reception in the hotel I stayed at. A plush clean place which was so cheap made it even better, one of the guys said he would take me, next minute I'm on the back of his scooter charging through Hanoi in torrential rain playing chicken with busses coming in the opposite direction. It was terrifying, all he did was look back at me laughing, glad I did it then as I wouldn't do it again. We got to traffic lights, the scooters out there are like mosquitoes all over the place one bike nearly hit us and I

On the back of a bike, in torrential rain which subsided as we approached the pagoda. The lightning hadn't, I looked at the structure and then pointed my camera. As I clicked lightning struck, this picture was the result. A lucky fluke to get the purple haze of the lightning. I was so pleased when I looked at it, blurry but that was my picture of Vietnam. Soon enough we were back on the bike and charged back to the hotel. I Left for Cambodia the next day, an interesting place and as we have seen reasons behind why Vietnam is the number 1 lowest adult obesity in the world.

pushed the driver. I realised he was braking so I apologised, that journey was something I had never experienced to that intensity. It's quite different using the roads in South-East Asia and I got used to it on my scooter in Thailand, almost too relaxed a lot of the time. With Cambodia's roads a race track too, it's amazing what you get used to when in the environment for long enough. Vietnam has shown us some very relevant clues to the way a nation and how an individual can have low obesity levels. My adventures in South-East Aisa were unforgettable and to tell the full story another time, suffice to say it created amazing memories and of the countries in that region. A real experience which I am so pleased I experienced and would recommend it to anyone. I cannot believe it was over ten years ago now as I write as I recall the memories it seems like it was yesterday.

I headed out on the boat to Ha Long Bay, it docked with a community that live on the water and have never been to shore, apparently. In the northeastern part of Vietnam and part of the western bank of the Bac Bo Gulf. Taking a small boat through the local area and seeing the locals, their floating school, their community, and local caves was amazing.

In Ha Long Bay, this picture I had taken during the trip. The rock formation to the right, is quite significant 'The VND 200.000 banknote has the image of Dinh-Huong Island in Ha Long Bay, one of the eight world heritage sites of Vietnam'[109].

Summary

We have looked at the most and least obese nations in the world. With all the countries involved there are now clear reasons we have seen what influences these results. We've looked at cultural influences, consumer demands, food preferences, geographical issues, and economic factors. How active the people are, how being obese is affecting their health and what access they have to resources, for the obese nations and with how much cash they may have in their pocket. Our Obesogenic societies are growing and has done consistently for a considerable number of years, package all the factors we have discussed. Environment, food choices, poverty levels, culture, learning what is going on with us as we realise now with this world view. We can see the main factors of weight gain across populations, and we are in our own unique situation, and we need to look at our own factors, our own reasons. I hope this is helping you, showing the causes and to look at your environment from your own perspective.

Country	Poverty rate	Most / Least obese
Vietnam	6.7%	Least
Cambodia	17.7%	Least
Bangladesh	24.3%	Least
Palau	24.9%	Most
Tuvalu	26.3%	Most
Timor Leste	41.8%	Least

From the world population review, six nations in the least and most obese doesn't directly correlate to the poverty of each nation. Nauru is also high poverty yet ranks as our number 1 adult obese nation. It's a combination of what we have seen creating the perfect storm one way or the other.

I would have assumed beforehand the nations with higher poverty levels are more likely to be in the least obese rankings and the reverse for the most obese. Across all ranked nations, yet Tuvalu and Palau are high in poverty rank and yet very high in the obesity rank, same with Nauru. The World Population Review[110] shows statistics of poverty levels to the right, but not for all of our ten nations, some observations are quite startling though. Nauru 67% of the population on less than $10 a day, which is not good whilst being the number 1 obesity ranked nation, high poverty and yet high obesity. If we consider height, my initial perception was that the obese nations would be shorter and heavier in accordance again with the world population review average height by country.[111]

Nation	male	female
Cook Islands	5'10	5'6
Tuvlau	5'7	5'4
Palau	5'7	5'3
Nauru	5'7	5'2
Vietnam	5'6	5'2
India	5'6	5'1
Cambodia	5'5	5'1
Marshall Island	5'5	5'1
Bangladesh	5'5	5'0
Timor Leste	5'3	5'0

Could nations heights affect the BMI score, hence obesity of a nation, the taller can be heavier with a shorter population yet equal weight would more likely be in the obese category. The most obese nations are also four of the tallest in a comparison. Interestingly the most and least obese, Nauru and Vietnam are closest in the graph height comparison. It shows height isn't an influence in the measurement therefore not an influence in the levels of obesity.

Looking at these obese pacific paradise islands of tropical rainforests and volcanos, there could be a sense of isolation or desolation possibly? Especially in Nauru, with its lack of work and prospects for the locals. We could take the view there that live for today's satisfaction as there's no guarantee what's happening tomorrow?

A combination of environment, how the people get around and preferred mode or access to transport. Employment and type of work being more manual or more sedentary, the wealth of the country can work for or against the level of obesity. Nauru being a relatively poor nation also in general choose a poor diet. We can also see culture plays a big impact in the results, especially with their view of body image in the Pacific Islands. Affordability & convenience / preference of foods, with the example of the Vietnamese people buying more affordable and healthier traditional street food. This being offset to South Korea where fast food is relatively cheap yet obesity is very low so they must be opting for the more localised traditional food options too. Japan being steeped in tradition too, looking at this factor, a key is the reward from food and their reward is tasty healthy food with spices to flavour. The preference between fats, sugars and spices appears to be a factor separating between examples of South Asia and South-East Asia, in those that adopt a more traditional diet than the push of western style fat and sugar in foods. Only in Japan, which brought in a specific intervention we've seen to tackle the issue of future obesity with their 'Metabo' Law. Besides the sugar and fat issue, much of the least obese nation's traditional staple of their diet is rice. We can see between the highest and lowest nations in obesity levels, the highest has adopted new ways of food consumption with the influence of poorer quality foods dense in sugar and fat. The least obese has stuck with more traditional ways, more natural wholefoods. That appears to be one of the biggest factors, sugar, and fat versus spices. It could be suggested one big reason Vietnam is at the top spot is the population prefers these traditional flavours to their food. Convenience and cultural outlooks as we have seen make an influence in this. On my travels in the South-East region, staying in Thailand for four months, I saw a real contrast of the population looking quite slender as they carried on with traditional ways of eating, but there was a lot of the western style treats coming in. I was in Chiang Mai, the north of Thailand, a lot of

This was my regular go to evening meal in Chiang Mai city centre, Squid Tom Yum and garlic chicken with rice. The Tom Yum was a party of flavours going on in your mouth. After this I would then onto a lodge for chicken kebabs and coffee listening to the Thai singer on his guitar playing American songs.

the more affluent schoolkids in outdoor classes were obese. Neighbouring Cambodia and in the region with Vietnam I assumed Thailand would have a similar low adult obesity population level. They are quite far from Cambodia and Vietnam, in at 53rd from bottom. A lot of western fast food is catching on, at the corner road where I was staying at the bottom of Doi Suthep mountain, a big Dunkin' Doughnuts was right on the corner and in town was MacDonalds, Starbucks and KFC then. The aim of showing you obesity from around the world is to be aware of different places and the influence on its people. This trend for the obese countries as we can see clearly needs to be stopped and the gears put into reverse. I hope this world perspective journey has been a bit of an eye opener. It opened my eyes as I was researching the countries and statistics, the influences causing obesity on the world scale we see today. Weight-gain as we can see it's not necessarily all our fault. If you may think so or others may suggest to you, it really is these factors we've seen in these world population examples. I hope showing these different nations and their individual situations highlights this. All healthcare in any developed nation in the world should be completely free, in my view. Would everyone mind paying an extra five pounds or dollars a month to ensure this? The fast-food chains make money as so do the medical pharma companies in nations, and so on it goes. The obesity figures are clearly an issue of concern, the best thing to do on an individual basis is to regularly make the right choices in food and drink, let our bodies adapt to a healthier routine and we will see a great reduction in hospital admissions. Less obesity, less heart problems, less metabolic syndrome, less circulatory problems, less nerve damage and eye damage through diabetes, less strokes, less liver problems, less kidney problems, and the list goes on. We will have less of this amongst our populations, more health, more time to do fun things, and choosing to do fun things rather than what is unhealthy for us.

Two Superpowers

We have looked at the top obese nations and the least obese, now let's look at the two worlds top ranking superpowers to see if there is any different perspectives to the overall picture. Let's look at The United States of America and China, see how their nations fayre in the obesity rankings.

United States

The overall unemployment rates are relatively low in world comparisons from the world bank, 2020 at 8.1%[112]currently its suggested to be 3.4% for April 2023[113] with a population of 334.7 million and a land mass of over 9.6 million square kilometres[114] they have the facilities and geographical means for people to undertake an active life, compared to the obese Islands. 'The United States of America comes into the obesity rankings at number 12, at an obesity rate of 36.2%'[115] The research furthers with 'obesity rates vary significantly between states, ranging from 23% to 38.10%. This is due to the same dietary, environmental, and cultural factors that cause variations between countries'[116] As we have seen with the most and least obese countries, with the States the impact of choices including all the fast foods. The advertisements constantly bombarding the population, with energy dense sugary, fat fast foods. However, this is amongst all the healthy stuff too. The five top States with the highest obesity rates[117], so why Is West Virginia in at the top spot?

The five states in USA with the highest adult obesity rates :
1. **West Virginia** (40.7%)
2. **Alabama** (40.4%)
3. **Kentucky** (40.3%)
4. **Oklahoma** (39.6%)
5. **Mississippi** (39.2%)

'West Virginia has traditionally maintained a poor economic position among the states'[118] A relatively poorer state compared to others, yet their obesity rank is at the top. A characteristic seen in examples of our most obese nations, as we see examples of both, poor and well off. Termed the 'Western pattern diet', it's suggested it involves the 'high intakes of pre-packaged foods, refined grains, red meat, processed meat, high sugar drinks, candy and sweets, fried foods but then continues with low intakes of fruits, vegetables, whole grains, fish nuts and seeds'.[119] Again, examples we have seen from the influences in our top obese nations, with their imported processed foods. We know the States is popular for burgers, hot dogs and the now global fast-food chains. Americans are known to work long hours and the reward being the time out of the office. The people do have their own unique views and individualism is encouraged. My experiences out there saw extremes in these areas, from the health fanatic, body beautiful people in Miami, to the opposing end of the spectrum and everyone in between. Having the high rank of 12th most obese nation does show the States is on the heavier end of the scales overall.

I really didn't think this would be appetising going for the most unusual item on the menu, I loved it USA is 12th from top in the obesity rankings. I couldn't find the kind of buffet food I wanted but there was just so much choice on the Las Vegas Strip and we had two days there before heading off to L.A, driving through the Mojave desert.

Heading to the States a few years ago a lot of their food is quite sweet with sugar and fats. Lots healthy but so much choice at each end of the spectrum. On one trip, breakfast in one of the big Las Vegas hotels on the main strip, we headed to was so busy and the portions were huge. Being packed, we had to wait for a seat, but it was worth the wait. I can't say I had ever had waffles, mash potato (other side of the plate in the picture above)

The Strip in Las Vegas, modern hotels with the two Cosmopolitan tallest buildings far left and designer shops in front this city centre area shows. Many food establishments are on the right hand side. Vegas I thought is like the modern day Pyramids. The buildings, restaurants, casinos, shops, bars. Pool party's in the Nevada Desert

and fried chicken with Ranch sauce on waffles for breakfast before, but I headed back there the following day. For me that's an unusual holiday treat, but is this eaten regularly by Americans? If so, then it's clear where the obesity is coming from. Prices were reasonable but I wouldn't say it was cheap, it was a driving holiday so making breakfast our biggest meal of the day for the travelling we planned throughout. Another example of the American view in Freemont Street was a restaurant that I had read about & wanted to visit, the theme was for the food to be as unhealthy as it could, full fat. Highly calorific and if the customer is over 350 pounds, they could eat for free. In the United States, 'From 1999 – 2000 through 2017 – March 2017 – March 2020, US obesity prevalence increased from 30.5% to 41.9%. During the same time, the prevalence of severe obesity increased from 4.7% to 9.2%'[120] In nearly twenty years that's a jump in over ten percent. At half-way in 2008 it was estimated that the medical bill of obesity in the U.S. was 'USD 173 billion in 2019 dollars'[121]. What is going on, America is one of the most advanced countries on the planet, yet they have a huge problem with obesity. As I look at the more common / popular foods of the USA we can immediately see some issues come to light as we can see with some of their favourite choices:

'Hot dogs, Tater Tots, Apple Pie, Barbeque ribs, Reuben Sandwich, Biscuits and gravy, Meatloaf, Grits, Hamburgers, BLT's, Po' boy' [122]

These are foods with a big influence in taste of fat and sugar to satisfy the American demand. Don't get me wrong if prepared right, the beefburger can be healthy, depending on the contents such as being 100% beef & no additives, a granary bun & salad with a bit of sauce. Low G.I. carbs in the bread and good quality meats. Ribs can be fine too it depends on the quality and that it's a natural product which hasn't gone through processes making it unhealthier. They will be far healthier if made from scratch, there are a lot of healthy choices, but this doesn't seem to be happening for everyone as we look at the obesity rates of the United States. It doesn't just stop there, one area we need to address is the soft drink industry. All their fast-food chains offer these sugary and 'diet' drinks, which are the scourge of society, and it cannot be denied contribute to what is unfolding.

Two healthy examples of restaurant food above, I would say they are more likely to have gone through less processes, less fast food. Fresh fish on the pier at Monterey on the Californian coast on the left and barbeque food from a barbeque pit in North Carolina. Both extremely tasty and little sugar and unhealthy fats. I couldn't choose between either, both were memorable.

More Barbeque in North Carolina, the deep friend choices a rarity and tasty. The hospitality and the friends I were with. I realise I am always mindful of what I am eating, it's a good habit I have created for myself over time. Eat healthily and treats are more enjoyable, more regular, the less a treat it becomes.

I was a big fan of the barbeque scene out there; I am more of a meat eater and like savoury foods rather than sweet. That kind of comfort food I really did enjoy, I could and did fill myself up on that and skip the dessert. Many do anticipate the dessert as their favourite part of the meal which can be a downfall to weight gain.

China

China's obesity ranking is way down the list at 169 out of 192 nations which sounds great, yet if we look at the population size its suggested from 2020 that 'Over half of Chinese adults are now overweight. That's more people than the entire US population'123and further reports agree with, '50% of adults were classified as overweight'124. It appears to be developing into a massive issue, and on an upward trend 'In 2002, 29.9% of Chinese Adults were overweight, including Obese. In 2012, that figure rose to 42%, according to previous reports released by Chinese health authorities'125 and now where we are more recently.

'The people's republic of China covers an area of approximately 3.7 million square miles, making it the world's 4th largest country by area. With a population of about 1.4 billion, the country has a population density of 375.5 people per square mile'126.half being just over the 500 million mark and at the 16.4% in China we are in the ballpark of 186.9 million obese

Chinese people. The Chinese population participating in regular exercise is said to be 41% in recent research[127].

As we had seen with Nauru and other examples where traditional diet was healthy yet the popular food choices in recent years is not. 'The main overall driver is likely to be China's exceptionally rapid economic growth. While this has created more prosperity and reduced poverty, the flipside has been an equally rapid nutrition transition away from more traditional and balanced foods to a gradual introduction of ultra-processed junk food products. Such changes in our diet are now increasingly being implicated in weight gain and obesity, as well as many other chronic diseases'[128] Following these trends of world-wide with increasing obesity, I am quite surprised at this before looking into it as I had visions that in the rural areas of China, it would show people eating far healthier than in the big cities. The Chinese would be very traditional with their food selections and tastes. It must be all the food videos I watch on YouTube one I find fascinating is of a generally the best street food or broth / noodles made from scratch a 200Kg street hot pot[129]. The scourge of fast food appears to be making an impact on China, as with much of the Orient and South-East Asia the traditional food all appears to be quite healthy, with fried rice, Peking duck, Chicken Chow Mein. More back to basics and less or no sugar and salt thrown in for taste, unlike our local western Chinese takeaway. Next time you head to the local Chinese takeaway ask for your dishes with no sugar or salt added, it will lose that zing and you will see how different it tastes.

It is suggested 'China's food system has moved from one based on rationing and grain coupons to one characterised by increasing choices, rising prices and growing concerns about food quality and safety'[130]. Here appears the issue with food becoming more choice based rather than necessity, which is the way it should be, but those choices need to be mostly right ones. With further influences in China, and this is nearly ten years ago: 'E-commerce grew by more than 52% in value between 2014 and 2016. Ordering lunch or dinner online became daily routine for millions of urban residents, despite the tremendous amount of food and plastic waste generated. Meanwhile, younger Chinese are distancing themselves from the origins of food and losing food knowledge and skills'[131] A valid point we haven't explored is the issue of food preparation and individual's habits, we are focusing on the adult populations yet what will the next generations be like. I want us to see where we are now and with your target people. Buddhism is a big influence in China with many Pagodas, ancient shrines along with their diet, with the quote below[132].

'Vegetarianism is perhaps the most important contribution Buddhism has made to Chinese cuisine. Today, Buddhist monks and nuns in China are expected to maintain a vegetarian diet, and as far one can tell, in general they take the prohibition seriously, abstaining from all forms of meat, fish, and eggs'. Inspiring vegetarianism across China. My experience of Buddhist monks was in Thailand, nice people.

Summary

We can see the obesity levels of the United States is right up there at 12th position and then the stark contrast with China being very low on the world rankings. It's worth considering the size of the populations, bearing in mind the country percentage of the population may be low but in China it's still potentially a huge future issue. The States with years of established fast-food outlets and China in more recent times starting to adopt these convenience food habits. We can say that as already seen, the level of poverty has somewhat of an impact on obesity, but affluence doesn't necessarily. As we look at both these nations the difference could be the culture as with such influence that kept Vietnam in the number one spot. The United States very much the more modern with more processed options being selected, and China seems to be well on the way. Obesity very much appears to be on the rise in China as they adopt the more western style of food consumption and the sheer size of its population and will increase the magnitude of the problem. Even though in the rankings they seem to be doing quite well, in the grand scheme of things their obese population numbers make the world's most obese seem tiny. An area we haven't really looked at as we could then compare obesity levels on number and not on the percentage of the populations. It could be suggested that a smaller nation with a far higher obesity prevalence is more of a concern due to the strain on services and needs of the people. In a far bigger nation with far more people and therefore more services, it could be suggested the likes of China can cope far better currently with their numbers, even though it is far higher than Nauru or the Cook Islands or any of the top obese nations.

It needs to change, of course it does as we need to see trends of obesity start to decrease over years and not carry on increasing. This growing trend of nutrient transition needs to stop and revert predominantly to healthy ways. I am convinced reward is the key and more to the point what we perceive as reward with our food and drink. Our relationship with food and drink needs to in some ways be redefined, and as I repeat again the likes of Japan, Cambodia and Vietnam are showing us what we need to be doing.

Nation Richness Offset to its Obesity Rank

Statements are made in research suggesting the more educated and individual is the less likely they are to be obese. It is not that clear, as we have seen looking at the nations obesity rankings when compared to the top 60 nations of the world's most literate, I have seen that of the top ten obese countries, none are in the top 60 rankings of most literate. Could this also be a driver, the level of education in a population. Let's compare add in the world nations obesity rankings.

If we flip the analysis and take the top literate[133] nations in the world could there be a correlation that way round ?

Top 7 literate Nations	Obese countries	Per capita	biggest econ. GDP
Finland no. 1	obesity rank 53	GDP 19th	42nd
Norway no. 2	obesity rank 54	GDP 7th	28th
Iceland no. 3	obesity rank 46	GDP 9th	105th
Denmark no. 4	obesity rank 64	GDP 10th	35th
Sweden no. 5	obesity rank 59	GDP 14th	22nd
Switzerland no. 6	obesity rank 111	GDP 6th	20th
USA no. 7	obesity rank 12	GDP 8th	1st

Per capita[134] means for each person, as in the likelihood of the population having more, more cash in their pocket so they can make more of the choices they want than just bore out of necessity. The top 7 literate nations being those most education / reading across a society. That pattern suggests of high literacy, these nations sit in the top quarter for obesity. Which sort of makes sense, these countries have an abundance of food and resources at the population's fingertips. Yet the previous statement of the more literacy the less likelihood of obesity. Well, this is not the case as we can see obesity in both literate and non-literate scenarios. There is clearly influence from the other factors we have seen, culturally & customs, preferred tastes and the environment people live in.

Per Capita Influences the Obesity Rank

Top 7 countries with the highest GDP			Obesity ranking *1
1	Monaco	234,317	very low
2	Liechtenstein	169,260	Not available
3	Luxembourg	133,175	rank 74
4	Bermuda	112,653	rank 62.5 *2
5	Ireland	101,109	rank 51
6	Switzerland	93,525	rank 111
7	Norway	89,242	rank 54

*1 Rankings are from the world population review, Monaco Liechtenstein and Bermuda are not featured so other sources are sought.[135]

*2 At an adult obesity level of 24% not featured in the WPR, this rank is where it fits in.

When it comes to the size of the economy the USA topping that chart. The rest bar Iceland coming in at the higher mean average. Many of the least obese countries are in general poorer nations, that correlation sadly would be a given. As we look at the world figures there clearly is a big problem with both starvation and obesity, being that there's rankings for both issues and clear evidence that both do need addressing. It is very sad that in today's world both are of real concern. We should be preventing world hunger whilst at the same time reducing obesity and promoting health and wellbeing, with literate nations we can see 6 out of the 7 listed are in the top half in obesity rankings and all high per Capita. Of the biggest economy rankings in the table, Vietnam is the world's 45th biggest economy[136] just below Finland, but their Global Hunger Index (GHI) is 55 in 2022 out of 121 ranked[137]. This may contribute to Vietnams lowest obesity figures. It would be easy just to say the richer, affluent countries are more obese well they are more likely to be in the top half of the obese charts and the more poverty stricken in the bottom half. Many are, yet as we have seen the top obese nations in our tour are not in the top ranks as economic giants, only the United States who comes in as the top superpower, 12th on the obese nation list and 7th for literacy does, being the home of many of the fast-food giants.

The Invisible Hand of Demand

It's not an accident in what's going on with obesity, they are making these quick convenience foods from the West cheap and easily accessible so people can afford to buy them. It's too easy to pop into a MacDonalds in any western world high street and in 5 minutes get a cheeseburger and coffee on the go (we saw the photos of American main streets and they are easily spotted) With the quick calories and additives yet crucially if we didn't buy it, they wouldn't be there, they have refined their products and processes over years & years to be one of the biggest fast food chains in the world. For lunchtime passing convenience there is sandwich bars, sushi shops, hot snack shops, and the like but what hidden sugar and fat are in these products too? A lot is pre-packaged and is likely to have additives and such. If we all took our food consumption and health seriously then a lot of these cheaper poorer quality foods would disappear, however there's the other factors to consider. As I write this piece in 2023 general food prices have gone up, fuel is up, energy costs are up and now interest rates are up. Shell just recently posted their profits are the highest in over one hundred years. We are having to pay more to live our lives comparatively in recent decades, rents and mortgages are not cheap anymore. We have so many things to worry about that what priority is our own health in what we eat and drink. As mentioned, there's profit in that too thanks to the Pharmaceutical Industry. We are being bombarded from all angles with our daily lives to have to do more to provide. Transport is another one, cars and insurance is so expensive along with the petrol or diesel to put in vehicles, now just recently the ULEZ scheme in Greater London boroughs has been rolled out. Another tax on people to just get on with their lives. Corporations want to make profit, that's why they exist, and they will go to any lengths to get it, legally of course. Think of everything, phones, designer clothes, the food, TV, entertainment, everything. What chance does our health have in the priorities of all these things, we must look to take charge of it. We must now make our own health, through our choices and weight management a priority for the good of ourselves.

From our Findings and Further Points to Consider

From our discovery of what's happening across the world and added practical points, we can go through each of the following factors influencing weight gain, I am sure there's a lot here we can all relate to.

- ### Obesogenic environment

Much of how we live is encouraging us to gain weight, we don't need to even head to the supermarket or takeaway anymore as it can all be delivered. Less walking around the shops as so much is being ordered online, with Amazon taking record profits during the pandemic and delivery companies business booming. Not even having to take a trip to work meaning less walking than before, to the station for example or even from the car park to the office. We are living in an increasing environment of convenience where less personal physical activity, the example of walking any distance is needed.

- ### Convenience food / drink

Fast food is on the increase in demand and supply, not only the fast-food restaurants but a lot of the pre-packaged foods we are buying and are not always clear on the packaging of the contents.

- ### Working longer hours

People may not have as much free time to prepare and consider the content of what they are eating at mealtimes. Giving less priority to more traditional mealtime routines and likely to snack on the go, means less chance of preparing healthy meals at breakfast, lunch & dinner time.

- ### More sedentary working environments than physical / Manufacturing jobs

Sitting at a desk all day won't burn anywhere near the calories of being on a building site or traditional manufacturing jobs. Maybe you do have an active job, many do not and there is some reflection of a nation's obesity levels in the main type of work available.

- ### Driving more and walking less

Has been a factor for years even with the high motoring costs in insurance and tax, its relatively affordable than 40 plus years ago. Now with the electric bikes & variations you don't have to walk to the station or to work and that's if you go into the office anymore. Along with Uber being the cheaper alternative to getting a cab.

- **On a typical train journey**

Temptation is everywhere especially on a train journey to grab a coffee and treat. A typical journey from the coast into central London could cause temptation at so many points, from the café at the station, at the destination, walking down the street to the destination. The times I grab a coffee and a snack at the station then at the other end.

- **Constant advertisements, locations and from the media**

We are becoming glued to our smartphones, with constant advertisements on the social media channels, billboard posters, tabloid ads, smartphone ads, tablet ads, TV ads, visuals, even smells, to think the times I smell chips passing a chip shop, suddenly I'm in there buying.

- **Our well know culture of socialising and drinking, even with the lockdown and pubs, bars**

Restaurants were shut, the number of yellow bins I saw full of wine bottles, beer and more on a regular basis. Could it have been linked to the stress caused by the pandemic (as I write this piece). Traditionally as the pubs open an evening beer session often causes people to have problems with their legs, they lead them to the kebab shop after.

- **The freely available supply of fast food / ready meals**

The result of fast-food choices becoming more regular isn't good. Rather than choosing what is better for us, being the natural wholefoods. We had seen in the United States street photo's where fast-food outlets are dotted, examples of convenience.

- **With less healthy choices available to us**

They are promoting us to be more sedentary through the whole day, meaning we are less active and likely to be more sluggish with a feeling of less energy after work. More sedentary will promote less burning of calories and promote weight gain.

- **Less traditional mealtimes and people are eating on the go**

Or in effect have no set times for breakfast lunch and dinner. No pattern and likely to chase calories into the evening, being one of many weight gain habits that can occur.

- **Prepacked foods which appear healthy may have to have added sugar and fats**

If something is low fat it could be high in sugar, check the contents not just the messages conveyed of the packaging images. Beware tinned foods as they can have high amounts of sugar added. The advertising can be very misleading, their aim maybe to associate with health yet the actual aim is to sell the product making profit.

- **The coffee biscuit crisps scenario**

As a snack socially say meeting a friend yet very energy dense same for a burger, chips, a sugary coffee scenario seeming less likely to contain so many calories, look again. Something on the go from a shop may not to be that healthy, only you know what goes into it if you prepare it yourself.

- **The aftermath of the pandemic**

From people spending more time indoors and less physical activity along with mental health issues and alcohol consumption higher during the lockdowns. Just walking along the streets seeing yellow bins full of empty wine and beer bottles. It never used to be like that. Resulting in more regular calories and health issues including diabetes a likely result.

- **Working parents**

More of a regularity these days is for both parents of a family to work. Thanks to ever higher living costs and a stagnation in an average wage both parents tend to be working and for longer hours. Preparing nutritious whole meals is not necessarily the normality it once was.

- **Good meals cost more, or do they (2023 UK price)**

Can you eat cheap and healthy, a one kilo bag of rice costs £1.20 one portion can vary from 60 to 90grams. Say we go down the middle and a portion being 75 grams. That's 13 portions at 9 pence a portion, add mushrooms and a chicken breast & soy sauce at most would be a couple of pounds. A quarter pounder with cheese meal in a main fast-food restaurant is £4.69. It's more in the time to select and prepare good food than the cost comparison itself, or so it would seem. With a little research it can be very cheap to prepare your own meals rather than eating out, the Vietnamese cheap Pho fast food being an example. We need to look at these things for ourselves make it priority.

- **Lifestyle from a young age**

I have seen a big link with client's home lifestyle, if parents are obese there is a far greater chance the children will also be. Adopting the habits of the home environment, this big factor moulding lifestyle in early life can lead to weight management issues through life. *The most significant predictor of childhood obesity is parental obesity*[138] a startling quote from my studies into obesity.

- **Level of physical activity**

What gets your heart rate up in the day, it could be moving furniture or mowing the grass, or walking to the station. If you are not at least walking daily, therefore not burning calories, offset to high calorie intake, then of course the weight will go on. I mean something to bring the heart rate up consistently for a minimum of 10 to 15 minutes, not just flitting around the house stopping and starting. We will go into physical activity more.

- **The effort needed to change dug in lifestyle habits**

Can seem like it's too much to change. Sitting in front of the tele, eating favourite snacks and treats, not moving from the hangover the night before, it's all extra calories with a lack of burning anything off being the triple whammy. Surplus calories intake, lack of movement and lack of exercise.

- **Cultural Influences**

With some interesting finds in the biggest and leanest nations, culture appears to be a big influencer. What do you find is a big influencer in this area for you?

- **Snacking**

We have so many choices through the day in the towns and cities of people trying to sell us food and snacks, as our lives are hectic a lot of what we do is on the go. Making quick choices for snacks on the go, many not ideal. The industry is seeing some changes with health and wellness considerations but so much more needs to be done. Treats when we really don't need them or shouldn't be having them, habits and we must register what's going on!

- **Having more money to spend**

We had seen in the world obesity section three of the top five obese nations are quite poor countries, yet in general the richer nations are situated in the top half of obesity rankings whilst the poorer in the bottom half.

Task: 1

•   Get yourself a brand new notepad and pen so it's dedicated to this YOU project.

Create a title for yourself, take a look at all these different points and see what makes a big impact on you. Write down each one and see how you are influenced involving each point. It's a great way to start to address whats going on for your own weight management plan, seeing where the problems are on a practical basis. Have a think about this, it will help to see what is going on and we are going to structure your habits for change. As these points show themselves this is your discovery to what needs to change and be honest with yourself as this is about you discovering what is going on in your life.

If you need to then yes feel guilty ! Show yourself what you really have been doing 😊

Where Did Fast Food Come From

Our most basic need, the fast-food industry is plying our temptations with desirable food and drink. We get it so much every day, go back 50 to 60 years plus, these fast food temptations just weren't there. The convenience choice wasn't as today.

We all need to eat, a basic need unlike the latest pair of Nike trainers that can wait if we don't have the money. Food being an integral part of society and fast food being a quicker way to cater for the masses. Going way back in history, 'the ancient Romans used to go to the so-called Thermopolia, some kind of fast-food restaurants because most houses did not have a kitchen'[139] in more recent times, the first fish and chip shop in England opened in the 1860's called Malin's on old ford road[140]. Even though records suggest fish was battered in England for hundreds of years, originally fish and chip shops were small family businesses setup in their house front room, these became very popular by the 19th century. There would have been setups going back to early civilisation of people selling food to paying customers, but the way fast food is setup, a more modern term. Originally it would have been independent business setup to supply food to demand. Our look at fast food is more of the modern processes of offering convenience food to customers. In the United States, from various sources it is suggested the White Castle in 1921[141] has been acknowledged to be the first regional hamburger restaurant chain, which went on the expand to its current size of around 370 locations in America. They didn't franchise the company so there's no further opportunity for further investment, but with 370 restaurants how much more would you need? In the United States, 'The term fast food first appeared in the Merriam –

Webster dictionary in 1951, but its roots are much older'[142] and started to take off. Macdonald's fast-food style established in 1948.

'In 1921, Billy Ingram launched a family-owned business with $700 and an idea, selling five-cent, small, square hamburgers so easy to eat, they were dubbed Sliders and sold by the sack'. I had never heard of a slider until a few years ago.

It Began with an Idea[143]

Is it Healthy? Supersize Me

Defining fast food could be anything quick to hand and from locations in a convenient vicinity. The food can be fast and healthy, as we've seen with Vietnam, unfortunately it can also be less healthy many of the big brand names come to mind. The foods going through many processes before it reaches us really isn't a good thing, but good for profits. This type of food cannot or should not be lived on, not eaten on a regular basis.

A documentary named Supersize me[144] featured one Morgan Spurlock who had set himself the task to eat, Macdonald's for breakfast then lunch and dinner every day for a month back in 2004. If they said at any of the fast-food restaurants he visited daily, 'do you want to supersize' he had to say yes. Even if he was sick of the sight of the fast food, he had to say yes. He would go for regular health checks, and it was his doctor that stopped him from carrying on, it was having huge detrimental effects to his health. Macdonald's hit back against the film, at the time in accordance with an article of the issue at the time, they stated they agreed with the films core argument. *"Where a man eats burgers continuously for 30 day's he will pile on weight to such a health damaging extent that his doctors order him to stop eating them."*[145] The Macdonald's ad placed suggests the film is flawed as an average customer would take six years to eat the quantity of burgers as the film maker ate. It also claimed the weight gain was exaggerated as the filmmaker cut his physical activity to a bare minimum, but that's no justification many people do minimal physical activity nor exercise.

I would agree with the chain as it's the decisions we make for ourselves, we cannot expect a business providing cheap calorie dense food to be too worried about its customers when their goal is making profit, there comes personal responsibility. Having said that Spurlock proved the food back then was not healthy if you cannot choose from their menu to eat daily just for 1 month, that surely indicates it's not healthy. Their potential worldwide contribution to the obesity epidemic is something that has been highlighted here, Spurlock put on 27 pounds and his cholesterol and blood pressure had risen after eating nothing but Macdonald's food. What was Macdonald's response? To remove all supersize options from the menu and added into the menu salads fruit and organic products. Sounds positive eh, well it was only a year later Macdonald's was sued and agreed to pay 8.5 million after the company reneged on a promise of reducing trans fats in their products[146]. Trans fats are evidently worse than regular fats or saturated fats, triggering this court case. There have been a lot of issues with fast food, the bottom line is that these corporations as I have mentioned are in business to maximise profit. Two years after the Supersize me film, in 2006 KFC was sued over the use of trans fats in its cooking.

'Trans fats were a part of fast-food meals in the 80's after consumer groups demanded the chains stop using beef tallow and palm oils being highly saturated. The trans fats were not known bad for health until years later. Now I wonder if the fast-food chains knew like the tobacco companies years ago. Profit before moral obligations seems like a regular thing, as long as the shareholders are happy, in my opinion I disagree. Now they are seen more harmful than saturated fat as they lower the good cholesterol and raise the bad[147]'.

Fast Food, Fast Profits

Another film based on Macdonald's was released in 2016 named 'The Founder' a biographical drama which illustrates the creating of Macdonald's. As the film illustrates, the original Macdonald brothers were about food to the customer, yet a travelling salesman persuades them to franchise the restaurant brand. To this current day Macdonald's is feeding around 1% of the population daily, and the original Macdonald brothers descendants receive no royalties, which would be around 100 million dollars a year. The motivation again, was and is to make money, the expansion of the business was a big influence of gaining real estate. From the fast processes the food goes through, could it be detrimental to the nutritional ranking of the food, likely. Examples like Spurlock's documentary did highlight the negative effects of our western style fast food but now it doesn't seem to have hampered in the growth of these chains. As we have seen with Vietnam, only the demands from a population can dictate how this works. If we don't spend our money buying their foods, they don't expand. Sugar is considered by many an addictive substance which is one big factor in fast food. These 'meals' are energy dense meaning for the limited size they contain a load of calories, that's thanks to the added sugar and fat. All part of the pleasure experience causing the reward sensation to the customer, wanting them to come back for more and this is well documented. I am not going to lie, I do like the odd fast-food burger or breakfast but as I research and find out just what is going on, with the health problems it can cause it will put me off the stuff. Shame as I did like a MacDonald's breakfast, we know the stuff isn't the best choice but with a busy day, sometimes fast food is that convenient choice or skip that meal. After we get to the bottom of it, I doubt it will be any longer the least we can do is cut back on its consumption and allow it far less and at most a very occasional treat. In the western world we are all too familiar with this sight, where I am in England so many high streets over the years have started to look the same. With the same chain retail places and restaurants.

A picture I had taken of New York's Manhattan up the road from Times Square. There on the left-hand side of the main street we can see the golden arches of the world's biggest fast-food chain. Fast food needs to be convenient, with locations in as many spots as possible, I bet if we walked down that main street, we would see many of the other western fast-food outlets too. What would happen if these chains were all about healthy low calorific food like Vietnam. It would probably result in some impact onto obesity levels.

Fast Food Locations by Country and Popularity, the Big Three

1. MacDonald's

'Macdonald's is the largest restaurant chain in the world. There are over 37,000 Macdonald's locations in about 120 countries in the world. The chain employs more than 1.7 million people and serves more than 70 million people[148]. The research furthers indicating that the company in 2019 full year's results they had sales of $100 billion and consolidated revenues of $21.1 billion. They are said to also provide different items at different regions, such as a Tempura shrimp burger in Japan and Bratwurst in Germany. Of the nations that don't have Macdonald's they are either a poor nation, have issues politically such as stability or the company's food won't cater for local tastes. Amongst these from the nations we have looked at, Nauru, Marshall Islands, Palau, Tuvalu, and the Cook Islands[149], all our top obese nations don't have any McDonald restaurants and out of the least obese only Cambodia and East Timor[150] are without, which is maybe surprising.

In the top ten, eight are in the top half of the obesity charts. Only two are in the bottom half, being China and Japan. Could it be the reward factor with preferred local tastes as seen with Vietnam.   S.Korea and Japan.   In accordance with World Atlas[151], the most locations in a country in the world, coming in at the top is, the United States, China is second and Japan third.

	Location	McDonalds	Ob. Rank
1	U.S.A	14,146	12
2	Japan	2,975	186
3	China	2,391	169
4	Germany	1,470	77
5	Canada	1,450	26
6	France	1,419	86
7	U.K.	1,274	35
8	Australia	920	27
9	Brazil	812	80
10	Russia	609	67

An alternative artwork piece in Coney Island New York when I was on my travels in the United States. Quite surreal and kind of a 'mind split' abstract art. The United States being the Headquarters of MacDonalds. In that area there was a lot of artwork bursting with colour.

Subway

The United States[152] is ahead by a country mile for subway locations, followed by Canada. Eight out of ten of these nations are in the top half of the obese rankings, again 80% are in the upper half, so could be seen as an influencer.

	Location	Subway	Obese Rank
1	U.S.A.	25,785	12
2	Canada	3,240	26
3	U.K.	2,380	35
4	Brazil	2,126	80
5	Australia	1,400	27
6	Mexico	1,012	28
7	India	621	188
8	Russia	616	67
9	China	598	169
10	France	458	86

Going through my Vegas holiday photos I did spot a Subway in this picture, on the right-hand side a few shops down. As with the Vietnam principle of convenience of their 'fast food' which are locations everywhere, and here's a Subway location. Spotted in the picture to the right side of the street.

2. Kentucky Fried Chicken

Next in is KFC, at number one with the most locations is China[153], followed by the United States two superpowers. Appears to be half and half, five of these nations are in the top half of the obesity rankings. Then the USA, Japan, South Africa, United Kingdom, Thailand, Malaysia, Indonesia, Australia, and Canada in at tenth.

	Location	KFC	Rank
1	China	7,166	169
2	U.S.A	3,943	12
3	Japan	1,140	186
4	S. Africa	960	30
5	U.K.	928	35
6	Thailand	853	139
7	Malaysia	770	124
8	Indonesia	742	163
9	Australia	699	27
10	Canada	601	26

In central Hanoi, the little girl was selling her balloons situated in the middle of the road. To her left was the KFC I headed into. The way it works out there is you walk into the road and people walk around you, I did it on that road and that seems to be how it is.

From these Big Three Fast-Food Chains

In accordance with the world health organisation, *'more than 1 billion people worldwide are obese – 650 million adults, 340 million adolescents and 39 million children*[154]*'*. We can be certain that this has consistently increased over the years.

With the ease of access to these big three fast-food outlets, looking at this data, the top two have most outlets in 80% of the nations that sit in the top half of the obesity ranks and then KFC is fifty – fifty, which is interesting. In total 21 nations within the top half of the obesity rankings have the most outlets of these top three fast food companies. Only nine countries are in the bottom half of the obesity rankings out of thirty. Let's be honest, these fast-food giants will more likely go where the perceived demand and money is, giving those with more cash in their pocket another fast-food option for the companies to profit from. They know what the

sums are and what places to target, looking like it's going to slow down anytime soon. These chain restaurants don't serve everything off the same menu in different countries. They do vary according to local tastes. To entice the locals yet the food all still goes through the fast-food processes to get their products to the customer to ensure profit margins are met. When I was in Thailand, the menu was slightly different than back home. They need to cater to local tastes ensuring sales are made, interestingly in Japan:

'The menu of KFC in Japan is one of a kind and has managed to blend in Japan inspired items like Wa-fu chicken cutlet, Natchan Sukkiri Orange, and Oolong Tea'[155]. Rice is big in Japan and is on the KFC menu, as it was also on the menus as I saw in Thailand. Subway do it, with examples being Brazil with their 'Smocked Chicken with Cream Cheese, Russia and the seafood sub and China with their Italian Sausage'[156]. All unusual combinations, yet if they sell well, then all the better for the business. MacDonalds also do the same, with Mc Spaghetti on the Philippines menu, Australia's Chicken Parmigiana Burger and Malaysia's Cookies & Cream Pie[157] being three examples. If anyone knows everything about their customers it's likely to be big

businesses, they will know everything about the customer to ensure they are making the profits for the restaurant in any location for a good chance to thrive. Many are franchises as the parent company became so big, so they adhere to the franchisor rules, policies, and procedures. One thing's for sure, these and similar food companies are here to stay, as long as people continue to choose their products.

The Energy Drink & Soda Scandal

As a youngster I only used to drink sugary fizzy drinks now & again, when I was allowed. Sports drinks were in the shops and advertised to TV, Ski brought out a yoghurt drink which I remember tasted so good. In my late teens workout / protein drinks were in the gym. Then the 'alchopops' appeared with two options, being quite a controversy at the time, in a few years the market was flooded with them. In recent times the surge in the energy drinks market is upon us, Red Bull was originally a big name but now the varieties of Monster alone I find unbelievable.

The global revenue in the energy & sports drinks segment of the non-alcoholic drinks market was forecast to continuously increase between 2023 and 2027 by 47 billion U.S. dollars (+24.32 percent). The revenue is estimated to amount to 240.24 billion U.S. dollars in 2027[158].

In an average high street shop, Fridges full of energy drinks, the main chiller for all the other soft drinks and all with their bright colour advertising to entice. Some of the designs on these cans is so eye catching, it mesmerised me as I looked to take the photo. The sheer amount of these on the shelves, it really is no wonder why the kids are drinking so much of them. We really need to get back to basics and to promote what is truly good for us, we are not designed for all these chemically manufactured drinks. All the sugar and the additives are not good, water is branded & healthier.

From the popular energy drinks that have all appeared in recent years to the more traditional fizzy drinks. One standard can of Coca Cola contains 39 grams of sugar, now let's get that into context. Try a little experiment for yourself, I have done this many times with clients. If you do drink these, look at the ingredients label. It will breakdown the sugar content but most likely per 100g not the full amount of the can. Let's say it's the number one soft drink sold in the United States and The United Kingdom is Coca Cola. A standard 12 oz can of the stuff contains 39 grams of sugar and 13.6mg of sodium. A teaspoon of sugar is the equivalent of 4 grams of sugar, so in that fizzy drink there is the equivalent just shy of 10 teaspoons of sugar. Do this for yourself, if there is cans or plastic bottles of sugary soft drinks in the fridge or cupboard get them out. Get a napkin and the sugar bowl or if there's a bag of sugar in the cupboard. Work out the amount in grams of sugar in the drink then spoon out the sugar with a teaspoon. This will show you just how much sugar you are consuming each time you have one can of drink. Don't think the 'diet' versions are much better as they are full of additives and fake sugar which is not good for us. The times I hear of people drinking this stuff daily as though it's such a treat, becoming a regular fix. It may seem like there isn't any sugar in the drink, it tastes great and gives a boost so it must be a win – win right, sorry no it's not. Taking in all that sugar and salt in each can, we must make the conscious connection of what is in these drinks. Drinking the artificial flavoured stuff as we see in that photo doesn't necessarily register with the individual of possible risk over time. Same with smoking, drinking alcohol etc it's what we really get used too. We're not here to go through those bad habits, just the ones making us and the world populations much bigger. When I worked in a local college to where I live one student I remember, daily he would bring bottles of energy drinks into college with him. He was always agitated as though either on an upper or downer with the drinks. We had a talk and he said how he just couldn't sleep, then got into a routine of drinking the stuff during the day to stay awake, then awake until late every night not being able to sleep. We wanted to get him off drinking these stimulant drinks, but he found it very hard.

What About Us

Junk Food Addiction

'Obesity researchers found fatty and sugary snacks trigger the same 'pleasure centres' in the brain that drive people into drug addiction – making them binge on unhealthy food'[159].

This has been known for years, so why haven't restrictions been placed on these fast-food companies. They are very rich and successful, but we do and should have the freedom to make our own choices, good or not so good.

'At the Scripps Research Institute in Jupiter, Florida gave rats electric shocks on their feet when they ate high fat food. Rats on a normal diet quickly learned to avoid the unhealthy food. But those used to junk food refused to let the shock get in their way of their high calorie food' [160]

The researchers found junk food altered the chemical balance in the brains 'reward circuits'[161] Furthering with the study took three years to complete and these results shows the impact of these foods. Personally, I tend to go through healthy phases, if I am training well then theres more incentive to be good. I do need a goal, that certainly helps but not by any means do I eat fast food regularly maybe once every couple of weeks. Some of the processed fake foods from the supermarket do make me feel weird and it must be all the additives, so I don't go near them anymore. I feel good for eating wholefoods, and when in South-East Asia I did get into the spices and exotic flavours. Fast food I tend to go for at convenience on a day out in London.

One of the big issues I find with people I meet who are keen to exercise as they are at the point of wanting to change but find it hard to change their lifestyle because so many influences. They prioritise the weight loss goal but there just doesn't seem to be enough hours in the day. If you can relate to this scenario, below are factors which can hamper setting goals, or we let them get in the way. The kind of obstacles I hear all the time, some we have already looked at and they are:

'I really want to lose weight, but I just don't have the time'

Yes, the odd snack / treat is fine, not daily. From the fast-food choices, . make it a rarity & put it into the same category with cigarettes and alcohol. We will feel better for it, as I state a choice meal at the weekend is acceptable. The less fast food the less need.

- It's the full-time job, the job is stressful and long hours.
- Getting the kids to school before heading to work to then be tired at the end of work and head home.
- When it is time to cook dinner, the kids as one likes one thing and the other likes something else.
- I don't have time to cook.
- There always sweets, chocolate and treats in the house for the kids.
- Your partner comes in and his dinner needs to be ready too, suddenly its 8pm. You have been on the go since 6.30am in your hectic daily routine, all you want to do now is relax for half an hour, then the kids go to bed which is another half hour of organising. Now its nearer 9pm, it's been another long day and exhausting.
- I don't like the foods that you have suggested (later we look at options)
- I'm so tired all the time after everything I do during the day.
- I like fried foods, chocolate, sweets, and it's my reward for a busy day.

How on earth can this person find the time or motivation in putting a strategy together to lose weight Being so busy every day, that planning a new strategy, sorting all the diet out and exercise is a mammoth task just how can it be done. The real question is yes you may desire so much to lose weight, but what action, what are you going to do to lose weight. We can be smart about it, looking at the strategies to do right now, which we will soon go through, incorporating physical activity to increase fat burning alone will get you on your way. Adding exercise sessions will increase the weight loss, even with such a long and hectic day we can build in the time needed for the physical activity strategies and exercise plan we will go through son. There is no quicker way to lose fat weight than combine fat shredding daily strategies with a consistently good diet and regular exercise.

I do understand this seems like a lot to do but I ask you the question again, how much do you want it. The strategies to incorporate into the day will give you good results straight away after two to three of weeks. This is about setting a goal, reaching it, and then maintaining your weight. It doesn't have to be hard, and it doesn't have to that time consuming. You won't feel hungry as this isn't a low-calorie diet, we will explore what your body is designed to do too. As you change your current routine your body will change and you will change, your food and drinks change, and it will get easier as you adjust to the new routine.

Habit

With sugar, our bodies send a signal to our brain to remember this nutrient and where we had it. We like the taste and get an energy boost from it and

Nibbles having a hard day

Many are emotional eaters, I have met quite a few that do use food as a comfort and reward. We know we have to break those habits, so replace food with something else. Make it a good habit though, not just another self-destructing one. There's a million and one good habits to adopt, from learning a new language, learning a musical instrument, even to exercise. Get down what you would like to do and do that instead.

our brains interpret this as a positive thing. We know what we really should be doing but it triggers a behaviour reward mechanism. This can link in a different way habitually, as in if you feel down then do something that makes you feel good. That is eat the food you like that is tasty to then you will feel better, if you're feeling down then eat the treat food, such as a burger & ice cream that will cheer you up. 'Once habitual responses are activated, people can act on the response in mind without making a decision to do so'[162], so it becomes an automated response. The interesting concept of mindfulness, 'mindfulness is a technique you can learn which involves noticing what's happening in the present moment'[163]. The problem solution of favourite food is it's a very quick fix, it doesn't last long then how do we feel. Well, the ice cream is all gone but do you feel any better? Weight is gained and then what, well that's not going to make you feel any better is it. As that pattern of behaviour keeps revolving, weight will keep being gained. Once a week treat is fine, that's going to be built into our strategy but if it creeps into regularly being 3 or more times a week must be reeled in. Seeing what we get from our destructive habits at a deeper level allows us to become aware. If we can rationalise that bad habits really do nothing for us except mask whatever the main issue is, it could allow us to not need that habit any longer.

The Chinese we get in the fast food form really is with added salt and sugar for the zing in its flavour. Lots of extra calories in this food, as mentioned. Traditional Chinese isn't necessarily unhealthy though. Home cook your Chinese with flavours from scratch much healthier and won't be a quick decision to just be a convenient treat.

We want the strategy of creating good new habits, which we are going through. Away from the comfort craving to a more constructive way. Soon we look at your habits and you will self-analyse what's going on, why you do it and we change it.

I looked at this too, as my habit was popping down to the local for a beer. When these social places were all shut during the lockdowns, I headed to the local benches by the creek water's edge after a few cans then head home. I sometimes head back to the creek then end up in the pub, after a few too many and too late. That is changing now, as I adopted this method of planning. As I review now, in 2023 that has cut down a lot as I am addressing the triggers to erase the habit. Clearly that repetitive behaviour became a habit but turning into a good habit in terms of my weight management with the walking. For some time, I would go down to the pub a lot, being a single man with evenings free it became too regular and the association thinking I would meet miss right. With the lockdowns and instability of work. Now, as of July 2023, one which I have consciously changed its not necessarily destructive any longer. What I found is as I kept thinking about the positive traits and in writing this book, my habits did start to change. I may have had spats where I wasn't as good but nothing like before. So new ways are formed and as I am finding the ways I want are happening and it is getting easier. Another example of changing the choice in a habit, I had a craving for chocolate and crisps over a couple of months, it was a Sunday evening. I had no beer on Saturday or Sunday and was really pleased with myself but by Sunday evening I'd had one packet of crisps then really fancied a chocolate bar and more crisps from the shop. I was ready to pop down there in the car but then I looked in the cupboard. There was a tin of Mackerel in a spicy sauce, I thought, 'oh I like that'. My craving suddenly changed as my focus changed, I had that with a piece of brown toast. Once full my craving was gone, the replacement option was much better. Lesson learned and practice what I preach, have more healthy things in the cupboard on standby for a craving, that's added to your strategy list. But was it really food or boredom that was the cause, making me think of the snack which I had got into the habit of popping out for, giving me a reason to not go to the pub. Our subconscious plays a big part in our lives, most of our daily routine we know how to do all of this from past experiences, making a coffee, preparing food, lighting the gas cooker, and boiling water. We know it all from past experiences, the same is said for what we choose to eat and our current routines. All from what we are accustomed to doing, especially all the bad habits. We are so used to certain patterns of behaviour that they become so ingrained that they are very hard to break. As we do them (the bad habits) more and more, our bodies change and we gain weight, which can become a perpetual motion of gaining more weight.

Now look at over the years what your regular eating habits and habits in general have been, can you remember? Probably not. This is not a test, just be truthful with yourself, how have you reached the point your body is currently at. Understand this is not a kind of guilt - punishment exercise at all, it is simply to make you aware what your routine, subconscious has been repeating 'habits' for you to gain weight. Reflect on the world tour of most and least obese countries and how people are affected with weight, their environment, the way they live, their habits. Now revisit how you live, let's look at how life and food impacts on you.

The Weekend Night Out

'Last night I had around 5 pints of beer, I think, two Popadom's, a lamb madras, mushroom rice onion Bhaji & coffee'.

A phrase all too common, that's around 2000 calories in total, then in the morning without a training session thanks to the inevitable headache. That's another possible 300 to 400 calories not burnt, we could say it's a difference the equivalent of well over half a pound of fat just in under 20 hours. Many would do that and then just think, oh well I've ruined all my efforts for the week in one evening. Wrong, that's a one off now get back on the wagon and make a difference, having a defeatist attitude will not get you or any of us anywhere. In my mind I would be thinking training session in the morning, then gym and then thinking of the weeks routine next week, eating healthily and cutting back on the beers. I'm not thinking, oh well might as well just eat and do what I want, for me that is not positive. I like healthy food and I like social drinks and I like to be in shape. I look better and feel better for it. It leads to doing other positive things, visiting new places seeing friends and getting out there.

Strategies on a night out :
- Plan to walk to the restaurant, even 5 / 10 minutes walk away
- Start off with a water then one in between alcoholic drinks
- Only allow two alcoholic drinks
- Drink slowly, two maximum over the course of the meal
- Go for healthy based dishes such as chicken onion & peppers or mixed grill, salads & lemon juice
- No dishes or sides heavy with sauces
- No Bhaji or fat / calorie ladened sides
- A rice is ok, boiled rice a staple

I know it can be easier said than done, after a busy week you deserve it but if you do over indulge, identify and address it. Following the points on nights out can be tough and sometimes a slippery slope but it does get easier in time. I find it's that 'three drinks and let go' scenario, enjoying the evening, then the drinks get flowing. Don't allow that to happen as you are in control, relax and enjoy but stay focused on your goals.

Binge Eating Disorder

'Binge Eating Disorder or (BED) was originally considered a sub-clinical derivative of Bulimia Nervosa (appetite of a bull) but is now considered a condition in its own right. BED can be mild or severe'[164]

Such characteristics include within a two-hour period eating a lot more food than normal, more than once a week. I have seen a client do this, others have explained they do similar & too often, there can be psychological issues at play here so further action in seeking doctor's advice is always recommended. Once I had got a client into a regular eating pattern, they didn't realise they were hungry as they didn't have a pattern with food. We focused on being active and a structured food plan, they started to see good results. It was hard for them to not fall back into the old ways, but they tried and persevered.

Causes of obesity, medical examples

There is some terminology which would be good to understand. Neurological refers to the area of the nervous system and secondly Endocrinological is about dealing with the endocrine system, which is our body's hormones. As we are looking more at general obesity due to lifestyle choices, below are factors which cause obesity outside of our control.

- **Hypothyroidism**
- **Disorders of corticosteroid metabolism, e.g.: Cushings syndrome**
- **Sex hormone disorders, e.g.: hypogonadism; ovariectomy**
- **Other hormone disorders, e.g.: Insulinoma; growth hormone deficiency**
- **Polycystic Ovarian Syndrome**
- **Hypothalamic Tumour brain damage or infection**
- **Congenital abnormalities e.g.: Prader-Willi syndrome**

'However, these represent less than 5% of cases of obesity in the UK, the vast majority of which is termed lifestyle obesity'[165] .

Rather than going into detail for each condition, if it doesn't affect you carry on. As we can see from the 5% statistic, the biggest portion of obesity is down to ourselves. This is the very people we are looking to cater for, if you are affected by any of these specific conditions, please seek the further advice of a specialist via your G.P. From the above examples I have worked with a client with Polycystic ovary syndrome, and regular exercise really did help them to lose weight, I see them in my local town and can see they are really making a difference to themselves, which is great to see.

Physical Activity Deficit

WHO defines physical activity as 'any bodily movement produced by skeletal muscles that requires energy expenditure. Physical activity refers to all movement including during leisure time, for transport to get to and from places, or as part of a person's work'[166].

There are numerous health benefits to us from physical activity beside exercise. It's all about the effect of getting our heart rates up (we go through heart rate zones in section 10) more manual work is likely to involve more physical activity when compared to an office job. Now as we rely more on technology with smartphones and the like we don't have to get about as much as we may have done in the past. A lot of our attention is taken by that gadget we carry around with us all day, (for so many of us) which doesn't need any physical activity to use, just a couch and to watch, same with the TV, games console and so on.

When I am out often, I might walk a distance, it can seem like such an inconvenience when the car is just sitting there making a quarter of an hour walk turned into a four-minute drive. I worked that distance out getting to my local gym, the walk seems like such a distance when it is fifteen minutes. But when you don't have the time, that extra 30 minutes overall does add up if that's how we perceive it. Then after the four-minute drive and not the walking for 30 minutes, the takeaway meal from the local Chinese adding a couple of thousand calories with high sugar content in the sauces adding to the calorie intake and less in overall calorie burning. We need to get everything going our way, so the weight starts to come off.

One way to think of it is a kind of life scales, tip the scales into your favour with regular physical activity added in with the other positive weight loss factors and you will be well on your way to reach your goals. Be aware of what you are doing, as you become conscious of your actions it will show you where the weight has come from, become mindful of this.

We go into Thermogenesis, with various ways we burn calories other than exercise, suffice to say as a nation and of the most obese factors such as physical activity are down the list and are likely to mean the populations are generally quite physically inactive. It's not about suddenly doing lots of physical activity as your body needs to adapt, so as we go through in the thermogenesis section, just become more active as seen in strategies to get you moving more soon.

'Experts have calculated that the extra physical activity involved in daily living 50 years ago compared with today was the equivalent to running a marathon a week, and in this modern-day convenience society it is extremely unlikely that those very high levels of continuous daily physical

A marathon being 26 miles, on average we can burn 100 calories per mile so over a marathon its 2600 calories. Consider that in a week, 1 pound of fat is 3500cal so it's not far off that in terms of overall lack of weekly exercise.. Consider a population which does less manual and physical work daily and an increase in automated and sedentary jobs daily. It just shows how inactive a population has become. It's showing across the developed world and needs to have a balance. As I write this it is Sunday 1st of October, 2023 it's just gone 2pm and already I have run 10k this morning. I had an early Saturday night and an early planned dinner.

activity will ever return.'[167] If you perceive it as too much to change your ways as with anything in life, nothing will happen and the next three, five and six months will pass anyway. A big desire to lose weight will still be there but with no sound plan nor consistent action to change, there will be no change. The negative cycle will keep going, if you go through this whole book taking notes to structure your plan, where will you be in one, three, six months from now, well you will be in a far better place for you. I have been a regular gym trainer and I do enjoy it. My level of fitness is good, and I push myself within my capabilities. After each session I feel relaxed and invigorated, yes as I have said I fall off the wagon like most of us as I am not some fitness guru saint who won't touch a beermat let alone go nowhere near a pint of lager. But I am healthy most of the time, so my weight stays in check, it's all about finding your balance and what your motivations are. I find a training session does invigorate me and help clear my mind, which helps. Let's be honest, we may have a model way we want to live our lives but with habits there we don't want but don't seem to change them. How do I want to be, I was drinking beer and eating too much fast food during the pandemic lockdowns. At that point, my weight hadn't really been affected as I had trained regularly and was walking a lot. Things are very different now, setting goals does help.

Food Routine and Habits

Task: 2

- **Let's look at your food routine & habits :**

Right now we are now going to look at everything you eat and drink over the next seven days. If you are unable to recall today's food & drink then start from tomorrow morning, on your pad write down absolutely everything you put into your mouth and what you drink throughout the whole day, morning until night for each and every day. Record exactly what it is and how much was there, was it the whole box of chocolates, all of the leftover cake? Write it all down and hide nothing there's no shame here in being honest with yourself. Record the time of the food you ate and the drink you had, was it early or late in the day ?

- *Over seven days write down everything you eat and drink*
- *Record how you felt at the time, what was your mood was you happy or sad ?*
- *What time of day was it ?*
- *You MUST do what you have always done, don't change anything for this record*
- *The record will show you what's immediately going on with your diet*
- *Appendix A is an example showing a full record (creating breakdown is optional)*
- *Appendix B is an ideal example of what a good daily record should look like*
- *Appendix C is a breakdown analysis of the full record A and comparative of Appendix A and B.*

If your first meal starts early in the day, then you have the day to burn off the calories. If it's later in the day, the next thing you will do is sleep so will only have your sleep time to burn those calories. No time of the day so the likelihood is you will not lose weight, more likely gain weight. Here we are looking at how you use food, is it to feel better? If you are unhappy, does the food you choose make or crave make you happy or is it something to distract your feelings? In these scenarios we are unlikely to choose foods that are necessarily good for us. I'm not saying this is always the case but there will be a tendency if food is being used other than hunger this is likely to be times when the doughnuts or favourite 'treat' foods or drinks are chosen. In your record Don't make any food or drink changes, do what you have always done, do not change anything. Don't suddenly change so that the record looks better than it might have been. That will leave you more confused than before, or more to the point it will not show to you what you are doing wrong, as you already are likely know what you are doing but don't want to admit it to yourself or change it as the naughty stuff tastes just too good. That's what I do see when people 'make adjustments' to their weekly intake record. Sometimes they are embarrassed to do what they normally do so change and start 'a new diet' as they are recording the information for me to look at, they are doing this to hide what is really going on. I have no opinion of someone's diet, the truth is there to be looked at and work with it accordingly to make the right adjustments. There will be eye opening truths you must face, which will present itself to you. It will show you answers straight away of what's really going on and will be the first part of your change. You can take this information on board and move forward to the next instruction. Look into each item of food and drink recorded and work out the amount of sugar & fat contained in it all, I bet you will be shocked. Look at Appendices A, B, and C for an example what an ideal day should look like and C the analysis. I hope you get an idea, and good meal examples we will go through soon. This will show you the daily habits, the extent of weight gain that has been going on through what you consume why am I saying this? I mean, you know what you are eating and drinking daily don't you? In many cases when I have worked with people, much of the food they eat in a day is simply not mentally recorded I mean all the snacks, coffees, handful of gummi bears, the doughnut at the office with a coffee as it's a colleagues birthday treat and so on. Record everything as well as main meals. Food used as a treat, a craving, a habit many other reasons than being its dinner time…. look at this and you will take the first step to altering this pattern you are currently in. Popping to McDonalds for a quick breakfast before heading into the office, as an example & ordering one double sausage and egg McMuffin is 551[168] calories of which 32 g fat and 12g saturated fat. For the size of the so-called food and with the hash brown in at 140 calories[169], plus large cappuccino at 128 calories[170] ,total calories being 819kcal. Also quite worrying is the total amount of fat in all three items at 51 grams but if the saturated fat the McMuffin contains is separate from the recorded 32 grams & is extra, then taking the total up to 63 grams of fat, that will bump up your daily calorie count.

'Food Diaries*[171] can give us a whole range of information, including:

Likes and dislikes	Shows how good, or bad the choices
Eating Habits – snacks/rituals/times/mood/etc	Shows to you habits you may not know
Social life – restaurant/pub/takeaways/etc	Is there big influences linked to social
Total calorie intake	Working this out shows excess intake
Amounts of carbohydrate, protein and fat	Shows an overview of your macros
Quality and types of carbohydrate protein and fat	Processed, fast food, poor choices
Portion sizes of different food groups	Just how much are you eating a day
Vitamin and mineral intake	Micronutrients, good choices are better
Fluid intake	Water, juices and how much sugar
Alcohol intake – habits, units etc.	Showing what's going on daily/weekly
Variations at weekends or during a holiday, etc	So 7 days represents our weekly habits,

While average daily intake for women in the UK is 2000 and for men it's 2400[172], that can be too generalised, we go through our own specific daily calorie needs soon. From my experience working with people this is a big factor. The size of that example fast food breakfast meal isn't very big. Meaning it can be finished off easily, with that total calorie amount of 901kcal at 63 grams of total fat is astronomical. Swap that for a home cooked two scrambled eggs in at around 80 calories a piece and one slice of thick granary toast at around 112 calories. Reducing the calories to a far less and better nutritional totalling 192, a difference of 702 calories. Now looking at the calorie content from your daily food record and you will see what has been going on. The first point to consider is the daily calorie intake of these fast food and processed food / high calorie drink examples. Weight will be gained without any comprehension of it happening we don't generally make the link between the food and weight-gain, we need to know what is in that stuff. The food can seem similar, but the calorie amount can vary so much between wholefoods and fast foods.   Added the factor of time of day you are eating / drinking is it early or does a lot of consumption happen late into the evening. Record, look at and consider why, if you are snacking a lot which is another habit which needs to be changed. To repeat the task from this point on for seven days make that record accurate to you. I would suggest you analyse and workout the total amount of calories you are consuming in a day, check the averages to see what is going on. Remember, don't forget ALL drinks, alcohol, fizzy drinks tea coffee, snacks, even sauces on food.

Everything with all the example guideline points, the more detailed info the more it will present to you what is going on and what needs to change.

If you are too busy to go through it during the week, just make sure everything is written down then give yourself Saturday morning to go through the details of your weekly regular intake. Analyse at the macronutrient level,

A drive-thru order for a breakfast, I took the photo a while ago after getting two extra hash browns for free. Good or bad, well the total calories there is the single muffin in at 423 Kcal and the three hash browns totalling 420 Kcal. All adding up to a whopping 843 kcals for a breakfast with a colossal 47 grams of fat. It's no wonder where the weight comes from if this kind of breakfast is normal for some people.

breaking down fats, with carbohydrates and protein. This will give you that clearer picture of what you are taking in, calories and all again refer to Appendix A, B and C. We will look at the Glycaemic index ranking of carbohydrates in the diet analysis section, but now we can only really go on all processed / convenience foods are of low nutritional quality and high Glycaemic Index the 'of which sugars' on their nutritional breakdown is an

extra bad news. Where the likelihood of sugar added to a product, there are apps out there and further guidance to show the presence of added elements. We should be having zero refined sugar as it's not good for us, but it just so happens its added to so much. Remember wholefoods, foods in their natural state such as apples, broccoli, cauliflower . With the seven-day record take ownership of this and work out just how much sugar, fat, empty calorie intake you are consuming. Read the food labels (which we will go through soon) and discover just how much sugar, fat and salt is in there. Now picture what has been going on in your body from food and drink consumption over say the last 12 months. It's more of all the bad things for use in sugar, fat, with salt and additives.

How did it go

What was your food and drink intake for the day, were they all choices you realise or was you shocked at exactly what you are eating and drinking over a 24-hour period. Did you work out the total calorie amount and if you did, was it what you expected? Did you discover what your habits are, what times did you regularly eat at do you have a regular eating pattern at all? Is there a lot of snacks in there? Is there a lot of processed foods, takeaways, late night eating? How was the drinks record, if you socialise regularly did you record exactly how many drinks you had? Seeing just what you are having on a weekly basis will present itself to you straight away as you then read through the record, self-disclosure, self-realisation. Has this shown you are a bit of a naughty porky, bit of a guilty feeling seeing just how much you are sneaking in there under your good consciousness radar?

This task is all about self-realisation and not kidding ourselves, our bodies don't lie.

Well done and if everything looks great food and drink wise then it can't possibly be your diet then, and I don't believe you. Weight does not come out of thin air I'm afraid, some naturally have faster metabolisms than others however, big rolls of subcutaneous fat don't just magically appear from thin air. If you are thinking that then no, sorry there's no blame diversion on this one I'm afraid, now take it on board and change your ways. If I'm wrong, then get a professional examination but as I have stated, the larger percentage of weight gain is all about the food and drink consumed. I don't want to sound harsh, but it really is up to you and please be truthful with yourself. Once you can admit it all to you that is a great start on the way to where you want to be. Wishing it all away with no real plan & affirmative action will be just that and will cause you more misery. Not linking your actions to results you are seeing of yourself won't change anything, we need action! If the record is not a full and true reflection of what you can been eating and drinking full over the week, the only person being deceived here is yourself. Remember this is not me having a go at you, it's just how it is. Be constructive and see for yourself what is going on in your life for the week truly, look at it and we move forward together. I hope there has been new discoveries / realisations in your food intake. That is part of breaking these now past habits and we are going to put in a new program which will allow you to create new habits of reward other than what has been going on. You need to be aware of the principles of good food intake not only weight management principles in losing the unwanted weight but the health benefits and these we will go into in detail along with the benefits of exercise. These three factors are crucial.

Food & drink choices / Environment / Physical activity / Exercise

Portion Size

One aspect which is worth addressing is portion size, we have looked at how much our individual metabolisms will need in a day in terms of macronutrients, but you don't have to fully calculate your daily needs. That is up to you, if you follow all guidelines then you will have great results anyway. The idea is for you to understand the quantity of food that you may need a day, another way to look at is through portion size. As I don't know your habits or see your food record it could be the portion sizes you have are very large. I have made it clear we don't want to feel hungry at all, we must feel full, and we must mostly go for the natural foods which are less calorific but will look like more on the plate. Also consider your portion sizes just to be aware if before any changes there was a lot more at each meal. A typical portion size could be considered the following from the NHS[173]

- A fist size of potatoes, bread, pasta or other starchy carbohydrate
- A palm size of meat/fish or poultry
- Two handfuls of vegetables or salad
- A cupped handful of fruit
- Top of your thumb size of oil or fat spread

A simple and clear analogy to use the hand to measure a portion size. Could it help to reduce what's on your plate, being a different strategy when you are on your treat meal at the weekends.

Label reading

Further to what we have just discussed, how often when you have bought your shopping have you ever sat down and read the labels on the foods you buy of the item's nutritional breakdown? We can be so busy with our lives that we race to get everything done and then there's more to do. We need to be aware on the back of the principles and choices we have seen and how to understand what a satisfactory option is or not in our shopping basket.

The example of tinned tomatoes, the total contents is 400 grams. Looking at the breakdown a lot of products do this, either 100 grams or half a can, not the full contents. Make sure you understand what the full contents are and just how much sugars, fats and salt there is. As an example, under the 'per 100g' it states 21kcal, which sounds fine. Also the 'of which sugars' is 2.7 grams also is fine, but as mentioned the can is 400 grams in total. So it's not 21kcal it's 84kcal per tin and 'of which sugars' is 10.8 grams.

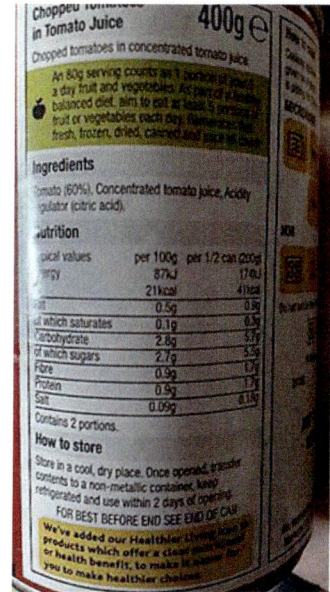

Get used to the way marketing to convey a certain message of health could be used to trick you into thinking something is healthy when in fact it isn't. Ignore the marketing promotion and go straight to the nutrition label. Make sure you understand what it is saying, and we need to have those 'of which sugars', and fat / saturated fat as low as possible. Start to read the labels, make it become more important and part of your shop, so you start to become more aware of where the extra energy, and weight is coming from besides the choices in poor foods, any tinned label that has 4 grams 'of which sugars' is the equivalent of one teaspoon of refined sugar. You will be surprised what you will find on your food labels, a tin of tomatoes can be a lot of sugar added. Check all contents, fat and sodium.

What's distracting Us from being healthier?

As with the perspectives we saw on the global fat finding mission, there are lots of reasons mentioned which are causing us to reduce awareness of our health through food and drink. Ok so I was a bit harsh about the results if you fibbed a bit, but for good reason. One of the distractions can be the powerful lure of the bad foods you really do like and maybe feel like you just cannot stop. Well, you can, and you know you can at least cut it in half straight away and gradually replace with good. As a general population we are working long hours for comparatively less wages, increased living costs over the last twenty plus years, technology is relatively cheaper, televisions, consoles and computers, smartphones, fast food all affordable and available to the western world populations. That's great but if its ever increasing costs to keep a roof over your head, rent or mortgage with council tax, bills etc then it's just not working out with a balance. More people are staying at home and increasing sedentary lifestyles, which only accelerated thanks to the two years of covid restrictions and the lockdowns of 2020.

These are acting more as a distraction to what we really need to be focusing on the main factor is our health. To achieve this, we really need to look at our lifestyles and just how much we are consuming what we are consuming and to get away from the 'treat' mindset. This must be raised in priority within yourself, these distractions can be getting in the way of much of our good intentions. Food has played a huge roll in giving us a reward as a treat rather than to give us nourishment to function at our best.

Modern life is at a fast pace as we link food and drink more to cater for us at an emotional level rather than just the essential need. The ways of South Korea, with Japan and Vietnam three examples showed their traditions with food resulting in their population statistics in relation to good health. A lot of that reasoning is we now have more choices and the fast food once a treat is getting cheaper. We want it all now, it does seem like getting to the end of a working week is enough and then to relax and do whatever which is understandable.

In my years of working with people in the health and fitness industry I have seen this too much, and I want you to understand what your body is designed to do. For you to fully control your lifestyle and cement good habits which become so ingrained in time you won't even realise you are doing the right thing. It will just feel and be the right thing. Friends / clients tell me they become more active daily, with say an extra walk to the train station but then reward themselves for it. An example being a chocolate croissant and latte at the station, a treat after the extra effort they put in to get active. The problem is those extra calories counteract any calories they had just burned on the walk and likely adding more. Now don't get me wrong, they are getting great health benefits for walking extra, but they are not going to see any shift in weight which is their main motivation to do it. This activity increase will stop sooner rather than later as they go back to driving to the station, having that extra 25 minutes in bed. 'That's a no to that walk, what's the point'. The real point is it's good for you, but the perception is 'will it lose weight, no I won't bother with this, I'm staying in bed'.

It may be a gradual process, not all change straight away. Ensure you are thinking what you want regularly and making changes, the more you think and focus on it and the more you act on it the changes will come over time. I find to mack such life changes just keep going, you may not be spot on all of the time but over the weeks you will adapt. You will change and improve towards where you want to be. The aim point here is to keep at it and have high expectations of yourself taking appropriate action.

What are we designed to consume

Taking a regular trip through the supermarket on a weekly shop, I am always aware of what people are selecting and buying. Mainly when I am in the queue waiting at the checkout. There is a clear correlation I have witnessed time and time again to the frame and weight of the individual to what is being chucked onto the conveyor belt, sadly I'm proven right time and time again. My regular shop involves fruits, vegetables, meats, fish, dairy and pasta, potatoes, oats, grain, bottles of water and tins of tuna. I generally stay away from pre-packaged, processed foods. Those I see consistently overweight their turn at the till displays all packaged foods, sweets, ice cream what I have mentioned and term 'treat based' foods. These lifestyle habits are built over time and much of that energy dense food is normal meals for them. Add in extra snacks and alcohol, Chinese, Indian & the calorie intake is much higher for them relatively than an average daily intake. It's no wonder the populations are facing real problems with this perpetual increase of weight gaining habits. If I look on a weekly basis, my breakfast, with lunch and dinners are mostly healthy wholefoods. Any flavour added to meats / fish are made from scratch or at most a sachet, and not a whole jar of sauce. Or spices to flavour meats, such as a hot sauce.

Rank	Country	Average life exp.
1	Japan	84.7
2	S.Korea	83.3
3	Norway	83.3
4	Switzerland	83.2
5	Iceland	83.1

See Japan & S.Korea also have such low obesity rates in our rankings....

I mostly I have home cooked meals, I don't generally do snacks like crisps or chocolate as if it's not there I won't have it. Maybe a couple of chocolate pieces out of a pack & only when it's there that's not a regular thing, ah you might say you don't have time to cook often. The message at this point is see and realise what you have been doing in terms of food and drink intake, eat wholefoods for most of the week and drink water. Increase your daily activity from now, the calorie burn will increase week by week, month by month then the difference you will see in yourself. As we will see, this can be done in any way with any activity as long as it gets your heart rate up consistently. The point I am getting across is it's a gradual effect, we need weeks for change not days or a week. We can see that Japan is ranked number 1 in life expectancy[174] their diet is one of rice, fish, vegetables, seaweed and more all being in their natural state, the article furthers. We will go through Ideal meal examples with the what's and why's soon enough. Taking it further, the source of the good food needs to be considered what conditions and the environment. How organic are foods, really and what chemicals are used to enhance production. It could be considered the less used the better to retain the nutritional benefits of good foods. I have noticed sometime when I get supermarket fruit for example, tomatoes have less taste than homegrown. The processes of growing crops are out of the scope of this read, but worth considering in the future as you progress in your weight management and onto a better lifestyle.

It could be said that the fresher more natural items are more costly than the pre-packed, processed. Meats from the fresh counter or organically grown produce. An area for consideration, yet items like bread from the supermarket and a lot of what's considered fresh items contain additives for prolonged shelf life. It then becomes practicality and cost offset to convenience and affordability. Having said that, we are focused on weight loss but Ideally, it's all considered.

Macronutrients

Carbohydrates

In all fruits and vegetables, grain and cereal and lactose in dairy such as milk, now it can be confusing as they can be considered different food groups in many examples, but this is the case. Our strategy is to stay away from the refined sugar, the high Glycaemic Index ranked carbs. Sugar and wholegrain bread both are carbohydrates but in different forms, the first is simple while the bread is complex. We need to focus on the complex and remove the simple like the stuff added in tinned items and processes, fast foods and drinks. It's all carbohydrates but different forms, the complex takes longer for the body to break it down needing more energy so less likely to be converted to fat stores than simple carbohydrates the 'of which sugars', as I do keep repeating, wholefoods especially carbohydrates are not the enemy but the refined sugar, simple carbs are. We must understand what carbohydrates are then it won't be an issue in weight gain. We will go through the Glycaemic Index examples of carbohydrates soon and that we should aim at only medium to low G.I. carbohydrate foods or more complex carbs. Not the high G.I. types such as sweets, sugar and the more in processed and tinned foods unless it's stated otherwise. In Vegetables, there are examples of vegetables being low G.I. ranking, such as lettuce' Spinach and Bok choy but yes all do contain carbohydrates. Many are high in fibre and with the good nutrients contained ideal healthy choices. Fruits, again all do contain carbohydrates, but as we will see soon good examples of medium to low G.I. choices.

Protein

We need also for muscles to repair among other benefits, and we also do use a lot of energy to break down and digest this macronutrient. As mentioned, we need to go more for the lean white meats, less processed and red meats. They're fine, once or twice a week maximum I do love a barbeque and during summer, I really do go for the meats of the grill, Fish is a great option too.

Fat

We do gain essential fats nutrients in different ways from our food especially from meats and fish. Cooking in good fats is fine too, the issue again is the hidden more unhealthy fats in fast food, processed food and the like. We do need fats in our diet and not to just stay away from it but we mostly should choose the right fats. The fats we get from foods should also be in as natural state as possible. Further examples being Avocados, whole eggs (protein), fatty fish too, nuts, cashews & Pistachios and in natural yoghurt less trans fats, hydrogenated fats (more in processed and fast foods) and those more solid at room temperature. Don't get me wrong a bit of butter in cooking on a jacket potato is ok, but mostly use Monounsaturated and polyunsaturated fats in cooking. Olive oil, rapeseed and sunflower oils are ok.

Micronutrients

Are the vitamins and minerals we need which come from a healthy well-balanced diet. Taking away a macronutrient from our diet, as many fad diets do suggest can cause deficiency issues like cutting out Carbohydrates, 'Starchy foods are a good source of energy and the main source of a range of nutrients in our diet. As well as starch, they contain fibre, calcium, iron and B vitamins'[175]. If we fully understand what our bodies need in terms of good macronutrients and micronutrients, then we have a better understanding in how to lose weight and promoting our own health.

Eating Patterns

A Big Influencer

A huge part of weight management in my experience is getting a sound regular daily eating pattern. Many of the clients I have trained and helped to lose weight tend to not have any kind of regular routine with food. As simple as a regular routine may sound, for many this isn't a normal thing. I have seen a huge correlation between the overweight & obese directly linking them not having an ideal regular eating pattern. Many seem to eat as and when they want, eating irregularly, grazing and all sorts but not regular mealtimes containing the essentials we need. A pattern they must have got themselves into overtime so we will now go through examples I have encountered and then an ideal pattern to adopt for losing weight and maintaining.

The Evening Eater

Some time ago I was working with a friend I used to regularly train, we could never get his weight down by the target three stone. His fitness was good, he trained regularly, and he was eating healthily, I would see him only once a week, so what could it have been?

I realised what it was on spending a few days with him and seeing what his daily routine was. Getting up at around 5am for work to load up the van and head out to locations over 2 hour's drive away. He didn't have time to prepare in the mornings for a healthy breakfast or lunch. His regular routine was to grab something out of the coffee shop on route to a project. Regularly skipping lunch because of the busy day, then would get back around 6pm or later then eat a dinner and then eat further into the evening. As I was with him only a few days, I would prep my breakfast and lunch the night before and take it with me. As I got up at 5am I would have a healthy homemade smoothie drink in the van on route & a breakfast being mixed fruits of grapes strawberries blueberries and raspberries with 2 tablespoons of yoghurt. The first day we did stop and as I have a regular eating routine, I was hungry by 1pm but I didn't get to eat my lunch of salad and tuna until 3pm. My friend wasn't hungry, grabbed a small snack and coffee at the petrol stop in the morning and that was it. We can see he's in a routine of no regular meals with one big main evening meal then snacking in the evening.

We did stop off one day at a petrol station on the way back after doing a hard day's work, still with nearly two hour's drive. He was looking for chicken bites, but the place didn't sell them, what was available was tikka bites. I checked the label, in a pack of 15 which wasn't big and could easily be eaten as a snack which contained 500 calories, from the size of the pack two could easily be eaten in no time. That would have totalled 1000 calories, with added sugar salt and glucose syrup for flavour & preservative it's a typical example of an energy dense snack. This kind of eating will not help weight loss, along with work it was physical but not getting the training effect of burning fat. The nature of the work was constantly stop and start, so as much as there is physical activity, if the lifestyle diet is not planned well then there is limited benefits for weight management. There is strength gains from the physical work which is a benefit. It is hard in many instances as our daily routines dictate when we can eat and drink, working out these obstacles can be done but it must be part of a planned and ongoing routine.

I have advised to prep good food examples the evening before and two to three days before the day's work and to get into that routine. Get regular mealtimes, start early and finish early with the last meal around 6pm there is plenty of hours / time to burn fat before the start of the next day. The routine here does seem to be eating later into the evening to compensate for the lack of food during the day. Take good calories in a drink on route to work, high protein low G.I. sugars, which we will go through and there must be time for lunch around 12 / 1pm. Then the final meal and no other calories after by 6pm which doesn't have to be gospel, just a guide if it's three out of five days is ok. If this can be instilled over the working week changes will start to take place in a few weeks. But again, as my friends work pattern and balancing with a family and everything else it's not easy, however that bit of prep and understanding what needs to be done means he will be on the right path to weight loss.

A similar scenario to above, another friend I helped with some training sessions and checked their daily pattern of eating revealed they skipped breakfast and lunch with only having dinner then eating late into the evening. Their physical activity was relatively low as they sat at a desk most of the day. The difference from the previous example is a lot was carb heavy, sweets and treats eating in the evenings. I helped to try and get them out of the pattern, as they sat opposite me at the desk where we worked. Just to have a healthy homemade breakfast drink of oats, milk and fruit was very difficult. A few mouthfuls and they were full, again the key is persistence. Over time the body will adapt to the new lifestyle, they wanted to lose weight and tone up, but this was their habit that needed addressing along with a regular exercise plan. To work out of such a pattern could take time, once the new habit is the norm it gets much easier.

Feast and Famine

One client I worked with over a few months was big, in the high 20 stone range. He had no daily eating pattern at all, going for 24 to 36 hours without eating anything. Then, and I was a witness to this, he would consume thousands of calories in one go. I worked it out to around 5000 woofed down in one sitting. Large chicken kebab, chili and burger sauce, a cheeseburger, mars bar then slices of pizza washed down with a can of coke then pints of lager. As I stood there watching my jaw virtually hit the floor and it was clear to see why he was so big. If you want to gain weight that is the perfect way to do it, all in one go then nothing. Talk about storing calories, we need calories for energy but doing that will store a lot of it as fat. Excess calories all in one go is not good, regular eating patterns is all about topping our bodies up with fuel, which is then more likely used by the body, much of it being converted to energy. Taking in so much at once means we are only going to use so much and then convert the rest to fat stores and more with not using any of the calories through physical activity nor exercise of the day. He was doing this in the evening too, around eight o'clock so also not a good time pile all this stuff in either. That took a while to try and unravel, introducing a regular meal pattern. Again, it's not easy but with persistence and being consistent then absolutely you can change such a pattern.

Through evolution, our ancestors are likely to have been in a feast & famine situation as they would have to hunt and only ate what they could catch. Not quite the same scenario standing in a fast -food restaurant moaning that it's taking ten minutes for your number to be called is it ....

The survival of Homo sapiens during evolution was dependent on the procurement of food, which in turn was dependent on physical activity[176].So less likely to be fat as they had to use energy to get their food through hunting.

Bit different to walking into Tesco's to the meat counter picking up a pack of chicken, sauce and then over to the till to pay. Total number of calories burnt, just above zero.

The night fridge - raider

Another friend explained their eating patterns to me, well again no pattern but they would feel hungry and get up in the middle of the night and eat. Having no set pattern day or night was stressing them out and they didn't know what to do. They are quite unhappy with this situation but as with any lifestyle pattern as we get ourselves into it so, we need to coach ourselves out of it. We do listen to our bodies when it comes to eating, but to get out of such a pattern you must create a new a set routine and follow it. You may not feel like you want food so light meals at set times first to get the new pattern going then as you start to feel hungry at these set times your body is adjusting, and it will get much easier in time. The hard part really is to make the change and then sticking with it once it's underway the new pattern can be created. Again, three meals a day the traditional style breakfast, lunch then dinner starting early and finishing early.

The Calorie counter / constant grazing

I had seen an individual weighing in at over 30 stone with a bodyfat percentage nearly one half of their total bodyweight. They gave me a day review of what they had eaten, and it was all based on calorie counting. It seemed that the calories met their daily metabolic rate requirements to not gain nor lose weight. Yet everything was sweet being high in sugar and or fat, cookies, chocolate bar, wine and small bite snacks. It revealed this person was just constantly grazing. All small amounts but no actual meals, it turns out this person also had a gastric band fitted. Clearly it wasn't or hadn't worked as that made no impact on their figure or the calorie dense food choices. They had been down the diet path for years and as a result went for bariatric surgery and the result was the point, they had now found themselves in. It appeared the band encouraged this grazing as they felt uncomfortable to eat full meals, which is totally wrong. To be the weight and size they were, this day record was clearly not an accurate account of their regular food / drink intake, only truthful in the food selections & total calories on that day. Don't necessarily worry about calories, it's the content as when you eat wholefoods there will be more on your plate but less calorific and you will feel fuller. Counting calories really is meaningless when it's rubbish you are eating, think health first and treat second. That's why ideally you would record all your food and drink intake for 7 days, one week as I want you to uncover everything that's going on. I got the impression this potential client didn't want to change their food and they ended up not following what I said but eventually going the gastric bypass route, which is unadvisable. The sad part was what I gave all my advice of what we should do about this, they totally agreed then a few days later changed their mind. They didn't even try let alone fail......

The Calorie Counting trap, (unless you have a sound plan covering all aspects) can become quite a counterproductive habit, the idea means well but people can get caught up with only the calories. My advice is don't do it, unless you are sticking to it and with good food choices. It does become counterproductive unless you are being truthful with it that is. We have looked at how many calories a day we need, but it only works if we are sticking to the plan with the ideal good food and drink choices. It was clear the individual I was speaking to didn't and with gastric bands it doesn't cater for drinks nor actual healthy food choices. I always feel full after a meal and don't focus too much on calories as I know what I eat is relatively low calorific and I prefer this kind of choice. When I eat fast food, which isn't often and energy dense stuff like chocolate I can only have a few squares, otherwise it's too much.

This type of counting calories I do not like as it does not differentiate what the macronutrient / food is, only the quantity of calories in whatever it is you are eating. It doesn't matter if it's protein or carbohydrate or fat, a chocolate bar or fruit and that's where the problem lies. Technically you can eat anything when calorie counting say you have worked out your body needs 1500 calories a day. If you count everything you eat and drink, first it can be quite a negative experience, you tend not to look at if you are being healthy or eating rubbish. Just how many calories are you having a day then the aim to stop when you reach your target number. How it tends to be is that the healthier foods are lower calorific when compared to a chocolate bar or high sugared coffee. For many people when they do calorie count it tends to be hard for them to stick to and can break the plan. Remember, your body will spend more energy breaking good food down than the bad choices.

Shift Work Pattern

This can be hard in terms of prep for your daily food intake, doing a 12hour shift or changing patterns and working through the night. It would still mean sticking to the wholefood choices and making regular meals as you can. When there is real disruption to try and create any routine, there tends to be a grab for convenience foods. Try and get a plan that stops this, get the fridge filled up weekly with good options and prep your food when you know there is disruption to a regular pattern. If you don't have a regular pattern, work it out to make sure there is healthy snacks and things to grab for when you are on the go. I would like to think if you are very busy and working long hours that you are earning enough, so you can afford food to be delivered. That would help in making the right selections. Failing that get a day when you are not in work to prepare food and into the fridge for a few days.

My Regular Eating Pattern

I have always had a set pattern and my appetite pretty much links to how much training I am doing. The more active I am, I tend to have 4 meals a day as I naturally feel hungrier. If I have time away from a regular training plan, then my appetite goes down to three. I do stick mostly to regular mealtimes, and it doesn't have to be set in stone as I have mentioned. For me it's around 8am start and dinner generally no later than 6pm, start early and finish early to then get the big break between the last meal and the following morning. I've never really been one for snacks but if something is there on the side, such as crisps or a doughnut I might nick one. For me there is no effort, as I feel hungry in the morning, then afternoon and early evening. This routine was the same growing up and I really don't have to think about it. Most of what I eat is healthy and yes, I will have a few beers at the weekend if I fancy it & a curry or fast food once or even twice a week depending on what my schedule is like. I do make sure there is fruit to hand as snacks. I do have to be conscious of that and it does become a regular thing, as I do tend to get into the habit and out of it sometimes. It depends what work is doing, as with all of us we all have our own routines and must adapt to them accordingly. When I am on holiday, I am on holiday I relax from it all.

Other examples could include fussy eaters, it is a difficult one and can be worked with if they try lots of new different foods. In different healthy combinations to find new choices is a strategy, experimentation is the key here and the will to adapt to change. Having food in the house for the kids, preparing theirs and then you own is another potential obstacle. The time needed and then maybe having some of theirs which is extra made. Ensure you stick to your plan and theirs, best off encourage the family all has healthy food and create this good meal selection and routine. These habits must be broken, as said it is hard at first when the body is so used to the irregular way, but a plan of eating a small meal at set times over the following weeks will gradually break this and your body will become adjusted to the new habit. Then as you do, over time it gets easier and becoming suited to your body's needs, your body will automatically tell you the new way when it's time to eat and so you will have trained in a good habit. We will look at good food options soon which is part of your 'new diet'.

Strategies to get out of the patterns summary :

Evening Eater
I introduced a healthy homemade breakfast drink for her to have mouthfuls of at the desk 8.30 / 9am then to finish at lunchtime. Record consistently the evening food and set plan to reduce over week by week and increase intake at breakfast and lunch.

Feast & Famine
Implement regular set eating times, if they wasn't hungry didn't matter it was about getting the new habit.

Night Fridge Raider
Only allow healthy options in the fridge and being night, healthy protein options. Enforce the daytime regular three meal pattern. Over time the night compulsions subside.

Calorie counter / grazer
Remove the 'calories only' view and focus on good food choices, with set meal times and if uncomfortable with the band then half the meal. Then finish off 30 min / hour later.

Fussy Eater
Try different combinations of good foods, build a repertoire of meal choices you like which fit into the good food plan (we will see soon)

Preparing different meals
Focus on your goals and do not be tempted by others or their meal options.

Sound familiar, all examples are from people I have worked with, seeing the changes has been a real positive experience. Witnessing the difficulty to break their own habit and adopt the new one and then the adaptation over time is an eye opener, knowing your own pattern to then see others having to change and for some just how tough it has been makes me appreciate the magnitude of the task in hand. The key starting point is knowing that you CAN do it, you can, and you will.

Popular Diet Plans Out There

Being on a diet can be perceived as a temporary change in lifelong habits to lose weight and sold to people their plan will fix the problem. A diet should be seen as what we are doing to consume food and drink ongoing in our lives, not just for a point in time. What we are doing is not the same kind of diet, it is a way of living your life and your relationship with food and drink. Any diet which is good will contain all macronutrients and sufficient micronutrients for your body to be healthy. Anything else is just short lived and not doing what your body is designed to do. We are now looking at examples of diets and what they mean, not to just sell the dream of losing weight.

A brief explanation of each example now and I will highlight what I see about each plan. Then we will have a concept which will take the positive aspects into a practical plan which really encompasses what we have gone through and making it achievable for you. The following examples have been looked at from an impartial viewpoint from my experience in the industry of over twenty years, with all the studying and so on. From numerous books I purchase in recent years from the charity shops, there is a plethora of good source information for 50p to a pound in those places. We are looking at popular diets which I am sure you have heard of at least one or two.

The Paleo Diet.

The term refers to the Paleolithic period of our history, stone age era. During the hunter gatherer time, we were out there with a spear in hand hoping to catch a meal for the day and get some berries & nuts if they can be found. The missus may be often back at the cave getting things ready and us fellas would go off hoping to find something so the family won't starve. We don't have that worry today and we do have the luxury of making appropriate or inappropriate selections for our health, courteous of the supermarket or local shop. The Paleo diet follows simple principles of being unprocessed wholefoods, which I constantly preach that should be of the majority in our diets, being less additives, less unhealthy fats, higher healthy fats resulting in lower cholesterol and less inflammation and no hidden salt & sugars. High in fruit and vegetables, gluten free possibly if there is an

97

intolerance, naturally low to medium G.I. (Glycaemic index we will look at) rich in plant-based fibre and antioxidants, further health promotion.

'Meat, Fish, Nuts, Seeds, Fruits and Vegetables are the foods of the Paleo diet', furthering; 'We have become dependent on synthetic and heavily processed foods that are leading to serious health problems (diabetes and obesity)' and, even when we think were being healthy, were often eating food groups, such as grains, dairy and legumes, which causes digestive distress'[177] It is suggested.

.   Just stating 'change your diet and you will lose weight' is simple enough but sticking to a religiously health-conscious diet ongoing is quite a big call, with no junk or processed foods such as it suggests avoiding 'jam, marmalade, ketchup, BBQ sauce along with ready meals and fast-food furthering with rice, buckwheat, cookies, biscuits, cakes, crackers bagels oats cereals and beer'[178] to name a few off limits things. This sounds like quite a call, is it that bad to have some sauce on food, the research promoting oats for health too is out there. Make sure the treats are in moderation, as we will look at which to be fair, they do go into after with a view of moderation after which may seem confusing. The Paleolithic diet does demonstrate one of the principles I do like that sticking to whole foods, natural unprocessed foods. Yet as for the grain causing digestive distress, more inflammatory disorders are not necessarily common for everyone, same goes for dairy and Legumes. Like any intolerance, we must act accordingly but it's not necessarily a general complaint. I do like the Paleo diet, promoting health and with some good choices, if it only concentrates on the food part alone.

The G.I. Diet (Glycaemic Index)

The G.I. diet, termed 'glycaemic index of carbohydrate foods, the effect this will have on glucose and insulin responses and how this in turn impacts hunger and satiation'[179] is the ranking of all carbohydrates. Using a traffic light signal as shown below, carbs isn't just sugar, it's contained within all complex and simple carbohydrate items. Examples include grain, bread, potatoes, pasta, vegetables, fruits, dairy, obviously also the sugar in sweets and drinks. I have always said fat isn't necessarily the main enemy, as sugar and fat both need to be checked in foods. This is due to the amount added especially into pre-packed goods, generally the G.I. principle ranks different carbohydrates in terms of how quickly the body absorbs them. The quicker they are absorbed then the higher the G.I. ranking, the body

Glycemic Index :

Red   -   High
Yellow -   Medium
Green   -   Low

doesn't have to put much effort into absorbing say a teaspoon of sugar so unless that is used for energy its more likely to put fat weight onto your body. A low G.I food item such as peaches will take longer to process through your body and with the fibre content is likely to absorb less of the fruit-based sugar or fructose and therefore less likely to be converted to fat stores. Dr Jenkins invented the Glycaemic Index back in the 1980's

'Dr Jenkins wondered if all carbohydrates are the same. Are some digested more quickly, and as a result raise blood sugar levels faster than others? And are other slow-release, resulting in only a marginal increase in blood sugar? The answer, Jenkins discovered, is yes. He published an index – the glycaemic index in 1980, showing the various rates at which carbohydrates break down and release glucose into the bloodstream'[180].

Glycaemic Index does look at the different macronutrient of foods. Where the G.I. might say an item is low G.I. which is good, it may be full of additives like a sugar free soda which is also bad. An example of a friend of mine who drinks nothing but diet coke, which is green on the G.I. diet, but unhealthy. It doesn't necessarily address the quality of the food such as being processed & full of additives green also is soft margarine and the artificial sweetener aspartame, no consideration of additives. It's only interested in the Glycaemic index. While it's good to know the G.I. levels of all the carbohydrates and macronutrients we are taking in, which should be far more medium to low and only a few high per week, we need to know about all aspects of what we are eating and drinking as in are they healthy or not being a kind of nutrient ranking. It does address the different food groups and the carbohydrate ranking present in those.

The Keto Diet

A big trend it seems, in accordance with the NHS, 'this is a medical therapy for drug-resistant epilepsy. The Ketogenic diet can be effective art reducing seizure frequency and intensity in all types of epilepsy.[181]' So the origins were not about weight loss, it seems to be very high in fat, adequate protein, and very low carbs. It seems the high fat content on the keto diet is advised healthy fats, yet per gram fat is higher in calories than carbs. Our bodies need carbohydrates, converted to glycogen to fuel all major organs of the body. To eliminate may work for some time in converting fat to fuel but not ongoing and this could lead to a loss in lean muscle tissue and as we know muscle burns calories and fat, needing that energy. Yes, the principles do work for some when removing carbohydrates or have a minimum intake for a period, it cannot be an ongoing trend, such as going into a state of ketosis which is not good. Yet 'common short term side effects resulting from the initiation of KD have been referred to as 'keto flu', which encompasses symptoms including fatigue, headache, dizziness, nausea, vomiting, constipation, and low exercise tolerance.'[182]

I mean to lose weight you do not have to deprive yourself this can lead to the rebound effect of going back to old habits in time and worse. I have known past clients who have used this or Atkins, known to be one of the most popular diets ever. Dating back to the 1970's, restricted carbs and high protein and fat. There has been changes or developments in the diet plans over the years, yet the focus is on carbohydrates. In some cases, this proved successful over the short term. 'However, in response of the body to the withdrawal of carbohydrate which is used for immediate glucose utilisation is dramatic'.[183] Keto is all about being low carbohydrates, again not necessarily showing the whole macronutrient picture. It's not necessarily selecting nutritious foods, across our daily macronutrient needs but focus on the carbs, less sugary items. If there's bad habits, as soon as the keto diet has stopped, what then, the individual goes back to their old habits? If lean muscle is lost, which is likely then fat weight can go back on easier than before. Due to the likelihood of losing lean muscle in the ketosis process, which as highlighted helps to increase our daily calorie burning. Lose muscle, gain fat more readily when the diet is stopped.

The Carnivore Diet

In this diet plan the focus is on protein, 'people following the carnivore diet eat a diet of meats, fish, including eggs and dairy products, but exclude all vegetarian, or plat-based foods'[184]. It appears this diet avoids fruits, vegetables and grains which means there are certain micronutrients that aren't being included.

'it's more likely that people who try a meat-only diet for an extended period may end up like the singer James Blunt, who revealed that he had developed scurvy after attempting a carnivore diet'[185] according to an article, following his own meat only diet at Uni, apparently. Scurvy was rife amongst malnourished sailors in the 16th to 19th century, it shouldn't appear in this day & age. This seems to be an extreme version of the keto diet as there is no carbohydrates at all. All meats and the suggested items, which surely can result in the lack of micronutrients again taking out key elements of our required macronutrients. Even more worrying is that 'The carnivore diet can lead to an increased risk of developing heart disease because it prioritises foods that are high in saturated fat'[186]. It will also be low in fibre which can cause issues when trying to go to the toilet. Considered an extreme Keto diet, there's hardly any choices and seems the main principle is protein which we use the highest amount of energy to digest, which is one main proponent of any protein focused diet plan.

Fasting

Has been quite a trend in recent years with apparent doctors suggesting how it's such an ideal way to lose weight and gain health well, from my studies fasting which is abstaining from food 12 hours & longer is not advisable. Especially for the obese who's metabolic rate is likely to be high. To then fast would be a shock to the system, I have had conversations with very big people, and they say 'I must eat, I'm addicted to food, it's not like smoking or alcohol. They can be stopped, but food I must eat', I can see the logic with fasting as it literally removes food, which is the craving for some. While evidence is given of drastic weight loss, from my teachings:

'Still widely used as a method of either weight loss or preventing weight gain. It involves total abstinence from food intake and only allows water to be drunk for prolonged periods of time (usually an excess of 12 hours) The regime is also linked with perceived detoxification and is used as a cleansing routine – but is not recommended. Fasting has been used for centuries and is often linked to spiritual or religious doctrines, some teachings suggest that fasting has beneficial medical effects over a wide range of conditions but again, as a practitioner, to suggest fasting as an alternative to seeking medical treatment is neither credible nor ethical and should never be encouraged under such circumstances [187]'.

I wanted to add this quote from my studies as I had an open mind with fasting, being that there is so much promotion of it, but it really is not as good as some make it out to be regarding weight loss. Especially if we make a comparison to a healthy balanced diet. Having the discipline to reach set goals and doing the right thing for us, not have some mindset of trying to 'cheat it' when losing weight. The attraction as with all diets is the potential results, to quickly reduce weight and eliminate the issue of food selection. Wouldn't it be better to change the relationship with food and drink for the improvement of our health, further the potential dangers of fasting include:

'Fasting is not without its risks and particularly for obese people who may typically be consuming anything up to 5000 calories each day to maintain their level of obesity. The drastic reduction in calories could be an extreme shock to the system. Severe calorie reduction carries a risk of sudden death and so long-term fasting should be treated with extreme caution. They should only ever be used under expert medical care'[188] If the fasting is done and weight is potentially lost what happens after, nothing has changed no pre-existing habits have been altered. The likelihood is the individual goes back to their old habits, the food they have been eating hasn't been considered, has it? If there is a food plan linked to fasting, then follow the food plan. The impulses with food must be addressed as this could lead to a pattern of fasting and binging which in the longer term can be worse.

Intermittent Fasting

Here is information in accordance with Bupa a private healthcare provider[189] on the variations of intermittent fasting:

1.   5:2 diets
Here you consume only 500 to 600 calories for two days each week. On the other days you would eat a normal, healthy, and balanced diet with your usual calorie intake.

2.   16:8 plan
This involves eating during an eight-hour window and fasting for 16 hours. So, you could eat from 10am to 6pm and then drink water, milk, tea or coffee for the remaining time.

3.   Alternative day Fasting
For this form of IF, you'd fast every other day, which can be very difficult to maintain over the longer term.

4.   24 Hour Fast
People following this diet would fast for an entire 24 hour period, perhaps monthly or weekly.

What's the appeal with fasting? It's got to be the 'wow I can lose loads of weight and no exercise or anything in a short space of time' has to be the motivator isn't it. Well, let's look at these examples all part of the same underlying thing.
Not Eating

5:2 diets

I remember a documentary that was on primetime television some years ago, friends of mine watched it and were convinced they could do this to lose weight. Eat what you like for five days and then for two days have restrict to very low calories. It seemed very convenient & it was really to compensate for the weekend excesses, all the food, beer, wine and so on. If they had, as the explanation say's 'a balanced diet with your usual calorie intake'. If it's a healthy, balanced diet, there would be no need for the two days of calorie restriction. As mentioned, such calorie restriction can be tough and as I have been told people who tried it feeling no energy later in the very low-calorie days, being overweight and need a lot of calories daily is likely to result in a high dropout rate as I saw with the friends that tried it. A few bits of fruit in a day will be tough to complete the day on

16:8 plan

Here they are replacing the traditional three meals a day principle with calling it an 8-hour window. This would mean eat all meals within 8 hours, an example being start at 8am and last meal by 4pm. It can be impractical if you finish work at 5pm and home before 6. I suggest starting around seven or eight am, depends on your day. Then lunch around midday to 1pm and aiming at dinner no later than 6pm. On the 16:8 for the next 16 hours a day this is said to be fasting, rather than part of a healthy lifestyle. It's discouraging late eating and snacking into the evening, which is a good thing, the calories consumed late are less likely to be burnt off as the next thing to do is sleep.

Alternative day fasting

Another arrangement of extreme calorie restriction, being in a regular routine one day to then not eat for a day, if the 5:2 VLCD days, which it is people find a struggle then not eating for a day will be tough. Could it be to try and get away with what they get up to at the weekends, compensating for the poor habits. It appears to be another angle on the calorie restriction principles.

24 Hour fast

Assuming alternative day fasting, and 24-hour fast are similar or alternative day fasting is like a '4:3, or 3:4'. The likelihood of sticking to it will be very difficult and the urge to snack will be high. As I have reiterated, I don't want you to feel hungry at any point. When you do the urge to just grab at whatever is in front of you becomes higher.

Fasting summary

Others use different strategies of fasting and then reintroducing foods over time, just another way to follow a low-calorie diet taking in far less than our daily maintenance needs. Many do use fasting, from my experiences to compensate for a poor diet by aiming to lose weight quickly. What about sorting out the unhealthy diet, that would be far better not only short but for the long term. I do say each to their own, but my focus is health and doing what our bodies are designed for. I don't agree with any kind of fasting when it comes to weight management, not only for what has already been mentioned for obese people's safety, the focus should be on selecting mostly good food and drink, not to simply remove it for any amount of time as the solution.

VLCD's (Very Low-Calorie Diets)

These refer to any diet that means you take in far less calories a day that the less 250 of your own daily calorie maintenance needs. Considered under 800 calories a day, the same issue here as with the fasting is the emphasis is on not getting the calories in, not necessarily what the food selections you have on a regular basis are. There is no management in terms of when you do eat, as I have mentioned the diet industry likes this as:

'VLCD's are likely to include meal replacement drinks which are designed to contain low levels of macronutrients but sufficient micro-nutrients so as not to induce micro-nutrient deficiencies. Dieters who choose unsupervised or self-administered VLCD's are at acute and intermediate risk of nutrient deficiency and malnutrition, which can have significant health implications.'[190] *'The risks associated with VLCD's are nutrients deficiencies and sudden death. In the short term, they encourage muscular catabolism and will force the body to slow its metabolism and reduce production of lipolytic enzymes while increasing lipogenic enzymes (less fat burning enzymes – more fat storing enzymes) acting to conserve precious fat.'*[191]

Summed up with the lack of real change again in the relationship with food and drink. Just a change from the normal habits for a bit and see what happens, then likely to go back to the old ways. Suggesting following these patterns can in fact turn the body into a perfect fat storing machine in this way. The statement of the body on a VLCD causing 'less fat burning enzymes – more fat storing enzymes' could be a big factor in how people over time seem to gain and store so much subcutaneous fat weight. From such a plan over time becoming the perfect fat storage unit, from meeting people in this situation and finding out they've been on diets for years, rebound and back on them. This could go some way to show the position some have got themselves into without realising it.

Food replacements, pills & drinks

Theres a lot of products out there & they tend to do the rounds for a while, most are just over the counter in shops while some have different marketing strategies for people to become sellers of their products. They all generally involve taking in less calories and relace the actual best option being a nutritious meal. A lot of the over-the-counter pills and such tend to be no more active than a placebo when the best effect on weight is changing habits, food intake and physical activity and exercise strategy that is advised with it. There are so many options in the big pharmacy style shops selling the same dream, then there is under the counter type products that for example can accelerate the heart rate to burn fat. Extremely unhealthy and counter-productive to the body, which can have very bad long-term effects.

All of these do not change the inherent issue of our relationship with food and drink, they offer a solution, and then what, just do more of it to lose weight? I am not a fan and I only use a protein drink supplement to make sure my calories are to my target levels after a training session or if I am increasing calorie intake during an intense training regime.

The 'Magic secret'

'In the heart of the Peruvian Jungle, there is a small white flower which grows high up on the Sumaumeria trees, up to 200 feet on a certain type of moss on the branches fed by the sun and jungle climate. The flower is known as the Rafflesia, one of the rarest and most endangered plants in the world, it grows in the trees as the average temperature is 77 degrees Fahrenheit or 25 Celsius, perfect for this rare flower. It is seen to have almost magical weight loss properties and in its completely natural form is almost priceless. Many have tried to seek out the flower. including one Chester Brinley in the mid 1900's there is papers documenting his adventure, but he went into the jungle and was never seen again. The aim is to fully analyse the properties, with today's technology it could transform the world, yet it remains in local tribal folklore. That could be a coverup as further information suggests It could even be destroyed or owned, patented, and locked away by big corporation to stop people losing weight and solving the obesity crisis in the world. That is until a month ago, these plants have sprung up in numbers recently and being cultivated by a huge team of scientists and experts as we speak, to become the magic we have all been waiting for'!

If you believe that you will believe anything, well not really, as if that's sold to you in the right way it can sound believable. That something

105

like this might be out there, the diet industry would like you to believe so. They don't go this far to tell a story and outright lie, but they tell you what you want to hear with just enough implication so you buy their stuff. The more you hear that 'big secret' style, the more it goes into your subconscious and becomes a belief. It's as real as Leprechauns, fairies and goblins. If this is something you have been hoping for, get rid of that in your mind right now. I have seen this viewpoint in people more than once, morbidly obese yet convinced they just haven't found 'the secret' yet. Have you or are friends in this mindset, deep down do you think there is an easy fix to melt away the excess fat while you sleep? I'm afraid there is not, and pills and weight loss surgery can have serious side effects. The diet industry's big motivation is for making money, with the weight loss claims being the hook. I just googled the main tree in the Peruvian Jungle and then the rarest flower. Yes, I can outright makeup a story, then aim to sell a product to you on half-truths and fairy tales. Most, if not more often in small print somewhere possibly to cover themselves is along the lines of:

'This product is to be used with a healthy balanced diet and regular exercise'

Which should mean really get rid of the product and go with this lifestyle change, not the easy bit that is the product, whether it's a shake, some kind of juice, or any of the over or under the counter -weight loss products. They generally mask what really needs changing in you. At least I was honest with making up the Magic Secret story then revealing it to be untrue, everything we are looking at is based on factual research and experience.

What a Carry on ….

We have looked here at the most and least obese nations in our world and now have a pretty good idea of what is going on, as I was researching these Obese Islands, I couldn't help but think of the classic 1960's comedy film 'Carry-On Again Doctor'. Jim Dale as doctor Nookey headed off to a mission in the south seas at the fictitious Beatific Islands he meets the local medicine man who has a magic weight loss serum. The locals prefer being bigger so there's no demand for it. Nookey then opens a weight loss practice in England to sell the potion. In the film this magic potion works and is a success in the western culture, with such a high demand. A fictitious magic secret the diet industry would love to get their hands on.

A fun film but with so many relevant points made, especially about the fuller figure being more favourable in the tropical island. We have seen the issue that has contributed in reality. The films serum does work and is a big success but as I've highlighted the various products out there tend to work as long as a healthy balanced diet and exercise is followed....... In the real world that could be any of the so-called weight loss products, if they sell it right as they would want you to believe they are the next elixir. 'Don't do a lot, use our product, you will lose weight. Or we will give the impression you will, just buy it'

KEEP CALM AND CARRY ON

Summary

From each of these diet plans, either focus on a past way of living (Paleo) or remove / reduce a macronutrient it seems mostly focusing on the carbs. Keto, low carb, or the extreme no carbs with the Carnivore diet, then with the G.I. diet focusing on the type of carbohydrate, then fasting and intermittent fasting & variations with no food or gaps in eating. Then the Very Low-Calorie Diet's drastically reducing everything daily. The meal replacements, being low calories and into the myriad of food replacement drinks, pills, bars, products all there to replace actual food. Looking at these, are they ideal for the long term or all there for a short time then once we do it for a while go back to old habits then regain the weight and go through the cycle all over again. In that group of diet's, the Paleo seems quite healthy yet no grain, dairy or legumes which apparently may cause problems, according to the NHS:

Milk and dairy products such as cheese and yoghurt, are great sources of protein and calcium. They can form part of a healthy diet[192]

With the least advisable such as the extreme Keto carnivore diet or fasting, which seems to be a growing trend likely because of the perceived fast results. As with the VLCD's, any drastic reduction in calorie deficit will slow the metabolism as suggested and once the reduced intake is stopped the weight is put on far easier through the issue of muscular catabolism and metabolism being in starvation mode will after clamour onto the reverted

107

normal incoming calories. That is why when I speak to people that are obese to morbidly obese, they have become the perfect fat storer from the numerous attempts of diets and rebounds which we must be aware of and how to break that cycle.

My experience of these and the clients I have discussed with and helped it's a sales pitch. There is undoubtedly going to be new twists on these types of diets in the future to entice people. Rest assured as soon as food is reduced, taken away or only one macronutrient is focused on in a diet then it's not a long-term solution. It's all very well focusing on the calories the dieter is not taking in to lose weight, well what about the calories they are taking in. Without addressing the regular lifestyle habits and what exactly our body needs how can we lose weight and then ensure it stays off. What happens after, with any of these or other diets, are you going to keep at it? People tend to get to a goal then stop, or do it for a while then stop, so what happens next. What's the strategy after, many regress to what they were doing before. We don't want that which tends to be the result for many opting for diet or surgery / procedure that really isn't what we are designed to do, it will likely be temporary. We must do what our bodies are designed to do and do it for the long term, that's what we are going to go through next. We are going to look at a plan, considering all the good factors the right way for us. Diet clubs or regular meetings are a good idea, as they can help with motivation. That sense of being accountable at the meet, weighing in and then the talks. I wanted to get my experience and the information across, use what we are going through to help with your overall knowledge towards meeting your goals.

The Modern-Day Diet

This concept I've used for some time with clients and friends, it's essentially proven best ways to be with food and drink and to cater to people's different work / life routines. The principles are sound with strategies that allow the treats and nights out. It's essentially an ideal relationship with food and drink for us, including the best bits from the diet analysis of Paleo, Keto, carnivore, fasting, intermittent fasting and VLCD's. When we have the mindset 'were on a diet' a lot of temptations are resisted to try and follow a fixed plan. I have a different view on this, you cannot deprive yourself of treats, but it must be now and again such as Friday or Saturday nights.

> **The diet has the best elements from what we have reviewed in :**
>
> - **Paleo**
> - **G.I diet**
> - **Keto**
> - **Carnivore**
> - **Fasting / intermittent**
> - **VLCD's** (only if calories followed then at most less 250kcal of your daily calorie needs)
>
> **Its' doing what your body is made to do and the best way to lose weight then keep it**

We need macronutrients being protein, fats, and carbohydrates which we have been through. The fats we also need being more liquid at room temperature, more natural state and less of what's contained in the poorer choices of processed and fast foods with an emphasis away from refined sugar and processed foods containing added sugars, fats, and additives. Choose low to medium G.I. fruits and vegetables to ensure we are getting a good regular intake of micronutrients, vitamins, and minerals while the food item taking longer to break down in the digestive system so less chance of adding to fat stores. Focus must be on mostly healthy choices, and we must never feel hungry. Stick to a healthy balanced and regimented routine with food in line with your work pattern for the days you are at work. On each day plan for three meals a day, start early, near time to get up and finish early as possible for your last meal at around 6pm. It's not regimented, if you are late home one or two days in the week & dinner is late then fine. Resist the urge to snack in the evenings but remember only a small portion of healthy snacks, natural whole foods too, fruit veg, nuts as per the example page. Monday to Friday regimented following all physical activity & home strategies, (we will go through) food & drink and exercise plans, once you get to Friday night have your takeaway, aiming at a less fat & sugar option and a couple of treats on Saturday. This is a simple routine which is easy and practical to follow, you will see progressive changes in the coming weeks and months, it's about living your life and your food & drink intake should be flexible around this yet well balanced. Focus more on the good food content than necessarily worrying about the calories. Yet the option is there for you to calculate that too (we are going through soon). Reason being not only can it be tiresome to work out calories but to focus on the good foods will change your palette and you are more likely to lean towards selecting those better options at mealtimes and that they are by their very nature less calorific. If you go off the rails on a big night out and a bit hungover the next day, skip breakfast and have a light high protein low G.I. carb good fats lunch and relatively small dinner featuring good food choices as the extra empty calories in beer added a lot extra to your system. Adjustments need to be made accordingly the next day, the better focus you have with all the advice I have given, and the Phase training plan will mean your weight loss results will reflect your efforts. I recommend you are doing regular physical activity from the strategy guide points we will soon go through and the exercise plan to suite you as will soon be indicated. The key to this 'diet' is that all the advice will be tailored to you. If it's all too much, do what you can and monitor your results through body shape. Use body analysis scales to get more information on your stats ideally every couple of weeks to once a month.

The strategy is if you do have a couple of indulgent days, it doesn't matter as you want to lose weight, but you also want to live your life. Provided you back into the regime the following day or as quickly as possible and the emphasis is 'now & again' for a treat. You must be good most of the time and over time you will lose weight. I would always urge constantly be mindful of the bad habits wish to reduce them, and then make sure you change it, and start to reduce them. As you take part in the exercise phases, rest and patience is as important as the effort. This plan is just as much about getting your mind right and to not be driven by 'results', such as what the scales say but the right actions you are making for your own health.

The training plan will be in phases, focusing on certain aspects at the start then add together a regular resistant / cardiovascular exercise phase, important which will add to calorie burning. Provided we can get you to the right phase to then progress, it will get the muscles working efficiently. Adaptation to your body happens at a cellular level, increasing your daily calorie needs, burning more efficiently to become a perfectly efficient fat burning engine. We must target the excess fat stores we have, not lose muscle. Many diets suggesting we consume well below our daily maintenance calorie target can cause muscle as well as fat loss. We will soon explore the metabolism and the fact that muscle to fat is a weight ratio of 4:1 muscle weighing so much more than fat can cause the scales to indicate we appear to 'not be losing' or with the VLCD & fasting route it appears we are, although short lived. Well forget the scales in accordance with the muscular catabolism principle, we want to change our bodies and not score quick brownie points on the scales. You will still have positive effects on your weight loss if you don't decide to add in the exercise plan, it may justtake longer to reach your goals and importantly be more disciplined with your food, drink, home environment and physical activity routine.

Path A: Lifestyle + food   =   good results

Path B: Lifestyle + food + exercise   =   good results quicker

As I have mentioned I find my clients all work better with simple guidelines than breaking down into detail such as working out the specific calorie intake of macronutrients a day offset to their BMR needs as there can be a lot of detail. Each of my client's weekly food habits are different calorie amounts, but we follow the same principles. As you continue reading, follow all the guidelines I have written on strategies to start the changes. Follow the guidance on increasing your physical activity and start your exercise plan. All midweek meals to be low calorie high content whole foods, nothing out of a packet or any of the 'weight loss' products. All vegetables, fruits are ok, lean meats and dairy, as long as it's not full of sugar & fat. Remember it's the quality not the whole meal itself, the guidance examples to get you going are in the next few pages.

Energy levels will increase, in time sleeping patterns should improve and you will be well on your way to losing the unwanted weight. If you are part of a weight loss group, they are useful for motivation and working with others so use this information in-conjunction with other initiatives but be aware we are going through how your body works. Those flogging their own food products as we have seen are unnecessary for you to lose weight. It's down to your own planning, cooking, and preparing meals from scratch. Following all guidelines and be consistent, make this diet your new life. I have added examples of the ideal kinds of foods in a following page, as I have repeated the term wholefoods / natural foods being food in its most original state. That is what we should be having the most of by far. The calorific amount in terms of the volume of food on the plate is relatively less than processed energy dense fast-food options. Feeling fuller for longer is important and the food selections I have added will do this, taking longer for the digestive system to break down the meals. We need good nutritious calories, not empty calorie packed foods which are more likely to be converted to fat stores. Follow everything with the lifestyle strategies and with the exercise plan, you will then see yourself progress and have every chance of meeting the goals you desire. They key is you understand the principles and how it works for your body, then you arrange it around your life and make healthy food selections that suit you more. 100% clean good food is great but not necessarily practical in our daily lives, so and 80 / 20 split is more practical. Some weeks it might be 70 / 30 or 60 / 40, which then means we have to change that as soon as possible and increase the good whilst decreasing the bad. Remember out bodies are using energy, burning calories all the time. We just need to make these wise choices to encourage the use of excess stored energy we want to get rid of. Patience is important, it may take a few weeks or longer to adopt this new strategy fine, you are in it for the long haul you are in it to change your ways. Not to just get to a point then stop, you are finding out a new way for yourself.

Believe in the Change

As with any goal, having the belief it will work. Keeping the changes consistent can be hard, I find when I have a goal as long as you keep thinking about what you should be doing and having the ongoing drive and wanting to reach that goal. My actions do make a difference and only with experience and hindsight can I then see how much it was worth it. This is the mindset you need to be in and to learn and develop. You will learn about yourself, we go through goal setting soon but I wanted to add this piece now from experience. We need to constantly remind ourselves what our goal is act accordingly and over time our actions will align more with our goals which in turn will more than likely ensure we do meet our goals. That can be in so many ways in life that can be positive for us. Here I just want you to have all the right information to allow you to know you can lose weight and it's all a benefit to your health all the way through, no side effects or sacrifices are needed in depriving calories at all. Follow all the advice, you will become consistent over time, and you will get there.

Guidelines for the Modern-Day Diet

These following 5 examples of breakfast, lunches and dinners are ideal choices to make when it comes to achieving our goals of weight loss. Low G.I, highest quality protein and all healthy fats used as it really is what we should be doing for ourselves anyway in terms of health. The examples are all ideal options to structure your week with and if there are selections you don't like then look on your phone / laptop at further good options based on these principles. Remember I am showing you the way and you have to walk your path. To ensure we are good, we must focus on following the routine to the letter during our routine working week. With our days off we can relax a bit, with a takeaway once a week and a few off-diet snacks. The following is an example of the MD Diet which uses all the good principles I have highlighted from the diets we have looked at creating the most flexible and weight loss for 'modern day diet'.

- *All carbohydrates to be G.I. medium in the mornings (small honey/chocolate added to oats fine) & medium to low lunchtime then low in the evening.*
- *Meals eaten to start early and finish early midweek 6 – 8am & last meal 5 – 6pm if later once or twice a week focus protein & a portion low G.I. Carbohydrates such as vegetables.*
- *All food and drink selection to be wholefoods, nutritious not processed in the week. Like Paleo but dairy, grain and legumes are allowed. Low calorific compared to fast food / processed.*
- *No refined sugar snacks, or processed fat (crisps) only wholefood snacks*
- *Weekend allowed a favourite meal Friday & Saturday or Saturday / Sunday*
- *If you go off the rails one evening / day, the next day no breakfast, light lunch, and Salad & protein dinner with low carbs. You feel compensating the day before and good to go again the next day.*
- *A couple of drinks are ok on a Friday or Saturday, live your life now in the modern day. Remember only a couple, preferably less is better.*
- *Be mindful of anything you buy convenience food in shops check the labels for added sugars and fats. Food advertising can be deceiving, appearing healthy but may not be.*
- *Make sure there is always healthy snacks / food in the fridge for convenience, the modern day is a busy one and planning is crucial.*

Remember this is flexible, you may have a couple of late evenings out after work and a late dinner back. That is fine, just don't eat later regularly. You may also have a big weekend away on a social one, that's fine get back onto the plan the following day. Look forward to the treat at the weekend, but don't go mad and keep your goals in mind. You will feel better for eating good foods and less of the processed stuff.

The Modern-Day Diet example page

5 Breakfasts

- 1 Porridge large flake old fashioned oats (1 portion), with 2 of blueberries, cherries, raspberries, strawberries & 2 tbsp of yoghurt
- 1 Granary toast and two boiled eggs, with rocket salad, small tomatoes pepper
- Mushrooms, low fat cheese & scrambled egg, whole tomatoes, 1 granary toast
- Two poached eggs, lean ham & 1 slice whole grain bread
   or just on the go opt for a
 coffee & fruit, apples, pears, peaches

5 lunches

- Tuna & Durham wheat pasta / normal pasta is ok, tbsp mayonnaise in tuna, pepper, chopped cucumber, sweetcorn, onion mixed in & sliced mushrooms with drizzle of olive oil. Chilli flakes for added flavour
- Wholegrain off the bone chicken salad sandwich, sliced tomatoes, lettuce, light mayonnaise
- Salad box of lean turkey slices, broccoli, wholegrain basmati rice, flavourings to suit such as onion garlic & spices
- 2 poached eggs, sweet jacket potato, low sugar beans, sprinkle mozzarella cheese
- Chicken salad, cucumber, olives, lettuce, lemon slice, pepper, sliced tomatoes, avocado sliced

5 Dinners

- Oven cooked roast dinner, chicken, parsnips, carrots, new potatoes, onion, garlic, seasoning in vegetable stock Kale boiled and gravy
- Pork chops fried, sliced cooked peppers, cabbage
- Linguine pasta, low fat mince in a Bolognese tomato sauce low fat good quality mincemeat with sprinkled Parmesan
- Stir fry vegetables, noodles, turkey added a small sachet sauce or small jar curry (check ingredients)
- Turkey, wholegrain basmati rice, assorted vegetables

Snacks: Five options
- 1 slice wholegrain toast with tbsp peanut butter
- 1 crumpet with low fat spread, as long as it's not lots, then any thin spread is fine, Nutella, honey
- Apples, plums, pears, cherries, blueberries, raspberries, strawberries, peaches, oranges, added bit of yoghurt optional
- Carrot, celery sticks, with humus dip, hazelnuts, pistachios
- What I like doing is cooking extra during healthy meals and leaving some in the fridge, so if I do feel peckish there is something there healthy to hand

Drinks: Good choices
- Water, from a good source water is my number one choice for hydration. Calorie free and really designed for our bodies, every chemical reaction in our bodies takes place in the medium of water
- Orange cordial with sparkling water, my version of orange soda with far less calories/additives
- Fruit juices, when I get fruit juices do contain sugar but aim at a least version possible examples of pomegranate, cranberry, orange, pineapple but I add a third juice and two thirds or more water to dilute. Less sugar per drink these are now & again and more likely at breakfast
- Smoothies, option as a breakfast option add semi skimmed milk, strawberries, banana, Oats.
- Another example I enjoy is milk, banana and a low sugar chocolate protein powder (optional) scoop after training sessions

Explanation

I have added these twenty-five examples of breakfast, lunch, dinner, with snacks and drink options to give you an immediate idea of what to do regarding food and drink Monday to Friday. Saturday night could be a favourite meal but look to healthy options as demonstrated with the curry night out example. A good Sunday roast is fine, aiming to stick to the principles as much as possible.

To add to the guidance points, the carbohydrates are mostly low to medium G.I. The protein is good quality mostly lean white meats, I would also suggest fish a good option such as Salmon, Mackerel, Cod. Lots of vegetables and the snacks including fruits as a replacement for the sweet fix in chocolate and the like. As with the guidance make sure there is wholefood options which can replace snacking in the fridge, examples such as chicken drumsticks or extras cooked from a healthy meal.

We should never feel hungry, as we must keep our metabolisms running efficiently. A treat or cheat meal is allowed once max two times a week, be mindful if it's with extras and what it is in a week it could hamper the progress of weight loss results you are looking for.

Remember you cannot out train a bad diet we really need to be conscious of what we are eating and drinking on a regular basis. That is crucial to good weight management and reaching the goals you have set. Over time creating your own structured meal and drink plan it will become a good habit and over time become easier to follow, repetition and consistency is key. The best way is to enjoy the food, if you find these bland and unappetising, look at how to spice and flavour the recipes up. Find similar examples that you would enjoy than given, then you are far more likely to do it and keep doing it. Look into different healthy foods, following the principles and see what you do like, and the plan then will suit to you more. A convenient fast-food snack is ok now and again, it just cannot become a regular part of the week. Adopt these guidance and food / drink examples for five to six days a week and rest a bit on the off days, but don't go mad. A couple of treats are fine but look for your own alternate healthy meal and drink options, a few drinks may be on a Saturday night, check out what are better or worse options, for all this the smartphone is in front of you.

Consider the foods from around the world, Vietnam, Japan, South Korea similar principles of what's here. Cook for yourself and try such different flavours of different cultures we've seen have such low obesity rates. Add a good number of new options to your healthy food choices and make them the norm. You now have the information on lifestyle / environment changes, the Phases training plan will be next and further guidance in your current diet analysis. With the five examples of weekly meal choices and snacks there is everything needed to really get started on your weight management voyage. The 'modern day diet' shows what we must do most of the time and will direct our relationship with food and drink into a healthier better and a longer lasting regular routine. As we see, it's not rigid in that you have to do a certain thing all of the time, as that isn't life. It's flexible to you and how you must get back on track as soon as possible. The goal is for you to lose weight through having a better relationship with your food and drink over the long term.

Task: 3

Is to now manage your diet with what I have advised. It can be you either get every other task in place then this or the tasks in an order that suits you. Rest assured as you adopt each task and get into place the changes will happen. Plan your first week of the new diet and look on your smartphone for options using the food examples I have given if that's needed. Increasing the options and more to your taste.

Cook from Scratch

Many clients I have worked with having weight issues, I have found as mentioned don't tend to cook for themselves. Opting for takeaways, ready - made meals, fast food all too regular.

Cooking needs to be a regular good habit it doesn't have to take long as many healthy recipes can be ten to twenty minutes to prepare. I do enjoy cooking and for all of us it should be a necessity, so please get practicing if you don't already. Using herbs and spices to flavour dishes, great recipes freely out there to find on your smartphone and It doesn't have to be broccoli fish and carrots all of the time, as an example I have just googled on my phone 'broccoli fish and carrots' and within seconds have found a tasty recipe of 'pan fried fish, spicy carrots and preserved lemon' the full ingredients are there and all the directions to prepare start to finish. Wholefoods can be tasty, get some flare, direction, and imagination into your cooking and the more you do the better you will get.

The low calorie and ready-made diet meals can contain sugar, or further additives. Stating 'low calorie' they should in many instances also add 'of low nutritional value'. Be mindful of the what's contained in the meal, read the labels. That's no good as you need to be full consuming the right foods as we have highlighted so you don't snack and grab the nearest convenient thing, whatever it is. As I have also mentioned, the foods we should only really be buying is what we have looked at in Appendix B and ideal examples are featured soon.

Companies, besides the supermarkets, delivery are out there that deliver healthy food items to your door with recipe cooking instructions, if it's easier and would work for you. The recipes use these wholefood principles as mentioned, the aim is to give simple tasty recipes which are also quick to prepare. A simple business idea but are great for weight management, and you don't have to spend the time in the supermarkets. I would suggest you do though, as over time you will get to know what ingredients you need, what is healthy and what is good for you, understanding good healthy nutrition as part of your life.

This is where I find clients do react with self-initiative in different ways, in terms of training some get hold of it and get into their own thing, and excel, this can the same be for the nutrition side. Will you knowing the principles then find you own recipes and take it all on for yourself, I do hope so as knowledge is key and we can all build on it, developing our lifestyle, exercise, food and drink principles and much more, so go for it.

I enjoy preparing food, a typical meal is lean white meat, here is pre-cooked chicken, lettuce sliced with a dressing lightly drizzled. Small jacket potato with a sprinkle of cheese and two to three tbsp of tinned tomatoes. A bit of barbeque sauce to taste. Takes a total of around eight to ten minutes to prepare. Small jacket potato may be high GI but the total meal is med.

Our Bodies, How Do They Work?

Metabolism

To understand how food impacts on us and how much we should be eating in a day we need to fully understand what the metabolism is. This refers to our whole bodily systems functioning to keep us alive. In doing so we all have our own calorie amount we need to sustain our bodies, meaning in neither gaining nor losing weight but to keep us at our current weight. How do we impact on our metabolism, how many calories do we need in a day and crucially how do we get our metabolisms to work more efficiently, to burn calories better, to lose weight. Our metabolic rate is a measure of how many calories we need to consume over a 24-hour period. Some conditions can impact on our BMR (Basal Metabolic Rate) but it is generally set by the energy needed by all or our organs and muscle tissue. There are several factors which influence the total amount of calories we need daily including gender, age, our daily activity levels, and our current fitness levels (which are a result of the amount of exercise sessions we take part in daily / weekly) and the amount of muscle we have, more muscle requires more daily calories. For someone that is very fat, there overall weight will need less calories than someone with comparatively more muscle.

'For example, in a normal weight woman with a body fat content of 25% the energy contribution to BMR from fat is equal to only 4%'[193]

This is one reason a regular and ongoing exercise strategy helps in losing weight. Increasing muscle and burning fat with an improved diet will have a doubling effect. You will naturally burn more calories in the day and lose fat weight as long as less energy dense processed foods eaten. It may be suggested if someone is obese, they are likely to have a slow metabolism as they overeat and low physical activity levels during the day and unlikely to take part in regular exercise sessions. Restricting food way beyond the minimal daily calorie amounts for an amount of time, (fasting / VLCD being two examples) could slow the metabolism. Meaning if such a restrictive regime is stopped and the individual goes back to past habits then they are prone to gain fat stores easier as the body doesn't know when the next meal is. We speed up the metabolism through being regularly active, eating good food at regular intervals and not feeling hungry along with regular exercise to stimulate muscle mass.

'Research has proved that obese people are high energy expenders and are hyperphagic (eat excessively). In spite of many years of research, the mythical obese subject with a low metabolic rate has proved entirely elusive. Obese individuals have a greater amount of both fat and fat free mass and therefore have higher overall metabolic rates'[194].

Ongoing calorie intake far exceeds the daily needs for such people, the metabolism does not need all the excess calories being consumed and therefore converts the excess calories to fat stores. Which, we know but I say this to make it clear and that we really are aware of it and the consequences of our own actions.

How much food and drink do we need per day

NHS guidelines suggest:

'Generally, the recommended daily calorie intake is 2,000 calories a day for women and 2,500 for men'[195].

That's an average across population, it doesn't consider the individuals muscle to fat ratio, the daily activity levels, natural weight to height, levels of regular exercise, health, or age. If we need to work out our own specific BMR so we have an idea calorie wise to the amount of food, we need. I would advise this but it's not essential to the plan. I say this as the 'diet' I put forward only considers good food choices as we have seen, and you need to feel full. When we are full there's less chance of grabbing the naughty convenience snacks. We must put all the guidance & advice into practice, then we really don't need to be hung up on calories, however if you are interested to know about it and the use of body measurement analysis, we can see. Non-intrusive and quick to use, it is likely your local state funded leisure centre will have a body fat scale in the facility, you could get advice from your doctor, or they're also often in large pharmacies / drug stores. That's easier than working it out manually, which gives a rating to your daily activity levels, age, gender, weight, bodyfat %.

If you can only get your weight measured, then here is a simple way to estimate your own daily energy needs. In accordance with my original personal training studies, it is suggested 'at rest we will use energy at a rate of 25kcal per kg of bodyweight per day. This is for our essential systems, 'breathing, circulation, brain and nervous system function, body warmth, cell turnover etc. This known as the Basal Metabolic Rate (BMR)'[196]

The equation is: Your weight in KG X 25 = your Kcal needs per day

As mentioned, 'one of the main influences on BMR is body composition. Even at rest, a muscle cell is metabolically more active than a fat cell'[197]. We will need more calories, burn more calories and / or get away with the extra snack as our bodies will need more relatively at rest if we add in an exercise plan, losing fat and developing muscle. We then need to know how active we are, now be truthful. If you do find it a struggle to walk and it seems a lot of effort, so you feel you are active comparatively you are not, be truthful with you.

Sedentary Lifestyle	**- + 20%**
Moderately Active Lifestyle	**- + 50%**
Very Active Lifestyle	**- + 100%**

Sedentary could be working a desk job, on the couch in evenings and not getting about much daily. Moderate could be some daily walking and weekly exercise sessions. Very active could be a more physical day job like builder, scaffolder, anything physical for the duration and with weekly exercise sessions. Let's say you are currently in the sedentary level and are now going to adopt a moderately active lifestyle, so we begin at the beginning.

Your weight in KG X 25 = **Your Kcals a day** + 20% on top = **total daily calorie needs**.

An example :   95kg X 25 = 2375 X .20 (**sedentary lifestyle**) = 2850

To gain weight is consuming in a day anything over 250 calories of the maintenance daily amount, then to lose weight we subtract 250 calories from the maintenance daily amount resulting in:

95kg X 25 = 2375 X .20 (**sedentary lifestyle**) = 2850

Add   250 = **calorie surplus and gain weight** 2850 + 250 = 3100

Minus 250 = calorie deficit and lose weight   2850 − 250 = 2600

We know if we overeat, but seeing it in black and white should help for self-realisation..

I do say don't get caught up in calorie counting as it's more our food & drink selections, but it is worth knowing what our daily needs are.

You need to know where the weight is coming from, and you need to have an understanding what your own daily requirements are. From this the three main elements of macronutrients need to be known, carbohydrates, fats, and protein. Remember this is optional, you can work out your own BMR this way or use modern technology as I have suggested which is quicker if you have access to a modern analysis scale. A percentage example of the three can be split below is the two examples of calculating grams of food[198] that can be consumed daily.

To maintain weight

Macros	Kcal		Grams
30% Fats	855 / 9	=	95g
15% Protein	427 / 4	=	107g
55% Carbs	1567 / 4	=	392g

To Lose weight

Macro	Kcal		Grams
30% Fats	780 / 9	=	87g
15% Protein	390 / 4	=	97g
55% Carbs	1567 / 4	=	357g

Rest assured, as you start the modern-day diet plan which we will go through, you will become far more efficient at burning unwanted fat stores. The more you do and over a longer period, if I then added in you've got to weigh / calculate all volume of food in your meals to your BMR rate it gets quite time consuming and loses the practicality I want the plan to maintain. If you want to try this, please do however there is so much to change already but for some it can be an added motivator to see how the scales, not just weight but body fat percentage changes. Fad diets tend to demonise carbs and or fats, but the right choices in all three areas are ideal for us and all serves a purpose. We saw in the Obesity world tour just how rice, a carbohydrate is a main staple in most of the least obese world nations. So how can carbohydrates be such a big contributor to weight gain, it doesn't have to be, provided we make the right choices. Remember, carbohydrates are present in salad, fruit and vegetables not just pasta, potatoes and bread and the macronutrient percentages aren't cast in stone.

Task: 4

- **Work out your daily metabolic rate, then the amount of macronutrients you will need in a day to function without gaining nor posing weight.**
- **Work out the macronutrients to lose weight on a daily basis**

    You will have an idea of how many calories you specifically need a day, just to give you and idea. If you want to go all in and plan meals, or if you just want to see how much is ideally needed and compare to your past habits / 7 day food diary.

Thermogenesis

Something we need to know about is Thermogenesis[199], it is the term for another part of our weight control during the day. How often do you fidget, walk round the house, get jobs done throughout the day. Or do you tend to sit still, not moving or fidgeting. In my mind, if someone is on the go, they are less likely to be morbidly obese and that bigger person is more inclined to sit around due to the weight they carry. Someone lighter will likely be more active throughout the day, up the stairs, into the kitchen making a tea. Go upstairs, forget something head down then go back up. All these fidgets and extra comparative movements in a day add up to burning more calories, with physical activity if you have an active job or need to walk about a lot at work and as well as any exercise sessions.

NEAT or non-exercise activity thermogenesis

Is different from structured exercise, it is all the daily movements we have just considered. Everything we do which will involve burning calories, however large or small.

'One study recruited 10 lean and 10 mildly obese sedentary volunteers and measured their body postures and movements every half second for 10 days'[200]

'The study revealed that obese participants were seated for 164 minutes longer per day than were lean participants. Correspondingly, lean participants were upright for 152 minutes longer per day than obese participants. Sleep times (lying) were not significantly different but, interestingly, the lean people lay down for longer[201].'

The bigger you are the less likely you are going to be moving around much during the day, adding up the daily, monthly, yearly lack of calories burnt offset to the calories going in and the result will be further potential weight gain. Where do you sit in this, look at your own NEAT activity. Any jobs around the house which could be planned to be done once a day or a few times a week? Then get cracking with them, are you a bit bored? Go for a fat burning walk rather than watching a new Netflix series, you will

---

Task: 5

- **Look at your own NEAT, are you active or more inactive from the examples given.**
- **Can you compare to others who may be leaner but appear to be on the go more ?**
- **Take a look at your daily routines and what is going on with your NEAT**

---

feel better for it. We are now going to look at the different elements of thermogenesis, just to show how it impacts on us and to go some way in possibly completing the picture more with people that may seem to find it easy to keep weight off the 'it's alright for you' scenario that many bigger people perceive in others. It's only a small part of the puzzle of us and adds to the overall picture.

Further examples of Thermogenesis[202]

Dietary Induced Thermogenesis – DIT
All food has an energy requirement needed to break it down and digest the various components to provide us with energy. Protein needs 25 – 30% of its own energy to be metabolised, Carbohydrates need 8% and fat 3%. So the net ingested from protein is far lower due to D.I.T.

Psychological Thermogenesis
Anxiety, anticipation and stress stimulate adrenaline, leading to increased heat production. A twofold increase in energy production can be found sitting at ease and sitting playing chess.

Cold Induced Thermogenesis
At low temperatures resting metabolic rate and hence heat production increases. Shivering from involuntary muscular contractions giving heat production and non-shivering by increased activity of the sympathetic nervous system.

Isometric Thermogenesis
Increased muscle tension but with no work performed. It explains the difference in energy expenditure of a person at rest, lying, sitting and standing due to the different muscle 'tone' required for each position.

Dynamic Thermogenesis
'Negative work' or heat produced by a stretched muscle – going down a ladder produces heat in the muscle but no 'work' is done.

Drug Induced Thermogenesis
Caffeine, nicotine and alcohol may all form an integral part of daily life for some individuals, and all three drugs stimulate thermogenesis. I can't say I would recommend these in any diet maybe a couple of coffees a day is ok. The impact really is quite marginal compared to the potential bad effects from the empty calories of alcohol and the effects of smoking.

This could explain why many current diets focus on including protein as it takes a third in digestion alone, stress can cause people to react differently, burning calories. Seasonally I tend to eat more in the winter and less in the summer, it must link to the cold induced. Isometric is an interesting one and dynamic, and to be in a certain shape from the jobs they do without realising it performing different movements. Whether it being on their feet all day or manual work on a building site, remember the body never lies. We need to understand and work out what's going on with ourselves. As for drug induced, it shouldn't be a factor to consider the health implications of caffeine, nicotine, and alcohol, apart from maybe a couple of coffees, then we need to remember the calories from purchases made from coffee houses.

Another area we need to be mindful in, a Starbucks bought Venti white hot chocolate comes in at 590 calories. That's more than many meals, it's a drink why is there so many calories along with 15 grams of saturated fat. So as much as these further examples of Thermogenesis may add to daily fat burning, we need to be aware of how we are topping up the daily calorie count too. On Starbucks own site a flat white[203] has 119kcal, 8 grams of sugar & 3.9g saturated fat. How many of these do you purchase or similar on a weekly basis? (All should be in your food / drink record)

Weight loss surgery

In accordance with the NHS, there are several different types of weight loss surgery[204]

- ***The gastric band***
Which is inserted through a keyhole procedure and over weeks is tightened to suit the client. The idea being they will feel full quicker.
- ***The Gastric Bypass***
Surgical staples are used to restrict the stomach and bypass a large portion of the stomach and again meaning you feel full quicker and absorb less from the food you do eat.

- *Sleeve Gastrectomy*

A large part of the stomach is sliced off and removed, reducing the new stomach size and again you cannot eat as much as before.

- *Intra – Gastric Balloon*

A soft balloon of air or salt water inserted into the stomach using a thin tube passed down the throat. (gastroscopy)

- *Biliopancreatic diversion*

Similar to a Gastric bypass but the new stomach pouch is further along the small intestine, absorbing even fewer calories but can cause more side effects than a gastric bypass.

- *Primary Obesity surgery Endolumena*

A private procedure which involves an endoscope passed into the stomach and the surgeon then passes small tools to create folds in the stomach in essence shrinking the stomach, making to smaller.

I have seen people go through many of these procedures with varying results. Many don't alter lifestyle guidance with the main view that procedure will fix it, in some instances there have been unwanted side effects. As specifically highlighted on the NHS website, suggesting people can achieve better results with a gastric bypass or sleeve gastrectomy than the gastric band, seeing that people could think, well, that's what I want, and I do understand. Yet furthers with 'the risk of serious surgery complications is generally higher for gastric bypass or sleeve gastrectomy' and 'weight loss surgery carries a risk of complications, some of which can be serious[205] ' It's stated on the NHS site, with such risks as blood clots, wound infections, Gastric band slipping out of place, Gut leakage, Blocked gut, Malnutrition, Gallstones, Excess skin (which can be more prevalent if weight is lost too drastically in a short space of time) Then the last risk :

Risk of Dying

'Weight loss surgery is a major operation and there is a chance of dying during the procedure or as a result of a serious complication afterwards, but this is rare'. Further complications from my obesity and diabetes studies highlight in random complications including 'unstable angina, deep vein thrombosis, pulmonary embolism, renal failure and stroke'[206].

I am also sorry to say but to have such intrusive procedure to somehow reverse the compulsions of eating or the habits, procrastination, lack of change or having no focus / plan to achieve what your body is designed to do can be a self-defeating trait. Is there any real change in the individual or is much just down to the surgery itself to change what has been done. Other examples include people regretting getting such a procedure as it transferred their compulsion of eating to another compulsion. Stories in recent national press of people travelling abroad to get such private procedures cheaper suffering the side effects mentioned. Surely it would be better to get to the bottom if there is a psychological issue going on or just if it's a perception that surgery is the solution. Rather than clients spending thousands on private procedures, including liposuction for more cosmetic reasons again they don't cover the real issue of lifestyle activity and our relationship with food and drink, nor promoting good health. If bad compulsions are too great, an ideal scenario would be to get focused and head to an ideal lifestyle. Life constraints can make these perceived easier options more inviting, but my recommendation is to aim and succeed from your own lifestyle change. It's also advised in the weeks leading up to any such procedure to follow a calorie-controlled diet, how about following a good diet and lifestyle, it will take longer but the results are far better. Or how about a remote facility where clients must stay and are trained in the ways of healthy living, weight management, discipline & spirit and they are away from all compulsions. We've seen the reasons for world obesity and these temptation triggers really don't help.

Meeting people who have had such procedures on the NHS and the conversations I have heard of how others are going to 'cheat it' as though having bad habits causing huge weight gain to then get NHS surgery and make no attempt to help themselves is such as shame, could it be they just don't think they can help themselves, are the compulsions too great, could it be a confidence issue, well I hope what I am writing here goes some way to at least help and offer some insight & way to at least help to address it. Offering any kind of bariatric surgery on the NHS is a difficult solution as for many as it could be seen as a last-ditch effort, even though it really doesn't have to be that way. I am not generalising, that's not everyone, but from my experiences with people there has been a mixture of such views, positive and negative. Primarily we must change our ways to promote our own health and wellbeing, procedures may help to lose weight, but they certainly are not a solution, doing what our bodies are designed to do for us is.

'Karen Throsby of Warwick University questioned 35 patients who applied for bariatric surgery on the NHS to discover why they felt it was the only solution. She found there was three main types of excuses used by the overweight' which were, 'Those reasons were some claimed they had a 'fat gene', being big ran in their family, others said it stemmed from childhood (well, habits and a lifestyle does but doesn't mean you can't change) the third reason was a stressful lifestyle'[207].

I hope what we are going through is really helping you for change. From this, my stance has always been for us to change ourselves without any such cosmetic procedures unless it's deemed by a specialist 'absolutely critical' to the client. Stress is a big factor in our lives, adding ingrained habits and not so much the fat gene, as it's other factors that may influence, we do have differing body types known as Somatotyping but not naturally to then need surgery from weight related health implications. What is the future of this now we are pretty much post Covid, will the service still be there? Would people want to go into hospital knowing that obesity is a big factor of vulnerability where Covid is concerned, even now being quite some time on. Are we possibly heading to an American style health service where when I have been in the states with clients, in Florida and Miami on South beach the body beautiful people take care of themselves more so being a lifestyle and possibly due to the high costs of health insurance. We need to adopt the same mentality over here but don't get me wrong my view is healthcare at this point in our civilisation should at least be free in the western world as we all pay our taxes. With such a luxury should come self-responsibility, we must help ourselves first. That is in the realm of taking personal action to help ourselves.

A brief word on Type 2 Diabetes

One crucial reason I would advise to adopt an exercise plan not only for weight loss, but also for the health benefits it can give you. Being overweight due to high bodyfat (visceral, the fat around our organs and the subcutaneous stuff, the other type that we see more visible underneath our skin) stores is associated in leading to metabolic syndrome type 2 diabetes. Taking part in a regular exercise plan will significantly lower the risk of developing diabetes type 2. As your muscles become more active, they will remove the sugar in blood to fuel the muscle cell far more efficiently. *People who are physically active have a much lower risk of developing type 2 diabetes than sedentary people*[208]. Guidance on physical activity levels refer to 30 minutes moderate activity on five or more days a week, ideally every day.

Insulin is a hormone which acts as a signal and is secreted by the Pancreas to alert the muscles to absorb blood sugar (glucose) to maintain good blood sugar levels. If someone is overweight and inactive there is a higher chance of the Pancreas becoming overworked. Secreting more insulin as the signal for the glucose to be absorbed into muscles. The reason being that someone who is overweight and takes no part in regular exercise is likely to be less insulin sensitive, meaning more insulin is secreted by the pancreas. If an overweight person does regularly exercise, apart from losing weight they are more likely to secrete less insulin for the blood sugar to be absorbed into their muscles. As this happens over time, for the less sensitive muscles of the sedentary person the likelihood to develop type 2 diabetes goes up. If the condition is not managed sufficiently it can lead to severe health problems. It is seen also that a high fat diet besides the sugar can also make an impact of diabetes occurring more prevalent.

'High blood sugar levels can seriously damage parts of your body, including your feet and your eyes, heart attack, stroke, kidney problems, nerve damage, gum disease[209]*'*

These are some of the dangers if the diabetes is not treated in the right way preferably early on. We have seen levels in populations increase a lot in recent years, so for this factor alone exercise should always be part of a weight management program. For anyone to dismiss exercise in weight loss are not looking at this direct health benefit, let alone all the other reasons to exercise. Forget the direct correlation to weight loss for a moment but how it can help to counteract type 2 diabetes, it's far too important to ignore. More poor health preventative benefits are made through regular exercise, physical activity, and the Modern-Day Diet. The Pancreas will reduce its workload and your body will be operating more efficiently to stave off the effects of type 2 diabetes, bringing the body back to a sense of normal operating.

Metabolic Syndrome[210]

> Metabolic syndrome is a multifaceted syndrome characterised by five major abnormalities:
>
> 1 **Hypertension**
> 2 **Atherogenic dyslipidaemia** (hypertriglyceridaemia, hyperfibrinogenaemia)
> 3 **Insulin Resistance**
> 4 **Glucose Intolerance** (type 2 diabetes)
> 5 **Obesity** (visceral obesity diagnosed by waist circumference)
> Of these five factors, large waist circumference is the chief predictor of the metabolic Syndrome. It is also suggested visceral fat levels are a big indicator too.

Hypertension, or high blood pressure with a likely build up of plaques on arteries. **Atherogenic Dyslipidaemia,** blood profiles with low HDL's and elevated LDL's and cholesterol also resulting a higher chance of atherosclerosis. **Insulin resistance,** the body not responding normally to release of insulin signalling the muscles to absorb blood glycogen which can lead to type 2 diabetes with **Glucose Intolerance** and the final syndrome, **Obesity.**

130

With diabetes type 2 exercise can really help reverse the effects and get you back on track. Once you go through the exercise strategy, get out there. Check with your GP, for blood pressure levels prior to starting a new program, I would always advise to have a chat first with them. Or before entering a gym, exercise can do so much for you, go get up that hill !

Moving Forward

Now you have an idea of how your body works in gaining and losing weight. Fix the strategies we've gone through just after seeing world obesity and you will start to see very soon and onwards. With the new healthy targets in place, we can look at the net part of your weight loss solution. As we will see in the activity / exercise plan soon it's ideal to combine cardiovascular work (walking / running / cycling / swimming) with a resistance program, so we work heart & lungs, promoting a more active lifestyle and you will feel better for it.

Right now, you're doing great, getting to this point we have been through a lot of info and I hope it's all making sense to you. Looking at yourself, your environment and what can be done to this point. You are in control, it may take some time and with the right planning, I have every confidence in You.

You now have seen the plan for your food and drink with the Modern-Day Diet. Soon involving practical weight loss strategies around the home, a regular exercise plan, strategy for your NEAT and your daily physical activity. With all these factors planned for this is the best way to lose weight with a focus on health and vitality, your body will love you for it. By the end of this book, you might only aim at the physical activity, better lifestyle, and your new structured food intake. Now we are going to look at how your body burns fat, a healthy lifestyle and then goal setting for yourself and how to go about it.

Goal Setting
& Getting The Weight Off

How does our bodies burn fat

Your body is a clever thing, knowing exactly what you need to do to start burning the extra fat off is important in reaching your goal weight. You need to understand the concept of heart rate zones, this refers to the number of beats per minute your heart is working during any kind of physical exertion such as the extra walk to the station or work. During a workout in the gym or outdoor session, it can involve any kind of activity but must be consistent, for a minimum of at least around 10 minutes continuously. You may have an active day in getting up early to get the kids ready for school, taking the kids to school, heading to the office in the day job. Getting back picking the kids up, getting dinner ready, washing up, cleaning, and getting them ready for bed. Yes, your day has been busy but unlikely to have any kind of training effect to burn fat. It has all been stop and start, that has little impact on burning fat. A simple guide to start with is knowing any continuous movement that keeps your heart rate up over a minimum of around that ten minutes will start to oxygenate your body, leading you to start to access fat as fuel. That's why I would say aim for a minimum of a continuous walk of ten minutes a day, better to three ten-minute walks a day. Provided you are at a level which you can sustain feeling your heart rate is up and you can complete it. The feeling is you are not quite out of breath, heart rate is up, and you are getting hot. As you adapt to the following plan, you will start to burn fat more efficiently.

> **80 - 90% MHR Peak Performance Zone**
> Think a player who can sustain a high intensity, in say a 100 meter sprint.
> **70 - 80% MHR Fitness Zone**
> You are at an intensity cant quite talk, breathing heavy heart rate up
> **60 – 70% MHR Fat Burning Zone**
> For you, could be a walk your hot, not quite out of breath & heart rate is up
> **50 - 60% MHR Moderate Aerobic Zone**
> A very low level of intensity but the body is working.

Equation to work out Your Heart Rate zones

220 – Your Age = Maximum Heart Rate

   X 0.80 = PEAK PERFORMACE ZONE

   X 0.70 = FITNESS ZONE

   X 0.60 = WEIGHT MANAGE ZONE

   X 0.50 = MODERATE AEROBIC ZONE

Standard Heart Rate zones from my Studies[211]

To begin with take the number 220 and then minus your age from it, the result is your 'theoretical' maximum heart rate. My age is 44 so 220 minus 44 is 176. In theory my maximum heart rate is 176 beats a minute, no its not a set number in that if the rate goes over that number the heart is going to explode, yes I have been asked that question in the gym and no it won't but what will happen is I will be breathing heavy to get oxygen in and I won't be able to keep going for long at all at that rate. We go with this simple calculation as it suits where you are right now. The low heart rate zone of 50 to 60% is known as the Moderate aerobic zone or MAZ, yet if you are very sedentary, trying to do anything about it your heart rate is more likely to shoot up. Even from getting out of the sofa and walking. Any form of exercise including walking that person is likely to get their heart rate straight into the next zone anyway. That is likely to be in the 60 – 70% heart rate zone or the weight management zone which again, is about you doing physical activity, a brisk walk or training session, breathing is increased, but don't quite feel out of breath, heart rate is up but most importantly you can keep going. If you feel it is getting too much, then slow down or rest to bring your heart rate into the 60 to 70% zone. After 10 minutes as your body becomes oxygenated from continually doing an activity, it will progress to increase the time you are doing it. You will burn more fat and you will access fat stores over a longer duration than carbs and fat. To increase your level of fitness the next zone is known as the aerobic fitness zone. This is at a rate of 70 to 80% of your maximum heart rate, the intensity is greater, and you will see your fitness levels increase in a few weeks. You will burn carbohydrates stored more freely during more intense exercise for immediate energy and fat which is accessed too. This leads us onto the highest training heart rate zone of 80 – 90% or the peak performance zone, this is for the highly trained person, it's any form of exercise when the intensity is high. Burning more immediate fuel, carbohydrates than fat. This isn't an area we need to focus on, but your heart rate may shoot up during intense parts of your training say when you are out walking and then hit a steep hill. Your heart rate will shoot up, you may need to stop for 20 seconds to recover but the main point is don't try to do too much too soon. In many very high intense workouts where you're pushing yourself too much you will burn far more carbohydrates stored than fats as the immediate fuel or glycogen in your system will be needed immediately for the high intense work. The justification from such training sessions is such as 'you burn more calories in less time' yes,

---

HIIT – High Intensity Interval Training

A popular trend, performing high intensity work in a short duration mixed with low intensity. A great concept as with any sound training formats but can be sold as an ideal fat burner / weight loss. High Intense, well is someone ready for that type of training ? A CD variation for home use was created years ago on these principles, yet the potential for injury could be high if your current level of fitness is not compatible. With a good foundation of fitness, go for it !

The issue with different training trends and effort needed to get the results in many instances takes the same route as the fad diets. In general, they are different repackaged training principles sold to people promising great results in a short space of time, just like the diets promising big weight loss in a short space of time. The problem is for many, their current fitness levels are not necessarily adapted enough to be able to complete such a session without it being hard, hence a high drop-out rate or potentially unsafe technique.

You need to put in the foundation of training to build to this level so that it becomes achievable. Too intense too quick and you are likely to not want to do it again. Another trap of exercise and physical activity in losing fat weight is that as people see results, they may get really excited & do too much too quickly, that's when there's a higher chance of an injury or fatigue and drop out. Be patient and just listen to your body, if it's tired then rest and go again when you are good.

Task: 6

- **Work out your Heart rate zones**

  It's useful to have a good idea how it works so work your out, if you go to a gym you will soon realise on the CV kit how to use the calculations. Outside the gym it gives you good awareness and if you look at the available heart rate monitors such as custom watches.

Near where I live is a coastal town, opposite the train station there is a very steep hill with 185 steps. It is very steep, but trying to do that in one go is a tough call unless you are conditioned to complete it already. When I use these to improve a client's fitness levels, I use a talk test and how heavy they are breathing, technique and other indicators like posture. I can tell how hard a client is working and have an accurate idea what estimated heart rate zone they are in.

How people are at the different zones :

80% - Cannot talk, the odd word & breathe heavy

70% - Can talk in short sentences, few words

60% - Can talk and heavier breathing

55% - Can talk not quite heavy breathing

An example when it didn't work:

Giving a fitness assessment to a client who's H.R. seemed to shoot up but they were very comfortable in the talk test. It was a concern as may indicate heart /

To make this part of the training session achievable we complete the steps in stages, if it is too much, complete a set distance then rest for 30 seconds and go again. There's no point forcing someone to complete it all in one go if it's too much for them. If the client's current fitness levels are not to a standard which they can complete the session for themselves satisfactorily, it becomes too tough, it's not achievable and they cannot do it resulting in a negative experience. They really ache after the session for a day or more then it all becomes a negative & unpleasant experience and unlikely to return. The result of such training is not good as it doesn't necessarily fit the individual. As we are at different points of fitness, some can hardly walk while others could do a marathon and everyone else being in between, one generic plan invariably won't work. You can do this estimated measurement of your levels when you are out walking, if at a regular pace you feel your heart rate & breathing is up but can keep going, then your heart rate is likely around the weight management zone. If you have a heart rate monitor on, tracking watch then use that maximum heart rate simple equation to get that maximum heart rate (MHR) number. Then multiply by 0.65 the resulting number will be your heart rate in the centre of the weight management zone. You will get the idea of this after a bit of practice, just another way of seeing what your heart rate is offset to how hard you are working.

Our goal is to lose fat in the most safe and effective way, the best perspective is to think of it in terms of health promotion and that each exercise session is a positive achievement. Build up over time in the weight management zone training and then start to add in slightly higher intense work. As the old saying goes, Rome wasn't built in a day and same goes for your plan, take time, be patient, stick to the principles and you will see results. With a far less chance of dropping out of the program leading to you to succeed and then keep it off. Remember, it's not a race but I do understand when people need to see results, following all the principles I am putting forward to you, you will. The key is the more positive the activity as in you know it's working then you are more likely to be motivated for the next session.

Voluntary Muscles

When I was teaching one of the gym courses in colleges one of the areas studied is known as 'Sliding filament theory'. It is the structure of our muscles at a cellular level, that allows us to move, flex and extend a voluntary muscle. As we exercise these muscles, they adapt and take on fuel more readily at the cellular level. The component known as the mitochondria adapts and aids to burn fuel more efficiently which links to our bodies accessing fat stores to convert to fuel more readily. Think of it as an efficient engine, as we add the right fuel it will work better, faster, more efficient. The more active we are, the better we eat, and we have more energy, our bodies work better and exerting more energy during the day, then helps us sleep better at night. The only way for these muscles to adapt is through regular progressive exercise, it cannot happen artificially. You most definitely will increase working muscle use and gradually burn fat more efficiently. There is no 'hidden secret' to this function, a combination of regular structured exercise and the right kind of eating will result in your body burning those excess fat stores and working muscles improve efficiency at burning energy all the time.

Muscle VS fat

From research it appears that muscle does burn more calories than the equivalent weight in fat, the exact amount is up for contention, it is agreed the weight ratio of muscle to fat is 4:1 so as you put effort in, and your shape begins to change sometimes the scales may show you are not losing weight. However, putting all the strategies in place and following everything know you are losing fat weight and working on the lean muscle from all your efforts. Fat takes up more space than muscle, so you need to check waist measurements or as advised use the body analysis scales. This will show what's going on and it's likely that you are losing bodyfat. As you lose more bodyfat and you gain lean muscle weight, the overall calorie burn in your body will increase.

Setting Goals

What is the goal you have always dreamed of, is there a body image you aspire to, a poster of your favourite pinup in your teens, an idol who has a shape that looks impossible to achieve or are you just looking to lose a few stone. I tend to find with many clients who are considerably overweight and what they aspire to would take a lot of time and effort, but they are so desperate to lose it all yesterday and it's got to all magically disappear right now. That is a big indicator to me that they are unlikely to be in it for the long term, I need to get their mind right of what action needs to take place and a realistic view of what they can achieve and in what timeframe. If they do then they can achieve what they desire, however if they want to follow the 'lose it all now' route they likely will drop out. They must break that and really listen to what can realistically be achieved with the right persistent lifestyle adaptations. The classic failure scenario is someone who has tried many times to lose the weight and perceived they have failed every time. That isn't necessarily down to them though, it can be a combination of poor advice, setting unrealistic goals to achieve, and in a very short space of time. Something which again, the diet industry is notorious for. As we have said, money comes first as with fast food, first we promise results but hey, it might or might not happen and it's

'Not our fault, it's yours'

As a rule of thumb, we can realistically lose around two pounds of fat a week, that's the equivalent burn of around 7000 calories over 7 days. That is an amazing amount of fat to lose, the equivalent of losing a thousand calories of fat a day. Look at it like this, what an achievement that would be to consistently lose that many calories in fat daily. Find yourself a bag of sugar of flour the equivalent of 2 pounds, look at the size and weight of it and that's what you will realistically lose every seven days. Remember we are targeting fat not just 'weight' as the muscle helps to burn fat. However, many very big people do have big legs, trained to carry around the weight constantly then over time as the fat weight is lost so will the muscular bigger shaped legs reduce in size, catering for the new slimmer shape which is developing.

A healthy Lifestyle

As you follow each aspect / strategy of your new daily and weekly active and more healthy routine the result will be weight loss. Focus on the changes you are making and not the result that you want and don't be focusing on the scales too much. Those changes you make are the crucial foundation in your weight loss. Let's for example say your goal is to lose ten stone. And yes, I have worked with a client following my principles lost over ten stone, this can be broken down into stages. That 2 pounds a week may not seem a lot where a goal of ten stone is concerned but as you make the lifestyle changes, becoming the norm the weight will come off without you realising it. That is when it gets easy, when the new habits become the normal daily routine and you feel rewarded for doing them. You will feel better and more alert in yourself and we will go through specifically the health benefits of exercise soon too. Back to the goal of losing ten stone in weight, say on average 2lbs a week is lost, now that is a great deal of fat as there's 3500 kcal to a pound of fat so burning off 7000kcals a week is a great achievement. You won't notice it off your frame initially as there is a way to go but make no mistake provided you follow all strategies accurately then we are going to turn you into a fat burning machine. In accordance with principals of goal setting:

'Failing to plan is a plan to fail'

What does that mean, well, for starters to get the end of this book means you are spending your time to get a good plan and vision together which shows conviction that you are ready to succeed. This being the initial stepping-stone in your preparation, follow the guidelines, go through this from start to finish then start again and make notes, complete the tasks as you go through a second time. If that seems boring, or too much to do then think about exactly what you do want. Skipping through the book because you want to get started 'as soon as possible' really won't help. Remember it's not a race against the clock to get going but more to gain the real belief that you can reach your goals, you need to see it, you must taste it. How would you feel if you had achieved your weight loss goal now. Take the time to really absorb the information I am putting forward to you. At each stage as you lose weight, a great way to acknowledge the achievement is to arrange a celebration of getting there (it will make sense as you read through the exercise plan stages). It could be a treat or anything which you really enjoy as a thank you to yourself. Even for setting up all the lifestyle advice points into practice. Does the end goal you have seem like a mountain to climb, in the past you may have started then slid back down? Tried to climb back up only to slide back down again, looking up at the mountain into the distance seeming like an impossible situation. Getting further and further away, then you stop trying, well what do climbers tend to do? They have camps at different stages, at each next height achieved. That's the same as how we are going to plan your goals, in progressive stages. With the aim to lose, say 15 stone, to think that can all be done in one go with such determination and immovable will is far harder and more likely to break down than completing one stage at a time. Rest, refocus and then aim towards the next stage. With weight loss as the goal, I would suggest you set a measurable time (as we will see in detail how to do) then have a celebration as you reach that goal. Something you really enjoy and to look forward to, being self-acknowledgement award of what you have just achieved.

Just like a mountain, Scafell Pike the highest in England, looking to lose so much weight can feel like a mountain to climb. With no real plan & strategy to get to the top, it won't happen. Plan & stopping at designated points will help. As with weight loss, any amount to lose can be achieved with the right plan of action. Scafell was a great day, picturesque.

Keep a structure of the plan in regular visible sight, it could be on your bathroom wall, or the fridge door. Be creative, it could be like a mountain, with the different stages or camps and what is measurable leading up to each achievement. It will be a real positive reinforcement tool to see the visible progress you have made, keeping the plan very visible and a priority in your daily life as a good reminder. A reminder not to fall back into bad habits that is and reinforce you to keep moving forward towards your stages and overall goal.

How about posters on the wall, find a great image to keep you on track. Have a positive image or message to yourself on the fridge door, to make you think if you suddenly have a bad snack how will you feel in relation in the goals. Remember small achievable steps are always much easier to get going than looking at everything all at once. Now look at this in terms of the mountain to climb, aim towards each stage rather than looking at the end goal. The end goal may be very daunting and possibly off putting, so maybe don't focus on that. If the goals you set seem to be too tough as you try and get to complete the stage, review the goal for the stage. Maybe you need more time to reach say the loss of a stone, look at the reasoning why you didn't achieve the first goal parameters. Remove emotional thinking, focus on exactly what you are doing and how you can achieve the short-term goal if it has not been met.

'Is it me, circumstance and or others', our goal setting we need to sit down and look at these three factors if the goals have not been met.

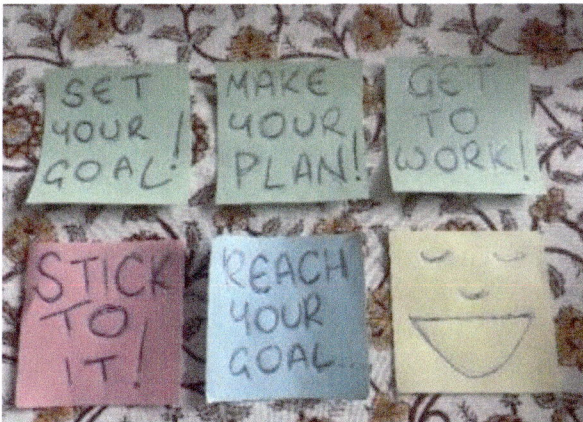

I am going through setting a goal first before you see the exercise plan as you need to know exactly what you want to reach. Could it be 6, 8, 10, 15+ stone to lose ? That's fine, then as we go through the 'phases' my training plan for you, you will be able to slot your goal into place.

One crucial aspect here, do not play the blame game really focus on how you perform day by day, week by week. Never try and point the finger everywhere else but from your own performance, be truthful with yourself.

This is a good quality to look at, if you always look towards everyone else and everything else as though it's never yourself you will never improve nor learn from your mistakes. Be critical of yourself but don't take it personally and beat yourself up about it, look to learn from any goals if they have not been met. Don't worry, but please learn and develop if you haven't achieved what you thought you should already. After this you will gain self-improvement and far more likely to achieve now. From experience, I generally find the people who don't achieve are those who don't take the time to plan, learn, understand and self -develop / reflect honesty of their actions. Especially those who seem to have all the answers and if things don't go to their way, in many instances they didn't even make a start. The main learning experience here is do not deceive yourself and only look at the facts of what is going on, as you get going how you have achieved a stage, or how you haven't achieved a stage. Analyse and go again. No success was achieved without focused and consistent work to improve on yourself, no this isn't down to luck either. You must realise this and what if this assisted you in other areas of your life, altering past patterns to then improve all in different ways. What will it really mean to you if you do succeed in each stage. Know you will get there provided you follow and take focused action on all the guidance. If you do not self-analyse without taking anything too personally or literally about yourself but acknowledge and change the action to succeed at the next affirmed action.

A Goal had Been Set

Back in early 2022, I had been asked to assist in a group of friends in working towards a challenge of completing a military fitness course later that year in 2021 and I was planned be taking part. The course, 10 miles wearing kit weighing 35lbs or 15kg. The aim was to complete this challenge, the PARA10 in 1 hour 50 minutes, I found the training quite tough but gave me a focus during that unprecedented time with lockdowns. The event represents part of the Parachute Regiment selection process with civilians and veterans taking part each year this is an event anyone can take part in, as a physical challenge. We had been working to motivate each other in a group chat, a great way to nudge each other for the event. I was doing well and had a focus after the lockdowns, but mid 2022 I had a sciatica injury in my back two months before the race. The last run I had completed was a

19kilometres without kit to see what the distance will feel like. It was ok, once I got going, I wanted to go further and went beyond the planned 10 miles or 16 kilometres. I was making short videos during and after these planned runs to send to the other group members. Then three days after my last run on a Wednesday I hit the gym, the next day I helped a friend I train with his day job, moving heavy equipment. Then hit the gym the following day and trained a client the following morning. By the afternoon I couldn't sit down nor stand for too long and started to get a pain in my lower back. The next week I struggled to get out of bed, the pain was excruciating. I went to an outpatient A&E who could only prescribe painkillers. As it was a bank holiday week all local physios and Osteopaths were busy, I found suitable exercises to help myself. This was a setback for the race and there was nothing I could do about it, I had to miss out this time. I was gutted but the team took part and did very well, completing the course in good times with one of the lads at 19 got the best time for his age group. It took a good two months before I could do a proper gym workout, I was able to train around the injury with bike work and appropriate exercises. Months later it got much better, but I was cautions with the exercises in the gym. I hope I don't need an operation to rectify the diagnosis of two affected discs it seems far improved now. It stems from an old injury when I was regularly doing high impact sports in my twenties. I was recovering well and training regularly months after feeling positive towards my goals.

Your sessions will be paramount around being safe and effective and as I say don't put too much effort in too soon. Let your body adapt the new lifestyle and you will be fine. Now as I was writing in May of 2023, I have been back training for over the last four months for the next PARA10 event, which is planned for next weekend. I have been able to train with an appropriate weighted vest & added kit. My last session was 13 kilometres and then rest until the event one weekend away. The original injury in 2022 and setback was disappointing, but I am much better now and have been able to train well. The preparation was all through a chat group again and to regularly get the distances up. The team started in October 2022, I was asked to help from February 2023, we would look to add 2 kilometres at each monthly group meet up in Hyde Park. Over the four meetups the group went from 6km to 12km. The extra distance needed we planned would be achieved on the day.

On Saturday 27th of May 2023 the team met up in Surrey, England and everyone that participated completed the challenge. It was a great day and a big achievement for everyone involved, over one hundred and thirty thousand was raised in charity donations for the charity 'Help for Children' and a great effort by everyone involved. Months of planned training and effort resulting in ten miles wearing 35lbs weighted kit, checked in at the start and at the finishing mark. It was a hot day and at the finish line as everyone came in, we were then all escorted to the local pub that had been arranged. With a great atmosphere and the good weather, everyone got a charity medal and gift. After all the training and the event, what happened after, well two weeks later I was back out with all the kit on a 12kilometre tab. I had reached a good level of fitness for the of event and am now looking to my next goal. I want that for you too, reach your goal and then look to the next.

An example of the domino effect, reaching one goal can lead to another. I carried on training at the weekends as we did in the lead up to the event. Then on October 22nd this year, 2023 I headed up to Brecon Beacons in Wales. The Sunday before I headed out locally and completed a distance over 17 kilometres and knew that following weekend would be an ideal time to head to Wales. I wanted to follow a path through all the mountain ranges up there which included the highest point Pen y Fan, this was different to the PARA10 event, instead of dealing with the heat it had other elements. Along with the contours of the land made it the solo event for me which really had everything, the steep climbs the concentration needed underfoot. Dealing with poor visibility, going up the peaks, wind and rain then navigating the region as my GPS would cut off at points. I found myself asking for directions off others I passed up there. As the weather and visibility got a bit worse, I followed a route along a ridge to the left of the last peak I headed to known as Big Y Fan. Then for the next 2.5 to 3 kilometres along a path which had a steep drop to the left a few feet away, at points. Getting to around 17kilometres I decided to keep going as I wasn't going to come back on myself, the route was pleasant, and I was happy with what I had done. Descending into lush woodland and the next 10k on flat road heading back in the direction of the starting point. A great experience and glad that I did it, as soon as I made it back to the car after over 7.5 hours, and a total distance of 28.13 kilometres or 17.4 miles. I then had a five hour's drive to get back home. I was so enthralled with the experience that tiredness only hit as I would try to get out of the car at services on route back, it must have been a sight for others around me.

Blisters on my feet and most of the aching in my hips from carrying the same weight as the PARA10 event and the terrain I had navigated, of sorts. How this can relate to you is reaching one goal can then give self-belief to get to a next goal you set. You only learn and develop as you follow the path you set, it won't just all happen.

For many people and possibly yourself, the effort put into the past attempts at losing weight may have had some success but didn't get to where you wanted. Try and seem to fail, as with my back initially. For some it can set up a perpetual motion of short-term success but long-term failure. This all becomes programmed into your subconscious over the time of these experiences in weight loss attempts, the feeling that this simply won't work yet you will make the time to purchase this or that diet plan and give it a go, but not really make any significant changes. With a feeling that 'you will try this time, but it won't work'. Now eliminate that from your mind now, easy for me to say but not easy to do, as you follow all my advice and are consistent with the daily, weekly plans and strategies you WILL see changes. This will spur you on, seeing more changes and following the guidance on breaks from the regime will then allow you to hit it harder on the next phase and go again. I had a setback and couldn't take part in the 2022 event, sat back recovered and got into preparation for that 2023 event. Looking back, I am pleased I took part and to everyone involved. Now get yourself into the mindset to know that you will succeed this time, forget all negative past experiences your mind is the best motivation for you.

Weight loss timeline

If we look at a timeline of weight loss it will take approximately 70 weeks to achieve a total loss of ten stone. 1 stone is 14 pounds so 10 stone is 140 pounds of unwanted fat to lose Now that sounds like forever doesn't it. Well, think right this moment just how long you have had this weight, how long in these lifestyle habits you've piled it all on with, how long has it been and what exactly would happen if you gained more weight. We must stop the momentum and get it going in the opposite direction. It may not take that long to lose ten stones your body may adapt quicker. The important thing here isn't to perceive all the 'effort' needed to lose so much weight but also that it will be much healthier for yourself. As you are empowered to make it happen, I hope you are starting to realise this is in your hands, as you really, seriously can do this. Again, think of what time is, we can't control it as we can't control the oceans, or how bright the sun burns, or how the planets are aligned in our solar system, but we can make the very best use of our own time. That time will pass regardless, and it is how we make best use of it which really counts. What are you going to do, what really is a year it will be the best way for you to use the coming time into a year from now. Now is time for you to take control, take control of your actions and be a better revised version of you.

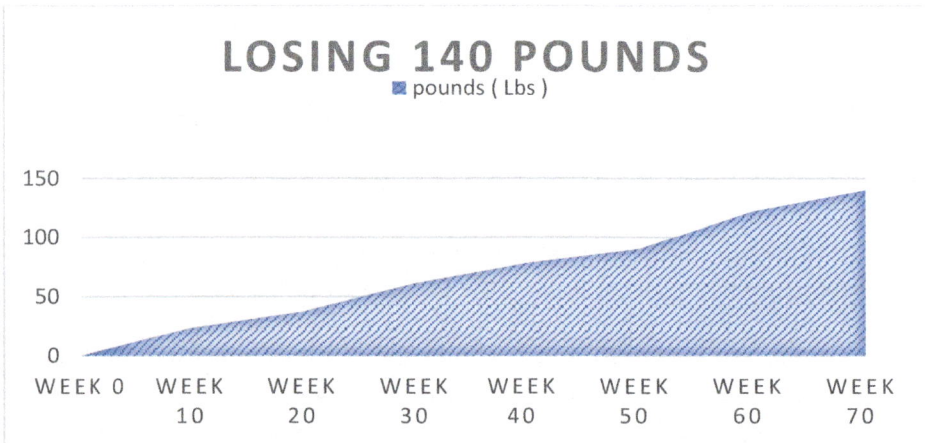

LOSING 140 POUNDS
pounds (Lbs)

How many times I have met with clients / people who regret not pursuing their dreams and goals. Don't let emotions of the past get the better of you. One thing I find very easy is exercise, eating well and following my principles of weight management. As mentioned, I do enjoy exercise and for me it is a form of therapy, clearing my mind while I exercise. For others that therapy can be counterproductive habits, remember that ten stone, losing calories daily, weekly, monthly. Forget the overall timeline but live in the now and make those changes I have already suggested. Lock in the new habits and then as we know the time passes if you take up the challenge, you will gain in so many ways you have not seen yet. In theory losing 20lbs every 10 weeks, but it won't be that straightforward and likely to be more one week or less another week. As you follow all guidelines your progression chart should ideally look like the above, consistent weight loss. Not always the case but your consistent habits will show results. This is an extreme example of a weight loss timeline, but if for you it's a couple of stone the guidelines apply the same, just over less time to achieve your goal. Week by week it can be mentally challenging if you don't see results, focus on the changes. The design of the phase exercise system is to show you how to tailor your own programme starting at the right phase for you. There should be a low chance of people dropping out as the exercise fits around your current levels, then you progress and adapt. You may have better results based on following all guidelines:

- Diet Changes
- Lifestyle / environment
- Physical Activity
- Exercise plan

We have seen the diet changes, with the new plan. All the lifestyle points for your daily routine, soon, the physical activity factors to follow and Exercise plan we go through soon

---

Task: 7

- **The big question, what is YOUR goal**
  What is it you want to achieve, what is the end game for you. Write it all down, what will it mean to you, how will it change you. Write down all the advantages you perceive it can bring. Let it all out and get it all down.

- **Get your set / target weight you want to lose**
- **Work out how long it will take to achieve**
- **Plan set celebrations at certain weight loss markers, could be at each stone lost**
  Or on a bodyscale analysis a percentage fat loss achieved.

Being A Personal Trainer

With supervision and progressive structure to every session my aim is for all clients is for their sessions be achievable, positive and to monitor their ongoing development. Everything done is to help the client is tailored to them and conducted in a non-judgemental and positive way. When training people, for me it's to make sure each client also gets the best information & appropriate guidance for them during their sessions. Each session is tailored to their current fitness levels and each session is very much achievable for them to progress. The regular clients I train are all doing great, they demonstrate good technique and I assist when there needs correction. Each repetition on each set of each exercise is all consistently observed. It's not only about the training but how things are in general, it's genuinely working with people and how people are doing does matter to me as much as their goals and results with the sessions. Many want a trainer but see the hourly fee as too expensive. Thinking that 'well I could save that money and do it on my own', I understand that the issue is that there's a high chance they just don't do it, the financial commitment then comes through in committing to the sessions. The amount of people I know getting annual gym memberships at good prices, which are ideal for full use of facilities, but never go. That's the ideal customer, full upfront payment and never show up, what a shame.

When I worked at a local college gym, my first fitness role people would commit to a monthly / yearly membership, stand there writing a cheque out then I might only see them a few times. From my perception, a lot of people want to take care of themselves but only jump into action when something goes wrong. Not in preventative change and make their week more active and healthier, not investing by putting the time into exercise food planning and activity, trying to juggle everything else first. The new smart phone, new pair of shoes and social spending at the weekend without thinking about it seems to be easy but when it comes to our health, for some reason for many people that's different and not as important, again when there's nothing wrong. Change your mindset and if you can't do it alone and with my help of this book then seek out a good trainer to help you along the way. Making that financial commitment as well as a psychological one knowing someone will be there and you have to be ready.

Not to mention saving that sixty quid from a boozy Friday night and then the Saturday and or Sunday afternoon drinks & fast food / restaurant spend. If that is part of a current lifestyle.

So many of us have the 'want it now' mentality, as we have seen a kind of well if I hand over money what do I get back out of it in a product-based kind of way. Being trained, getting inspiration, sound guidance and a plan in how to progress forward to achieve goals is all part of the experience. Others and I have mentioned are great with a bit of advice of a couple of sessions, they take on board my advice and really go for it. That's the great part of the job to see when people really transform themselves and have nothing but praise for it. Then the others who dip into being active and out, that's far better than doing nothing and works for some people to manage their schedule. I do have other clients like this, and that's fine.

I really do enjoy training people, it's a social job and is really rewarding to see people changing and meeting their goals, it feels like I am making a difference. I like the fact that a lot of the people I work with do become friends, I cannot work in a toxic office type of environment which from my past experiences I was all too familiar with.

Training Clients

I have worked with lots of people over the years, different aims, goals, views yet all getting positive results. Others just want some advice which is fine, and they do well with that. An example of great commitment was with a client, in three sessions at the local gym I worked at the time, some years ago, he took on board everything he needed then was happy to do it by himself. After some months training, he then went up Mount Kilimanjaro, and was over the moon, he had accomplished a dream he'd had for years. After that he stayed part of a running club, I still see him out regularly running and taking part in local events.

Another success story of the friend / client losing 12 stone from sending some tailored information for them. They knew me and wanted advice, so I said that's fine in a few emails they took on board what I had explained for them how to lose weight and the 12 stone came off over the next 16 months. I was really pleased for her, and it seems to work either some need you there or others take on board the info and really go for it. Others are motivated for a few months then take a break, its usually a goal to lose weight for a wedding, for the photos or to getting ready for a holiday.

Only a few meetings I have had with potential clients had ended where they don't want to take part in a planned routine. It has been with very big people, in their minds exercise sounds terrifying and I can understand that. From their experiences of watching TV shows of big people getting pushed too hard by drill instructor style trainers to the point of collapse that would put off most people. I do explain that is just for TV ratings and not real life, some do see it as that impossible mountain to climb, some finding it just too hard to take that first step. I am here to explain that this plan is for everyone wanting to lose weight and learn about weight management. Especially if you are considered severely overweight or to the point of having difficulty being mobile and beyond. Bigger clients have explained how daily life can be tough with their weight, the discomfort of being so overweight. Just to move about with so much weight is tough, I have not been in that situation but part of a study course I completed years ago was to experience this very feeling. One part of the course was to wear an obesity suit to demonstrate the struggles of dealing with lots of extra weight. Soon it becomes apparent being very overweight really does have a negative impact not only on your body but on your mind. It's always there, from the moment you wake up throughout the day up until bedtime. I have heard many suffering with sleep apnoea, people needing a mask to help them breathe. Regular broken sleep being normal then feeling tired and lethargic the next day can be a real drain. Being more prone to sugary foods giving an energy boost, then a dip feeling tired, and many carry on like this. As we go on the idea of promoting health, it will give you more energy and as you gradually change that feeling of constant struggling and negativity towards changing your ways, you will start to experience more positivity. So many negative aspects can and likely do impact on your day, not only the discomfort and tiredness feeling but possibly a dissatisfaction with how your body currently looks, anxiety and a sense of low self-esteem, guilt complex, with the potential social stigma in the western societies, which doesn't help anyone, and this will all change. Which partly inspired me to write this book, so you can really help yourself.

Why do people say one thing and do something else?

I have had a few clients & prospective clients that have been in such a state over how desperate they are to lose weight, I was quite convinced they would be amazing people to train as they appeared they wanted it so much, they came across so determined. From their talk and conviction, they were going to be the best clients I have ever worked with, literally in tears they were so desperate to gain control and lose all the weight. Disappointingly it was all talk, they go through the emotions but when it's time to walk the walk they didn't want to do it. Some didn't even let me demonstrate to them what their ideal plan would be, just meetings with words and emotions, they didn't really want to do anything. It all seems to become a self-destructive cycle which they are less likely to get out of. One example of someone so desperate to lose a huge amount of weight, near half their bodyweight they wanted gone. Being in and out of diets for most of their adult life. They were desperate, I spent hours going through exactly what would be ideal for them. How it would work, all relevant information they were unaware of, at the end I recommended I see them soon after and go through exactly what to do. I was convinced again this was going to be my 'best ever' weight loss client, in several days they replied that they had decided not to pursue what we discussed. Not only had they had not achieved their goal ever, here they didn't even want to try. A big influence is decision making, did they believe what I was saying, I doubt it from their final reply. I got the impression it all seemed too much work ahead and they didn't want to attempt it. It can seem daunting, I do get that, but over time as the body adapts, with the changes and the ongoing weight loss, improved well-being It really does get easier. Seeing a mammoth task in its entirety, as maybe here can be extremely off putting, maybe that's what happened.

Another view is when people know better, there's not much you can do to try and help because well, they know better. That's all fine, I wish them all well and hope they find what they clearly are looking for. This is another reason for me to get writing, so that I can help by people reading and taking in what I have to say, and it really is up to them how to move forward. It's like having the desire so badly to be a top professional sportsperson yet without putting in the hours and hours of practice & dedication after the regular training sessions have finished. It just won't happen, no matter how much in your head you desperately want it. If you don't put that desire in your head into reality and act accordingly it has no chance of happening. A huge emotional turmoil of really wanting something but not really knowing what it takes or just not wanting to go to that level of dedication to achieve that goal. Or their perception of the effort required seeming enough to them for what it takes, but unrealistic of what is really needed to get there.

We all get into habits, good or bad. This can be done with anything, our subject matter is with food, or activity, exercise & lifestyle. I really hope this information I am putting to you is helping and you are becoming more self-aware. I Know you can do it and I am telling you that you can do it. Now start to realise that you really can do it and you will get self-belief that you can do it and take the action required to make it happen. This is far more important than going into a 'new plan' with a simple instruction to follow giving you motivation to do it and you 'hope to do well' no, you will know exactly what's needed and then it's up to you to take the path.

To those that say exercise is futile in losing weight

I have read books of self-proclaimed experts in weight loss who state that exercise as part of a weight loss program is futile. The problem I have is that they do not go into any detail whatsoever to back up their claims apart from statistically there is said to be a high drop-out rate of individuals to continue any form of exercise to contribute to weight loss. Having said this I fully understand why there is such a high drop-out rate, being in that 'want it now' and not knowing what is best for them in so needing a tailored plan, and we have just seen. As you learn of the benefits to your health and body from exercise this element is just far too valuable to your overall health and wellbeing besides weight loss alone to ignore and skip.

One main factor of health in exercise is the direct protective effects of exercise on your heart. Appropriate sessions will allow the heart to become stronger and function more efficiently, now considering people that are considerably overweight and have been for some time wouldn't you want to have a stronger heart to operate the rest of your system? I mean, we pay for our cars to run properly and have to maintain water, oil levels, MOT service, checks and so on to ensure its working properly. We must do this with ourselves, but we are less likely to unless there is a health problem that we then seek to try and get fixed. Many of us just simply don't register it and only when there's a problem, we then look to change things. I am pleased you are looking to address and focus on your goals and taking the time to go through this. Emphasising prioritisation, working hard, paying the bills, and everything else before you consider yourself. What is your favourite possession, is it your car? I'm sure that will be serviced, cleaned and valet regularly. Well, why not yourself? The money and time people put into their hobbies to enjoy and relax, I get that. But why do we only look to invest into ourselves when there is a sudden change in health? We need to be serious about this, as you are looking to lose weight see yourself as your next favourite project or hobby. This way it may be less of an obstacle and more a challenge to enjoy and achieve. As I will reiterate it's about you are in control, being in control of both your exercise / physical activity and your regular routine with food / drink. As you master these factors then weight loss is inevitable. As I have stated, and as we will look at all aspects, if you focus on food drink and physical activity alone you will lose weight, but adding in a tailored exercise plan will allow you to reach your goal even quicker and boost your metabolism. Not to mention the positive mental wellbeing it can offer.

2 Examples: A 19 stone man completes 50 Sessions once a week over one year, that's a burning of an extra 18,000 calories[212] besides the better foods and physical activity plan & lifestyle followed. Not to mention all the added health benefits we are going to go through in the next section. I weekly train on distance walks, 96 minutes one session 762 calories burnt according to my app walk tracker. I have said that following the exercise plan

> 19 stone man completing a 30 minute weight training session bodybuilding or power lifting Total Calories Burned :
> **360 kcals**   360 X 50 sessions = **18,000 kcals**
> In one 30 min session a week over 50 weeks
>
> Weekly calories burnt on 96 minutes:
> **762 kcals**
> 762 X 40 sessions = **30,480 kcals**
> In one 96 min session a week over 40 weeks

is an option as if you are following all the lifestyle environment changes, (we see shortly) the physical activity guidelines and the food plan as you will see great changes anyway. The exercise as I have explained above will give added benefits to you, if it all does seem too much to do at once then that's fine. Do what's best for you and see the changes in the three of the four strategies to weight loss.

Health benefits of exercise.

Exercise is so good for us, as categorically stated on the NHS website and I quote:

> *'Exercise is the miracle cure we've always had, but for too long we've neglected to take our recommended dose. Our health is now suffering as a consequence, this is no snake oil. Whatever your age, there's strong scientific evidence that being physically active can help you lead a healthier and happier life*[213].

As we have mentioned, it has a protective effect on your heart the organ & walls get stronger and as with any muscle it will adapt. Exercise promotes better circulation throughout your body and reduces the chance of atherosclerosis which is hardening of the arteries or artery plaque build-up. If you have been unhealthy and sedentary for years and do have some partial build up, exercise can assist in it not progressing and promote circulation accordingly. By producing HDL'S or higher density lipoproteins, these are created in the liver aided from exercise and they help to keep clear any potential further arterial build up. From taking part in regular exercise your body's metabolic rate will increase, meaning you will be more alert as well as burn more calories daily. As you exercise and use more energy in the day it will help you to sleep better at night. This in turn will help you burn fat in your sleep over a longer period as you are more likely to have a full night's sleep. As you exercise regularly either with walking or in the gym it will help with connective tissue at your joints. In losing mid-section weight can help further with joints especially knees. As you perform regular resistance sessions more voluntary muscle will need more calories so in turn it's easier to burn more calories. There is a reduction in the risk of Tumours & various illnesses, it will help you gain confidence and have a more outgoing approach to life, as you can do physical tasks more easily. As this develops you will see you are doing more without realising it so burn more calories and move around more. Your lipid profile (blood) will be healthier, more oxygenated and you will head towards having a healthier fat content. Combining exercise with the healthy regular diet will reduce your visceral fat stores, that's the fat contained around organs within the body and the more visible subcutaneous being our goal in weight loss. It will help to reduce blood pressure and help to remove toxins from the body. As we see a lot of people in the western world developing type 2 diabetes, exercise will help the body to become more insulin sensitive so the sugar in blood or glycogen is removed and absorbed easier by muscles, as we have already highlighted. With the exercise and resistance training, the result is stronger muscles to support the body and a potential to reduce the chance of an injury. If you are less stable and weaker there more chance of falls and bone breaks. Better support of the mid-section posture and with appropriate exercises supporting the back decreasing the chance of back pain as many bigger people have a lot of weight at their stomach which can cause spinal problems. Exercise helps to reduce stress, with the positive natural chemical rush after exercise, endorphins will increase a sense of wellbeing. It's potential to swap the pub / fast food for the gym and being more outdoorsy is a financial as well as a health benefit reward. The calorie difference could be removing poor food choices and adding exercise will be a big difference in calories take on than those burnt off from the exercise session alone. There are more examples of the benefits of exercise, but I think you get the idea, it's good for us. I have read from many different authors, medical journals, documentaries, and health programs. Some of which have categorically stated if they could create a magic pill which can give their clients all the health benefits of exercise, that is the elixir. The problem is this simply cannot be done, we cannot mimic the positive effects of exercise on the body. Facebook, You Tube and many of the huge corporations are pouring millions into just this idea. However only exercise & doing what our body is designed to do will we get these positive effects, so I would advise you now create a training program for yourself which I can guide you through in the coming information.

Create a fat burning weight loss environment

1. Remove All crisps sweet snacks and any rubbish from the house because if it's there, you're more likely to eat it. Replace with fruit, nuts, vegetables, and salad options to be within reach, check the examples we've gone through. I tend to use fruits to replace sweets, mango is very sweet, strawberries, raspberries, pomegranate. Making these as now your regular snacks, your pallet will change over time away from the sweet treats of the past. Fruit really should be our way of having a sweet treat, slice a mango up and leave in the fridge as a snack. Have strawberries and raspberries in the fridge as a snack, you will get used to the flavours of these natural foods and you will feel good for it. Make it a ritual sacrifice, get an empty bin, get hold of all the chocolate, crisps and the like, look at all the stuff knowing it's not good for you. It's your call.

'I cast thee into oblivion, begone'

Once everything in your house is in there go and straight away put it into the bin outside, there must be no temptations to go and bring any of it back indoors. An alternative is to ensure you significantly reduce your weekly intake. I just don't want the temptation to be there.

2.   Plan a weekly shop to include all natural snacks for the week as above, so these are the only options that come to hand in doors. Also have cooked chicken, turkey, protein-based snack options in the fridge. As per the diet plan, ideally protein-based snacks or extra foods / evening eats.

3.   Everyone in your home environment need to assist you and to work together. From past clients the urge of temptation as other house members eating whatever they want can be hard. This must be a team effort, if you can resist temptations put in front of you then kudos to you. If not, it really is down to you so if there's others in the household don't make that as an excuse as to why you cannot follow the plan. If your kids eat different to you, that's still no excuse to graze on their stuff. Give them the same as you're having, it's ideal to get them into good healthy eating too.

4.　　Learn to cook from scratch, many of the clients I have trained over the years with weight management issues didn't cook for themselves. They would often opt for takeaways and pre-made food. When you cook for yourself, you know what's going in, other than the examples in the diet plan, there's plenty of different healthy recipes online, have a go. It's not hard, just follow the instructions, the more you do it the easier and quicker it gets.

5.　　Add in this physical activity stair challenge straight away:

Week 1: up and down three to five times every day / other day
Week 2: up and down five to seven times every day / other day
Week 3: up and down seven to ten times every day /other day

You can increase weekly, if a few is very comfortable then start on ten as you can do more, you get the idea. If it's too much, then reduce the number of times up and down so start with one or two. Being consistent and building over time is key, five a day is far better than none a day and don't look to build it to 50, or 100 a day within a couple of weeks. Just manageable and convenient if it gets continuous to 5, 10 or 15 minutes a day then great. If you ache, do it every other day and see the changes.

6.　　Get rid of the sugary soda soft drinks and focus on sugar free only, cordial with water and with the fruit juice strategy & drinks we have gone through. The sugar in the big brand juices is unbelievable, remember to look at the labels and make the connection. The diet drinks are no good thanks to all the fake sugar and further additives, remembering your taste buds adjust over time.

7.　　If you love tea and coffee, and you do add sugar from now gradually reduce the sugar amount each time. From now if you have two sugars, in your next cup only have one and a half. Do this for a week then go down to one sugar. The following week reduce to a half, then look to remove sugar from your tea. Over time your palette will get used to the new taste, the two sugars won't be missed, and you won't miss the extra calories that used to be in your hot drink. One teaspoon is about 16 calories, so say six cups a day with two sugars is an extra 192 calories or 1,344 a week. The calorie equivalent of nearly half a pound of fat there just in sugar.

8.　　Get all the tinned foods out of the cupboard and look at the labels, use tinned foods but be aware of the content. Look to reduce if you do have a lot regularly onto fresh wholefoods. Or gradually reduce the tinned stuff, just make sure you are aware of the contents. We have been through in the label reading section.

9.   If you are peckish into the evening anything protein-based and no sugar snacks / chips / carbohydrate loaded. Salad or vegetable style is fine, aim at the Low G.I. examples from the diet.

10.   If you like smoothies or never made your own before a good habit is to create your own, with semi skimmed milk or almond milk for example, and low sugar substitutes add half a pint and add fruits of choice like bananas, strawberries, blueberries. As we have gone through, they're Ideal as a quick breakfast or meal substitute if you don't have time to prepare properly. Do not buy the smoothies out of shops as they are often from concentrate and likely contain a great amount of sugar, contrary to what the marketing of them implies.

11.   If you eat regular white bread replace this with granary and or brown bread again over time you will prefer this as your palette changes and won't miss white bread. I can't stand the stuff now, only granary or wholemeal are preferences.

12.   When eating at mealtime take your time, enjoy it and don't race to get it down. You will start to feel full rather than rushing and getting more food in before it registers.

13.   Drink a glass of water previously or with each meal, it can help with reducing the food portion size you then eat, also hydration is good for us in general.

14.   On your smartphone if there isn't an app recording your daily steps then download a free app to track walks and distance to add to motivation aiming at an increased amount every day for 3 weeks then progress. If you struggle to get about, try to be more active one day then look at how many steps you did. That will show you your current capabilities, don't change for a week and look at the results and improve from that. Look to gradually improve daily or if it's too much to begin with then every other day. If you start the stair activity keep your phone on you for record. This is besides exercise, just daily steps, increasing daily physical activity. There are many free apps out there which are useful to record your workouts outdoors, tracking your route via GPS, distance and calories burnt this helps to give a physical record and add to motivation. 10,000 is a lot of steps, if you are doing say 2000 then aim to consistently add a thousand daily for a couple of weeks then increase that.

15.   When you go to the supermarket park your car farthest away from the shop, yes you will have to walk adding to your daily physical activity. It may not be the most convenient but helps to your daily step count. Look

at this for other scenarios when you park your car or look at planned walking routes for daily tasks if possible.

16.   Get yourself a list of physical jobs that need to be done around your house / where you live. From regularly cutting the grass to clearing a room, tidying up. Fixing and painting the fence, it could be to rearrange the garden. Aim at one different thing every other day, not only are you doing a good job you will be adding to the fat burn.

17.   Check sauces if you cook with them. Possibly lots of sugar and or fat, but again just make sure you are aware, there's no need to live like a monk on just cabbage water. Also don't have food swimming in sauce, if you don't know what's going in then treat it as fat & sugar.

18.   To help with motivation theres lots of content on smartphone apps like YouTube and there will be social media setup from me.

19.   Look at who you mix with, if they are a negative influence on what you want to achieve for yourself then limit the time you spend with them. Identify with what you want and then seek out likeminded individuals. It will help with motivation in general, it could be going to the pub or eating the wrongs foods etc.

Task: 8

- **Environment preparation:**

Before you take the big step to start your upcoming exercise action plan, I would advise to make these environmental changes, it could be you implement that for some weeks first. Get your environment, habits, and mind right to encourage the next stage of the body transformation. As we have gone through lots of strategies to put in place which will lay a foundation in aid to your weight loss. There is a lot to take in and things to do which may take that extra time to get it all in place and for it to become a new routine. Follow each point and implement it into your daily routine and be consistent before you look to start the next phase. If you try and do everything all at once it could be too much. You could take a week or a few weeks to implement everything up to this point before the next tasks. It's all a big step, so plan how is best for you, as doing everything at once could be too much of a big step.

---

20.   Look at new different things you would like to try, jot down 20 things that you have always wanted or look to new challenges / experiences you may like to have a go of. Make plans as you lose weight to encourage you to reach your goals.

Beginning Your Exercise Plan

There are two options on starting your plan, if you are very big and find it hard to walk any distance and I mean as soon as you try to get out of the chair it is a struggle then start at the Phase foundation stage. Here we will be looking to get you mobile enough in preparation for phase one. If you can walk a short distance then need to rest, go straight onto Phase one. This is all a gradual process of change over time, read through all the phases and take in what the training system is all about. This has been in development based on the experience from working with clients, giving you the best scenario to make sure you can achieve and get to where you want to be.

Up to this point the content has all been about getting you right in your mind, showing how we have been impacted and influenced in gaining weight. How our bodies work and where we may go wrong, not necessarily through all our own fault but more a result of our environment. Don't look to cut any corners such as jumping phases ahead. You will only be cheating yourself out of the good work and results you deserve as this is not another quick fix this is your strategy to change and meet your goals.

Follow everything to the letter and in the weeks and months to come you will look back at just how much you have achieved. At the end of each week keep a diary of how the week went what you did well and maybe what you could improve on for your plan. If you really do want your goal, then you will put the effort into this part and then all the phases. If you go into it thinking, 'oh I'll just have a go at this and that and hope it works' then you are likely to do the same with the phase plan and then the results won't be what you may hope for. I do repeat myself but please, do not kid yourself as you are in control because you can change the way you are to what you really want to be and only your actions will make it happen.

- *Take a photo of yourself.*

In shorts or under ware in front of the mirror or get someone to photograph you at the exact same position and the same time of day once a week every week from now on. Do so when it's convenient for you, maybe right now for your first one? Maybe a Saturday morning at 9am or just as you get up. Save and date each picture into your smartphone as you take them. As you look back over the coming weeks & months you will see the transformation and it will be motivating to see how much you have achieved. Reaffirm to yourself whatever shape you are in now you ARE going to change. Really look at yourself, think how you want to be in the time to come. Take your time and then take that picture (do a full torso front and side, same positions pic)

Be accountable to you, don't think of this stage as a weight loss stage, more a health encouragement & preparation stage for the upcoming phases.

- *All non-exercise strategies in place from the previous instruction on your home / work*
  Environment as mentioned.

- Seven-day diet sheets done & new habits adopted.
- All guidance points put in place in your home.
- Regular physical activity added in daily with a progression strategy.

Task 9
- **From now keep a weekly diary of progress and self analysis, as long or as short as you want**
  - What you did well, changed
  - What didn't go to plan & why (if needed)
  - What you are going to change / focus on
- **Take the weekly photo of yourself for reference of your progression**
- **All up to scratch with all previous tasks complete**
- **We are now going to go through the tailored exercise plan, once you are confident in your lifestyle changes and progress then move onto either the phase foundation as appropriate or onto phase 1.**

Start to really think about weight loss and being healthier, read into the benefits of it and visualise where you want to be. Our minds are such a powerful thing so as you act on your goals switch onto it and make it a kind of hobby. It shouldn't be seen as all an effort as this really is going to benefit you. Consider warm ups and cool downs for the sessions, the more low impact less intense will result in less chance of injury (which is unlikely) however a warm up is advised. To mimic the exercises with no weight targeting the muscles for reps is fine, shoulder circles and knee raises are advisable. Being big is touch to stretch so the preliminary focus is on getting the heart rate up and target the weight. For static chair exercise monitor heart rate in how you feel. When walking, warm up incorporate a slow walk 3 to 5 minutes.

Foundation Phase

The foundation phase is about getting a foundation of fitness, if your current situation is one of finding it hard to get about around the house then this is for you. To build up and progress so we can then get you going into phase one. We need to get you to a point of being able to get around the house without discomfort, being able to support your own current weight for short consistent periods of time. That means starting a regular plan which is achievable for you. If walking any kind of distance is not an option at this moment, we will start with seated chair exercises. I have added in some standing exercises and leg movements to assist. Focus on your daily food, home strategies and the physical activity you are only capable of. In your current state carrying all the weight is likely to be tiring not only the weight itself but your heart rate is likely to shoot up when you are just trying to get up and about. The exercise we are going to do here is controlled and you will be able to do it. It's about getting active in an achievable way for you, and with all the other weight loss strategies in place.

Safety points:

- **Breathing during a resistance training session, breathe out on exertion & don't hold your breath.**
- **Tempo, count 2 up 2 down on speed of the movement**
- **Any light-headed / dizzy feeling, then stop**
- **Don't lock the elbows or knees fully out on any resistant exercise just before they do then return to the starting point**
- **Maintain good posture throughout the movements**
- **Warm up can be mimicking the movements you will do with no weight**
- **Further guidance will be on Facebook 'The Obesity Secret' group for warm up / cool down and exercise demonstrations.**
- **Seek professional guidance in a trainer or gym instructor to aid**

The Chair Exercises

We are going to focus first on raising your metabolic rate / encouraging calorie burn working on lean muscle through these resistance movements, so you will start to burn more calories ongoing over a day period. Aim at a minimum of two sessions a week, up to three sessions a week. An example of this being Tuesday & Thursday or then Monday, Wednesday, and Friday. As this happens regularly over weeks you will gradually be able to get about the house better and then you are ready move onto the next phase. It is crucial you get into a regular routine with completing these movements. It's easy to have a negative view of exercise as maybe it's not your thing but is in the past now, see this as rehabilitation to get you away from your current position and free from the weight you must carry around with you. Get this positive mindset before and during every session. Remember, this is good for you this is how you are going to change this is how you are going to get there. Between each set (doing the movement eight to twelve times) rest for thirty to forty-five seconds. If you are struggling and your heart rate is up, then rest a bit longer. If you have any heart issues seek the advice of your GP & don't do any movements overhead such as the seated shoulder press.

Technique

Take a seat at the edge of a chair which you can sit upright in, and feet are flat on the floor, with a weight in each hand. The weight needs to be light enough so you can perform the exercises but heavy enough so at the last few repetitions of each set you feel fatigue in the targeted muscles. The weight could be dumbells, or a can of beans, anything comfortable to hold really and giving resistance. If you feel your arms are currently heavy enough to perform the exercises with no weight, you be the judge. On warm ups, shoulder rolls & performing the exercise movements without weight beforehand is ideal as a specific warm up aim for 3 – 5 minutes.

Seated lateral raise 1 x 8 – 12 reps.

Seated in an upright position, good posture and raise your arms slightly bent outwards holding the weight or just arm weight if they feel heavy enough to your side to shoulder level and back down to your side, repeat for the target number of times.

Seated to standing 1 x 5 – 10 reps.

Seated in an upright position, aim to stand without any support. (If you need to at first then fine, over time look to stand up without assistance) Feet shoulder width apart and aim for your bodyweight to go through your heels, meaning not onto your toes. If it helps hold your fingers at your temples (side forehead) elbows out to the side, as you progress to stand unassisted. Tense your midsection and aim to keep your torso straight throughout. You will lean from the waist slightly forward as you get up, that is fine.

Seated bicep curls 1 x 8 – 12 reps.

Seated in an upright posture, Arms positioned to the side, palms facing slightly outwards. Curl the arm to chest height, keep the upper arm in a vertical position throughout, wrists locked straight if holding a weight.

Alternate knee raises 1 x 8 – 12 reps.

Seated in an upright position, good posture chest out shoulders back and alternatively raise each knee up, foot off the floor and down then the other. Your heart rate will go up as you do this, as it's a big body movement, that's what we want.

Front raise 1 x 8 – 12 reps.

Seated or standing, try both and see what suits you better. Arms to the sides with palms facing down in front and raise the arms up in front both to shoulder level and return down to the front. When seated same position but arms starting down at the sides, same action. Either at the same time or alternate each arm, see what works for you.

Leg extensions 1 x 8 – 12 reps.

Seated in an upright position, both feet flat on the floor positioned hip width apart, raise on knee so the foot is slightly off the floor and extend the lower leg out straight in front. Raise the lower leg up just before the knee joint locks out, return the foot to the ground and alternate. Alternatively, to make it a bit harder raise both at the same time and grip the chair for support keeping the torso upright, this could be a progression exercise after getting use to the single leg movement.

Frequency

To start we are looking at one set of each movement per session of the indicated rep range. If you feel you can do more than the total of six sets then go for two sets of each exercise. Go with how your body feels in terms of fatigue so if it's too hard, even with only bodyweight then reduce the range of movement. Make it a partial repetition on each exercise so you can complete on or near the targeted repetition amount. Gauge this yourself as only you know how easy or hard it is, we are targeting the voluntary muscles and you will know it's right if you do have some muscular fatigue over the next day or two. Visualise the muscles you are working and feel them contract and extend on each movement, this is to get you more in touch with this resistance training and know it's working.

- *This chair routine for 3 weeks + all planned eating points & physical activity then 1 week rest*

A.VERY LOW FITNESS	B. LOW FITNESS	C. THIS PHASE FITNESS
Two weekly chair sessions	Three weekly chair sessions	Three weekly chair
One/two short weekly walks	Two short walks a week	Three short walks

Workout time of chair fitness and the walk 10 – 20 minutes Include all the lifestyle factors, physical activity where can be and the new diet in place

Aiming at this for three weeks then the one-week rest, you will not stop losing weight as your body is adapting. If you need you can do another three weeks of this at two to three sets per exercise. That's six or nine weeks of good work, you should start to see changes in getting about the house. If you feel you can do more now, either do two or three sets per exercise, or complete all the exercises once then do all the exercises again. See how you feel, as this is all about your fitness levels and how hard you find it to complete. If you see good improvements in the first weeks, such as being able to get about better. If you want to invest in home kit look at a recumbent bike, rowing machine and an indoor walking machine. The kit is not essential as it can instead be short walks in the garden and not forgetting the lifestyle physical activity of incorporating daily, every other day stair climbs (Here for you it may be to take a few steps up, rest and go again depending on your current levels).

- *If interested in home kit look at recumbent bike, rowing machine, running machine*

No, you won't be doing any running but short achievable walking distances and build on it. This would be a great indicator at your progress. As you complete each week, starting with two short walking sessions a week added after the chair exercise after say the Monday and Friday sessions. If you start on two sessions a week as three seems too much, then add the short walks in after both those sessions. If walking is too much of a struggle, don't walk yet. On the three sessions, see how you feel and if you feel you can do a third walking session after a week then go for the next two weeks at three full sessions a week of chair exercises and walking, if not indoor kit, then go for the walks using distance indoors or an outdoor area. If very unfit you may want to start at A, onto B then C. Try out any kit options from a superstore before you buy, don't just go for cheap online, but if it's in the local buy n sell ads in social media or local paper go and try it before you buy. If it's not a good sturdy bit of kit you are likely to use it a handful of times and it soon becomes a clothes horse to dry washing, I have seen that a few times. Find out your local big fitness store to go and have a look, you may have to spend a bit but for this to help towards your life goal it will be well worth it, demonstrating to yourself you are willing to commit to the plan giving yourself every chance. The convenience of being able to do the workout in your own home, with a treat and incentive another way to motivate would be to only allow yourself to watch a favourite TV program, boxset, or film while you are on the kit or during the chair exercises. Have it on while you exercise, as a kind of incentive to help with consistently doing the training sessions.

Example :
Start with 1 lap of the garden to walking or to a point it becomes too tough and you ache but don't push too much. If you struggle, rest and go again an example:

| Week 1 | - | 1 lap | week 3 | - | 3 laps |
| Week 2 | - | 2 laps | week 4 | - | 4/5 laps |

Aim for whatever you can do to start then build. If with everything you are doing you may stick at say one lap for more than one week.

The clear results of being able to gradually do more for longer as you'll see will show you what progress you are making. Forget looks and bodyweight for this part (there will be changes) as our goal is to get you ready for the phases. Be under no illusion, to go from struggling to walk (if this is you) to phase one will take time. Do not rush, crucially be consistent & as you put the effort in following all the strategies and now with the exercise plan you will gradually come out of the confinements of your body as you start to really burn the fat stores over the weeks. It's a real balance of being consistent, knowing you are working just hard enough to make a difference but not too much, resting and repeating the process. As you go through and review your daily food and drink intake along with this phase you will likely see some great changes in your capabilities.

Remember don't kid yourself, your body weight loss will be the result of the ongoing structured effort you put in. Following the training principle of three weeks structured exercise and physical activity with food checks then have a week off is achievable and allows your body to recover, don't try to keep going and going. You will start to see your clothes getting bigger over the weeks as you are burning the fat off and in no time, you will be telling yourself - great work.

On the week off your metabolism will still have the training effect but you are letting your body have an adequate rest. Allowing muscles and joints to recover from the good effort you have put it. (You could add in one walk/swim preferable low impact cyclical exercise if possible, during mid rest week). Go for another three weeks of training and following the principles, repeat this process until you can complete ten + minutes of continuous unaided walking. At that point congratulations, you should now be able to get around easier and be able to do more daily for you increasing your quality of life, you are now ready to progress onto phase one. Remember, if you do fall off the plan for a few days that's no worries. It may happen don't just let it go but get back on plan straight away. You want to be able to look back at all the good work you have put in and feel more positive that you are going to achieve than let go and think 'oh well, I'll do it another day'. Have a good time, but make sure you are on plan straight away we do need to live our lives. It's all about balance and we are looking to create that good balance here between living life, helping your health and meeting your goals. For some this can truly seem like a mountain to climb and more, you must know that every positive action you follow is making a difference. Self - belief is a tough thing as how can you pluck it out of thin air, I can say that you are doing the right thing and you will lose the weight get more mobile and progression is inevitable, but you must do it. To just exercise with no self-visible results is a tough one, many use the scales as a way of motivation, but your weight won't necessarily show how much fat you have lost. Seeing your progression is you witnessing yourself being able to become more mobile, that should give you the positive feedback and spur you forwards. I believe positive reinforcement is needed, self-encouragement, and seeing results.

Why many find it hard who fall into this category is that getting into finding it tough to get about took time and getting your body out of it is a gradual process and will take time. I would say try and forget overall time and change on a daily / weekly basis. The results will come as a side effect of what you are changing in food physical activity and exercise.

Self-reflect and be honest with yourself, read the next section which is phase one and really ask yourself are you ready for this phase. As I've mentioned, it is not a competition to get to the next phase as quick as possible only the truth in your own achievements will see if you are ready. It is all a journey and if you need a couple or several more weeks doing what you are doing, revisit and go through the foundation phase again, its ALL progression, read through Phase one to decide. You are achieving and the journey is all about what you are doing and seeing how your body is changing. We cannot speed up the process so be thorough in your planning and if it's too tiring then listen to your body.[214] If you have put in place the lifestyle strategies, physical activity, food guidance and with these sessions you really are making a difference to yourself. Give yourself a huge pat on the back, it's not about lifting loads of weight for an hour or more at this stage. It's that you are making a difference to you, you now know you can do this. You have already succeeded if in your mind you know you are going to take this seriously. Your weight management guide is here.

Phase One

Phase One is your exercise plan for the next three weeks, your fitness levels are adequate to start at this level then great. This phase is focusing on cardiovascular exercise, this first three weeks is for you to complete 3 to 4 sessions a week, walk for a minimum of 10 to 15 minutes away from where you live and then aim to walk back in the same amount of time, totalling 20 to 30 minutes per session. If you struggle fine, slow down and break up the selected time with one or two rest periods and aim for the minimum ten minutes out and ten minutes back. You will only know what you can achieve when you are out there trying it. As you walk you need to feel not quite out of breath and you can keep going, (refer the heart rate zones) your heart rate will be up, and you are likely to sweat. If your heart rate goes up too much and you are fighting for breath then slow down, if you ache / fatigue too much then rest. This is a simple way to set an achievable goal and then look over time to increase it. Work out at a time when is most convenient for you, build it into your day when you are most likely to do it. If being outdoors isn't your thing, arrange it indoors or in the privacy of your back garden. You might work from home or don't want to be outside, so complete the sessions how they would suit you the most. It could be twenty laps of your kitchen or hallway, does it take twenty to thirty minutes. Time a route you set, provided you are continuously walking for the 20 to

30 minutes you really can be anywhere. Should you be fatigued and tired the next day or two after a session, then aim to complete the same amount of time a day after that onset of muscle soreness and don't worry it's a natural process. If you try to repeat your sessions every day or too often, too soon you may feel too much fatigue and drop out so listen to your body.

In this first week Phase One see what time is achievable for you and repeat for three times that week. In the next week aim to add 3 to 5 minutes on the outward journey, so it will naturally be the same heading back. If your initial time was a minimum 10 minutes out now aim at 13 to 15 minutes. Then the next week add again 3 to 5 minutes, aim for this increase every week for the three weeks. Obviously if you are using indoor kit complete

Phase 1	Duration
Week 1	20 to 30 minutes
Week 2	+ 6 to 10 minutes
Week 3	+ 6 to 10 minutes

At a minimum of 20 minutes 3 sessions a week to 50 minute sessions by week 3 maximum.

each workout on the full planned times, or maybe you feel you want to mix it up by having an outdoor walk and then two indoor sessions. Do it however you feel comfortable, over the weeks you will gradually feel more awake during the day and connective tissue at knees hips and ankles could improve and be more supportive. If you do have issues with walking because of any joint problems, then the indoor kit is likely a better option for you. In the gyms for people with joint / weight issues I always would start them off on a recumbent bike, check it online. The back support and pedal position, allows comfortable pedalling and promotes good circulation. Running machines & cross trainers are good (as mentioned in the foundation phase section). Do not try and do the maximum I have said unless you really have the fitness to do it. Most importantly see how you go any session is far better than no session, again listen to your body. You will see how your body quickly adapts to the simple and measurable routine. You will be calorie burning while doing this but also creating a foundation of fitness to progress onto the next phase. If you own a smart phone have a look at the free apps out there that can keep a record of your progress as it will record your map & route, distance, average pace, and calories. This information further adds motivation for the plan showing you further information of completion and the info and maps do look good, giving that kudos appeal.

As you complete Phase One give yourself a big pat on the back, how do you feel now after three weeks. Also following all lifestyle strategies adding these new active sessions. Have you been weighing yourself, how do your clothes fit I bet they are looking big on you and don't forget to take that weekly progression photo of yourself & diary of your performance in the week. Well done on this completion, now have the seven day's rest, not only for your body but psychologically too. It doesn't mean now rest from all the other lifestyle and food strategies but relax from training sessions in preparation for phase two. A pointer for Phase One rest week, you could decide to do something completely different like an easy swim or just something away from the plan once or twice in the week. We don't want to cause any injury or fatigue through overuse of your body and as mentioned rest is very important. Remember in all these phases the week time frames are not set in stone, if you feel the next stage is too much for now then go through the current phase cycle again. Have the planned week off to recover and then go for another three weeks at this phase. The better you follow the plan being consistent, the better results you will have to then progress. This is down to you and the actions you take will yield the results you want and remember we are looking at around 2lbs a week or 7000 calories targeted fat loss. With following all guidance, it could be more weight loss. With the added mobility from your physical activity and exercise this is all a gradual process to get you in the right direction.

Phase Two

We now are going to add in a simple exercise routine which can be done at home in a small amount of space. Now you will be aiming at around 15 to 20 minutes per workout and a minimum 30- minute brisk walk after. The full session time progressively increases with resistance and walking is around 45 to 50 minutes in total, resistance movements and then the cardiovascular work incorporating a cool down. The exercises are a mixture of compound and isolated muscle movements meaning working many voluntary muscles in one exercise or focusing on one muscle area to ensure muscle activation across a lot of the body and therefore a good calorie burn. This will be further raising your daily metabolic rate. The movements that use a lot of muscles at once will likely result in your heart rate shoot up, this is fine but take care not to overexert yourself and keep it sustainable. The 12 to 20 rep part means aim for a minimum of 12 repetitions, and if you can only do 8 to 12 reps fine. If you're struggling with the squats then complete partial reps, not thighs parallel to the floor. I repeat, it's always advisable to seek professional guidance to assist in your form.

Exercises:

2 sets x 12 – 20 reps Wide Stance squat

In a standing position, place the feet shoulder and a half width apart and feet pointing slightly outwards. Fingers can be placed on the side of the forehead at the temple, elbows pointing outwards and parallel at shoulder level. Lower your body and stick your glutes slightly back and out, knees not sinking forward past the toes, your back will naturally lean slightly forward from the waist. Keep the back straight, meaning don't arch or round the back and only lower at the hips with the thighs parallel to the floor at your lowest point. If heels come off the floor, then to prevent this just perform partial repetitions. As long you feel the quadriceps and glutes muscles working also bringing in some Hamstring work.

2 sets x 12 – 20 reps Knee press ups

Press ups are a great movement, and this variation is all about building up to a full press up. The knee variation positioning start is to lay face down on the floor, hands placed out to the side in line with chest level palms on the floor & elbows out with upper arms parallel to the floor. Now raise your body up and keep the torso taught from the knees on the floor to shoulders. We are reducing the movement intensity by not performing a full press up, and from knees to shoulders keep the body in a straight line. Bending at the elbows for the press up and the knees pivot on the floor.

2 sets x 12 – 20 reps Regular squats

In a standing position, position feet hip to shoulder width apart and feet pointing straight ahead. Fingers back on the side of the forehead at the temples. Lower the body from the hips & bend knees, as with the sumo squat stick the glutes back & out and knees not sinking forward past the toes. Again, keep that torso straight don't round the back, lower to the point of thighs parallel to the floor and return to the start position.

2 sets x 12 – 20 reps Standing Front Raise

In a standing upright position, feet shoulder width apart, use weights for this exercise. Hold in each hand palms facing down. Hold your arms down in front of you to your sides, keep them straight at the elbow throughout the movement and raise them up in front of you to shoulder level, then return down to the start position in front.

2 sets x 12 - 20 reps bicep curls

In a standing position hold the weights in your hands, down at your sides palms facing out & in front. Keep your upper arms vertical and bend at the elbows in half a circle bringing your hands up to chest height. Keep the wrists locked straight and return half circle motion to the starting position.

2 sets x 12 – 20 bent over row

In a standing position and bend from the waist aiming for the torso to be near parallel to the floor. Keep the back in a straight position with the weight you are holding in both hands, arms straight down near the floor. Draw the elbows up to the sides up past the torso until hands are close to the body. Return the arms to the starting position and repeat. You should in this position feel the legs, glutes supporting your position isometrically. The main muscles targeted are the back, with some bicep work, another compound movement.

2 sets x 12 – 20 Standing Shoulder Press

A big movement as we are activating a lot of postural muscles to hold the position. Stand feet shoulder width apart, with the weight you have hold in each hand at shoulder level, upper arms parallel to the floor with palms facing away from you and knuckles parallel to the ceiling. Start at this position and raise the weights up overhead high just before the arms lock out and return. Safety point here, keep it nice and controlled and emphasise you are well within your capabilities of lifting the weight. It cannot be heavy, but you are confident to perform in a safe and effective way. The shoulders targeted and working in the set.

That's a good start for muscular movements in a full body approach session. Another option is to seek out a good Personal Trainer as mentioned for sound assistance & visual demonstration, it could be your local council community gym and instructors working the gym floor there could help you. Don't be afraid to ask, as I always said when working in gyms and the like the facility is there for you. Forget about what everyone else is doing in there and focus on yourself. To reiterate, ensure the weight you are using is heavy enough for you, this can be quite confusing as what does that actually mean, well it means you can complete each repetition with good technique and on the last few reps muscles are starting to fatigue, I prefer using kettlebells indoors as they are so versatile and can be used in a small space when compared to barbells and dumbells. These are fine also, if you have any existing kit dig it out and have a go. Even two cans of baked beans, items that are practical safe and effective. Remember this is down to you, I'm giving the guidance for you full plan. You may find your bodyweight is enough for the squat movements. With the knee press ups you may struggle with those, ok then start with a few repetitions and build up over time. Have a thirty to forty-five second rest between each set and a minute or more between each exercise. The important factor for each workout is that each repetition is spot on, each set is technically correct with a feeling of muscular fatigue. Not complete failure and so intense, struggling like Rocky getting ready for a big fight. No, it should be controlled, smooth and result is muscular fatigue, you are not trying to max out each time you do it. Straight away you are getting your body on a path to become gradually stronger and operate more efficiently, also you will be increasing your daily calorie burn. This in turn will allow you to burn more fat stores and add to ongoing weight loss. Now combining the brisk walking with these resistance sessions starting with three times a week will help accelerate the weight loss. This Phase Two is both resistance training and Cardiovascular work with fat burning.

The phase Two walk

Aim at 30 minutes per session minimum, a progression from Phase One complete straight after the resistance component. You will naturally get walking faster and for longer as your body adapts to the ongoing sessions and with the base fitness from Phase One. Phase Two combines the indoor resistance exercises and brisk walking, aim at this for the next three weeks then the week four rest. You will gain so much in health benefits and be able to do more during your days. The reason people generally drop out of any such program is they really didn't want it that much, or as mentioned try and do too much too soon. Or is it, a big part could be they don't believe it will work for them, everyone wants it, but the work, the time, and the effort does get the results. It's an opportunity cost for many who want to just relax after a long day at work and I get that, I really do but this is how it is......

I maybe repeating myself but having patience and persistence is key, everything must be achievable and positive. Wanting the results but not actually having to put any effort into making any changes is as we have discussed, won't yield anything just more frustration and misery. This is a shame, as it shouldn't take a lot of will power but effort over a consistent period and then maintenance. As you do more it will become a real positive part of your life, you are less likely to think about it in terms of being hard as you adapt. Far better than just sitting in front of the TV and eating fast food wishing your life away. The inner positive feeling exercise and being active gives you, you will experience over time as your body is adapting,

174

changing. You will be working with gradually increasing intensity and not going 100 miles an hour with the 'to lose as much weight as possible, as quick as possible' approach. This strategy is more of a steady one, making sure you are changing lifestyle habits than just focusing on the perceived results you want.

Well done for completing Phase Two of the plan. How was it, did it seem a bit more taxing to complete the three sessions a week of 45 to 50 minutes a time? We have increased the duration and now using voluntary muscles working and the fat burning walking combined to use different energy systems in your body. That way we get a better training effect and the results to your fat burning will be better. How are other areas, better balance, coordination and getting around I bet your daily quality of life has improved. Do you struggle to get up the stairs, did you before? You must be seeing good improvements overall, how are the photos looking now from your starting one you have taken over the weeks, I hope you are feeling positive from it all.

Now have a deserved week break before we move on, again optionally you can have an easy swim or relaxing bike ride once or twice on this rest week.

Phase Three

At this point you are now a minimum six - week veteran of brisk walking. You are hopefully getting used to the compound movements in the phase 2 resistance sessions, it's only been three weeks so is all still relatively new. If you are happy & can see progression changes you are seeing over the next three week's you can either:

Increase the sets of each exercise in the resistance sessions to 3 sets per movement and with the brisk walking add in jogging intervals of say 3 to 5 second bursts to start, back to walking for 30 seconds and do that several times added into one session, gauge yourself and build in bursts or just keep walking. As I do say don't go overboard with it, look to increase these intervals gradually, all done so it is manageable for you with progression in longer jogging interval bursts, remember a gradual process as we need to get the joints and connective tissue stronger and weight loss to reduce any chance of an injury.

Intervals can be whatever time and number of bursts you like, again listen to your body and give it a try. 5 seconds might not be enough, and you can do 10, so do it and see how many intervals you're good to do, it might be 3 it could be 10. Just don't do too much too soon and the key is making it achievable. The recovery time could be extended on the more intervals you do, see how you go.

An example of adding intervals :

A. Walk 5 minutes, 5 x 5 second jog 30 second recovery walk

B. Walk 5 minutes, 7 x 5 second jog 30 second recovery walk

C. Walk 5 minutes, 10 x 5 second jog 30 second Recovery walk

You can combine the resistance session then the 30 minute or longer brisk walk or alternatively change the walk for a bike ride, or swim. What do you want to do, what is your preference, it's always better to mix it up so you don't repeat the same too much. We have emphasised walking a lot as it's safe effective and for convenience but remember don't try and do too much as you will feel more fatigued after and the next day. It is important to follow the gradual increase principle and remain consistent.

OR

Stick to another 3 weeks of a similar plan to Phase two of resistance and brisk walk sessions and one session of either a big longer walk, cycle or swimming. Hitting the body in different ways really does get the best benefits and variety for you than doing the same thing repeated over and over. There is less chance of overuse injuries, meaning an injury occurring from repeating the same movements such as consistent longer walking. I hope you are keeping up with the daily calorie burning strategies and the initial advice on practical strategies. Remember if you are feeling too achy after sessions, days after then reduce the intensity at your next session.

Don't forget for safety :

- **Don't go too intense and then stop, incorporate a cool down of five minutes gradual decrease back to a state of pre-exercise.**
- **Stretches can be found on 'The Obesity Secret' Facebook group**
- **I always advise seeking a trainer or gym instructor to help you**

Well done so far

Now remember again, forget all the empty promises of fast weight loss in low calorie diets and fads. Yes, I do keep repeating this but for good reason, it can sit and fester in the back of your mind (if you have done before) that oh this is too much effort, too much planning too much to do. Learning new ways does take time to adjust and it is really for the better. Here we are looking at consistent and gradual weight loss and promoting a healthier lifestyle through proven tried & tested principles, resistance training and fat burning strategies. Ensure you are following all the advice up to this point and you will have seen big changes in yourself in what you can now do, how you can get about and how you feel. Your environment now is far healthier for you, and a result of this you really do deserve a medal, know that it does get easier now as you are creating these new 'good habits'. That is a big key to the maintenance phase and keeping the weight off as you start to really progress and reach your goal. What you are hopefully experiencing is the rewards of your structured effort from this guidance. Looking back at the effort you have put into phases one, two and three it must be a good feeling, a real sense of achievement. How have the scales been, I have mentioned about weighing yourself and not to worry too much if there isn't a constant weight reduction on a weekly basis as there is a good reason for that. The equivalent weight of fat to muscle is 4:1, muscle weighs four times the amount of fat, the best way as I have advised is a body fat scale measurement. To check bodyfat levels just as much as weight. There will be weight loss but checking size changes, waist measurements is a key indicator. Fitness centres and big pharmacies such as boots have these facilities as mentioned you can use for good info & make sure they explain the results to you, this can then be done as a monthly benchmark along with your weekly selfie-photo record.

The scales just to check weight might not reflect exactly what is going on in your body as in you are losing fat but not in overall weight regularly, don't worry about this you will notice mostly in these ways:

- **How your clothes fit**
- **People that haven't seen you for months**
- **The transformation seen in taking the weekly selfie photo**

You will get some great feedback from those that haven't seen you in a while, but to you it's such a gradual process that you won't notice much difference. You do see yourself every day and that's why others will see the changes far more than you. You will notice how some clothes now don't fit.

Only you know if you have really followed everything to the letter, the more focus and more action taken then the better the reward of weight loss you will experience. If you have followed a handful of the home strategies and done a few walks, a few resistance sessions but still eating a lot of high calorie foods then be honest with yourself. You have put some effort in to change but your body doesn't lie, this can also lead to dropping out.

Have things gone to plan

At this point at the end of phase three, well done great work. I hope you are seeing yourself change in many ways, all the new habits, lifestyle choices and feeling fitter and more alert in yourself 😊

If you are not happy with your current progress reflect, and see just what is going on has there been obstacles which have not quite been overcome?

- Is the lure of fast food / sweets / chocolate just too great?
- If there was before has alcohol been cut back (remember around 200cal a glass of wine)
- Was you consistent in completing all planned sessions in phase one and two.
- Have you been able to follow all guidance strategies and put in place.
- Have co – habitants been assisting you or have been an obstacle?
- Are you doing more positive things than sitting in front of the television or PC?
- How do you feel?
- How has your sleep been?
- Eating pattern, is it at more regular set times now?
- Have you been motivated to complete all suggested sessions?

Really ask yourself what has been going on during the phases so far, it's a good way to clarify how to move forward and what areas need focus for change. I will say it again, if you haven't followed everything, don't worry be truthful with you and look to focus and improve each day. Following this guidance is down to you, you need to put the structured effort in to get the results you really do want. Have these changes been hard to make, has it been a bit of an emotional roller coaster. If there is a lot that needs to be done to change onto the right path, don't be hard on yourself if so. Focus to be persistent, be disciplined and make the changes and gradual improvements in all the areas and it will happen. Habits do take time to change, it may not happen overnight, and we need to be aware of that. As I have said, the time will pass anyway so why not try your best to make the changes, learn, refine it and go again. Then the reflecting part will be really enthralling for you.

Let's say you have put all effort into the phases one, two, and phase three, you may be raring to keep going but again remember those built in 1-week rests are just as crucial as putting the work in.

TASK 10
- *Check your waist measurements and how your clothes fit*
  To reiterate, you should see noticeable in your waist circumference. Again, remember this is about health promotion and new habit formation, not only about weight loss.
- *Go through all the review points highlighted, have things gone to plan*

Phase Four

Now you have a foundation of fitness and if you feel ready could you now look to take part in a set challenge, it could be to build to a 3 kilometre or even a 5Km walk. This phase is your call now, what you found enjoyable and stuck to or would like to try something altogether new. A bike ride / swim / gym cross trainer twice a week aiming at 30 to 45 min duration is a great progression on from phase 3, with two to three 25 to 45minute resistance training weekly sessions. Or maybe a 60minute distance walk, see how consistency leads to progression and then the workout times can go up provided they are within your capabilities. In this way the fat burning will increase relatively too, whilst also sticking to all the fat burn guidance points. It could be three weeks of every other day walks / cycle / swim / whatever suits you now. The more structured planned action / rest you take consistently will yield great results and you will feel good for it.

This 12-week system then can be mixed and matched for different weekly exercise activities. You will continually see the weight come off, if you are considering dropping out of the plan at any point just remember to emphasise

> **3 / 5 / 10 Kilometre walk example :** Aim for 2 x weekly walks building distance. Start with the longest duration of your phase 3 walks and add each time. You will surprise yourself at your distance progression, see what you can achieve in three weeks. Adding in more intervals too if you want to.

that time will pass anyway. Remember you are looking to lose weight and keep it off and be healthy, this is an ideal way how to do it. Once you follow the phase plan system, it may take two three or more cycles in one phase I did say at the end of the phases:

If you feel you want to go through the phase again, that is fine. To repeat, it's not about just progressing to the next stage as quick as possible, as that's perceived to be better, no it's all about your effort and how your body feels as adaptation and fulfilment from the new structure and work you put in that's important'.

As you are creating a fat burning environment for yourself. I'll repeat, it doesn't really matter what phase you are at, it's not about 'phase 4 is better than phase 2' It's really all about your body and where your fitness levels currently reflected in the increased fitness levels and fat weight loss. Provided you are putting the effort consistently in, you might do phase one repeated a few times totalling 9 weeks with the three weeks rest periods, then feel good for the next stage that is fine. It's better for you than to just rush onto the next stage. You may complete the plan, then for example if you then have a month off, go back and judge how you can start in terms of how much you can do in a session. I'm sure it will be far more exercise than when you originally started, then you will lose more weight over that next 12 weeks and so on. As you reach your target weight, by then the good habits and guidance is more likely to be fixed in place and you are aware to not just revert back to your old lifestyle habits.

Now you know the principles, so create your own plan.

When on the plan always have a stop lock, if you do have a couple of bad days then bring it round and have good days after. As you continue this way of thinking it will become easier and your norm. The result is the weight will then stay off and never return to the original levels. Remember you must act then keep those structured habits going to make them your new normal behaviour.

180

Rest weeks are so important.

Rest allows your body to recover and for your immune system to not weaken. You are now changing and leading a far more structured & active lifestyle, your metabolic rate is increasing and with the rest week from the exercise but keeping all other weight loss principles you will still be going in the right direction. Many I know that start up new gym classes with lots of motivation, then suddenly going three four or more times a week from nothing will likely fatigue, come down with a cold or under the weather and stop the unrealistic plan soon enough. That's a classic of doing too much too soon, there's a reason I have structured your training plan emphasising physical activity and food as much as exercise as well as rest. If you focus too much on one area you may lose sight of the whole picture, do it in a balanced way and be consistent, too much physical activity and too much exercise could lead to quick burnout. Same with the intensity of the exercise sessions, we are introducing you gradually to bigger and longer exercise sessions over the phases. As you get more active and fitter you will be able to do more. Your body needs the time to adapt to the new way of living and the new habits. The rest also helps mentally, the week away from the routine will help your outlook towards it all. Coming back after a rest week feeling fresh and a new energised approach will help motivation to get things done and encourage you moving forward.

Don't Overtrain

The main factor with training is to follow your level, allow progression and adequate rest. If you do, with the subsequent fatigue then there's the high chance you will drop out of it altogether. As with the proverb of the tortoise and Hare, don't rush but build adapt and progress as you want to make sure you get there in the end. Focus, dedicate, be disciplined and patient in the effort you put in as well as the discipline of rest. Be patient, be consistent with gradual adaptation over time, longer more intense sessions your body will be able to cope with. You will be able to do more which will become evident, and you will get there.

At 19 I experienced what is known as chronic fatigue syndrome from trying to do everything with not resting enough. I had a full-time job in London, yet my dream was to be a professional Rugby player. Part of the development team at Saracens, the premiership London based club. If I wasn't at work, I was on the training grounds or in the gym and if I wasn't there, I was playing a match. Also out socialising too, burning the candle at both ends as the saying goes. I literally just kept going with no rest, one day

I woke up and felt very different. A weird kind of fatigue, but this was totally different to feeling exhausted, as it lasted 18 months and wouldn't want that ever again. Psychologically I couldn't rest as I would be out of the team, so I thought but I wasn't aware of what I should've been doing. All the motivation was there but not the self-guidance, it just seemed to be more and more training. I tried to train and run but it left me feeling exhausted and really fatigued. I couldn't sleep and if I had two or ten hours sleep it made no difference to how I felt the next day. I learnt after and that sense of competitiveness was out of me over 18 months later. That was my lesson in the importance of rest, discipline isn't only about training and putting the physical effort in, it's about having a plan and following all aspects including planned rest periods and listening to the body.

Another example of overtraining, but to a far lesser extent, working at a college years ago myself and a colleague took a group of students to a fitness expo in Excel London. The event was huge, with all sorts of fitness companies selling products, supplements, gym equipment and training products of all kinds. The event was great, so much going on, there was a strongman competition in the event centre and then downstairs was the preliminary heats of a bodybuilding competition. I had never seen either in person before, it was quite an experience. We were given a lot of freebies in fitness magazines, supplements, t-shirts and more. On the way home the students reading one fitness magazine explained about Arnold Schwarzenegger's regular workout routine of training twice a day for six days a week. We were all motivated by the experience of the big event and I accepted the challenge. I said to the students I will hit the gym before I start work in the morning and then head into the gym after work every day from Monday to Friday. Each workout was around 45 minutes long and by Friday afternoon I was absolutely shattered, after work I couldn't complete the last training session. I headed home, ate dinner, and went straight to sleep around 7pm and was up around 8.30 the following morning. It's ok being motivated, but as I experienced trying to workout at that higher level was just too much. I trained four mornings a week regularly, and I never tried those double sessions again. It's too much to expect your body to adapt to an intense regime straight away. It is a gradual process allowing your body to adapt over time increasing intensity of exercise and physical activity. Starting with deciding to walk a distance every day can be tough so follow the guidelines and don't overdo it yourself.

Maintenance

Wanting to reach the goal you have set yourself, say it's to lose seven stone or 98 pounds, it will be amazing getting there with the sense of accomplishment, but then what. The focus then is on maintenance, we must maintain and look to improve our position in relation to meeting that set goal. We therefore change the initial mindset from a goal weight then switch to ongoing lifestyle maintenance, so the weight doesn't all go back on. We can put strategies into place to counter any potential weight regain. If you gain say five pounds, then make sure you are then back on an appropriate phase / check your habits with the guidance. We now have a strategy here which can be used as required once you meet your goals. The more weight going on, is potentially harder to then get it all off as psychologically it must feel like starting all over. Like digging a hole then to be told to fill it in, then told to dig it out all again. So have cut off points if you find yourself starting to re-gain, such examples could be:

- Don't just 'let go' when you reach your goal
- Check weight regularly say once a week, a target range
- Set cut off points once you reach your goal, it could be if you re-gain 5 – 10 lbs start a 3 week exercise Phase. Then review
- The lifestyle and physical activity keep going
- As mentioned in phase 4, now look to new activities and goals to set yourself

'Draw a distinction between weight loss and weight maintenance and ensure the client considers the two aspects as separate challenges[215]

As we know by now consistent exercise will boost our metabolic rate and aid in some compensation of extra snacks, depending on what the snacks are. If physical activity and exercise is stopped along with any kind of structure to eating habits and choice of foods, then weight can and inevitably will pile back on. Adopt this idea of cut off points, getting to your goal you may have stopped with all the structured lifestyle & exercise habits. No, that's not the point and the idea is to change the lifestyle and keep the guidelines going now. Follow the points on the left, weigh yourself weekly, be aware of what's going on and for example if there's a 5 to 10 pounds gain after goal reaching, get right back on it. It's easier to lose at this point than to ignore, let go and then do it further down the road once pounds have been put back on. The longer it's left the harder it will be to get back to what you want, physically and psychologically. These fail safes need to be in place to ensure you stay in a maintenance phase and not slide back to gaining weight.

Weight loss Example

John he is 37 has a full-time job working in construction. He works long days is up at 5am Monday to Friday and is very overweight, he currently tips the scales at 22 stone at 5'11. He has a goal of looking the way he did at 21 years old when he was around 12 stone. John has a target weight loss of ten stone. With our principle of losing around 2lbs a week, at 14 pounds per stone John needs to lose 140 pounds. If we work that into the weeks then its 63.6 weeks, or just over a year. Does that sound a lot, well this is a realistic timeline for such weight loss, he could lose more in that time reflected through the effort he puts in with all the guidance. What is a year, John has been overweight for a very long time we need his body to adapt to the new lifestyle and new principles he will follow. This is a change which will suit John, yet it can be quite discouraging thinking of such a long timeframe to reach his goal. Focusing on the positive changes, focusing week by week and not too much on the end goal is a good way to go. It can be discouraging to think of the entirety, a year to get to the goal. That's an issue of today's society, we need to overcome, we want it now. Put the time and structured effort in then as the saying goes:

'all good things come to those who wait'

John's work is long hours, but he has two days off at the weekend and we need to ensure his diet is consistently good that he is getting adequate calories from wholefoods during the working week. Along with all the lifestyle factors we have looked at. To build that into the routine, then a treat meal Friday or Saturday night along with a few snacks and a couple of drinks is fine. John needs to add in on Monday to Friday physical activity at an extra 15 to 20 minutes daily where he can. On a break use a portion to walk daily, I would say set progressive targets like the stair climb physical activity. It could also be increasing the distance weekly as his body adapts to it which will show progression. Then training sessions at the weekend Saturday and Sunday mornings, only two a week but it's workable, then as he hits the appropriate planned phase he will progress. John does get about on site which we can say is physical activity provided it follows the principles we've been through.

> **Johns points to consider :**
>
> - **7 day food diary – self analysis**
> - **Calculate own calorie needs**
> - **Modern Day Diet plan**
> - **Times of eating**
> - **Physical activity / NEAT**
> - **Home fat burning environment**
> - **Exercise session plan**
> - **And all tasks we've seen to cover**

Phase one aiming to do the minimum 30minutes walk on Saturday and Sunday when is convenient. I would suggest early is better to discourage a late night out before. After the three weeks have the week rest from the exercise sessions physical activity then into phase two then three. Three weeks of the consistent good weekly food, physical activity and the two weekend sessions of then into the longer cardio and resistance sessions. I always advise to plan it early so then the rest of the day is free to do other things, for John again early at the weekends. Managing the three areas is key to the plan, listen to your body and if John is overdoing it then bring the sessions to a lower intensity and reduce the training times. It's all manageable but as we have said it needs to be achievable for the individual. He works long days so possibly short sessions in the week watching the Television as an incentive. An example at around 20 minutes of extra physical activity a day will total 100 minutes in the working week, it's all a gradual process. With John focusing on having three regular healthy choice meals a day at right times he will burn the calories throughout the day and not add to his weight going into the evening. As he is big, he needs to feel full earlier in the day, so he doesn't chase the calories into the evening or more chance of snacking. This is where quality meal preparation is important, so the part of becoming aware of what good meal selections are is important to then become a good habit.

Don't get Lazy

Here I am writing this passage in my gym gear, and I haven't gone to the gym. It's a regular Saturday morning I had planned to head there for an hour after having a couple of weeks off exercise. I had renewed my membership three days ago and just rationalised to myself 'well, I do have to head into London for 11am and I'm now pushing it'. I decided to sit here and write for half an hour then have a bath to then head into London. When I am in a routine I crave the gym, but I also can get out of the routine when I have a break. I will get in there tomorrow morning after training a client early. Training good habits into your weekly routine can be an important part in your weight management plan as we know. Yes, I did have a few beers in the local pub last night then a curry and it's why I was up late and had less time and enthusiasm to get to the gym which then clearly didn't happen. The beer and curry not being on the menu every Friday and I will get straight back on the wagon in no time. Tomorrow morning will be an hour's brisk walk with exercises for my client then an hour in the gym after, I planned to then go to a Sunday buffet at the local Nepalese restaurant. it's all about finding a consistent and manageable balance to it. I'm about to have a bit of food, two eggs on brown toast before I head up town. This afternoon might be a few beers too as I am meeting a good friend I used to train. If your pattern has been late nights and no exercise just think again of the calorie difference 12 hours can make. I hope by now you have realised you cannot fake what we are going through to transform you and the health benefits gained in the process are far too important to ignore. From all the clients I have trained and for me it's all about being realistic and practical to be able to live your life, socialise, feel good and be positive. It may also be you quit other habits too, you may cut right down on the drinks or foods you may have regularly once had. Let's be honest, we are in a socialising and somewhat drinking culture, looking back to see what effort and discipline you have demonstrated must be a real proud thing. I have seen so many different situations with people, their food relationship, their exercise, managing weight. When the penny drops and they see exactly what they need to do to help themselves and how it's going to work, it then is a great life altering experience for them, and I am happy for their new discovery. An iconic rapper from the 80's Flavour Flav in one of the world's biggest rap groups at the time Public Enemy, this quote I found quite insightful and important to hear. He would always wear an oversized clock around his neck. His reference to wearing this as he stated is:

'it's about time. Time is the most important thing and it's how you use time to the best of your ability. Don't waste time'

Joining the Gym

Training outside where people can see you, or indoors at home where there is no motivation to do it? Bit of a tricky one eh, for a lot of people the gym can be a real intimidating place, from years of working in gyms, I've seen different environments and different types of people frequenting the gym floor. Regardless of how others are, the focus is on what you are going in there for, you know exactly what you want and as we look at goal setting and with a focus you will know what to do. Forget about what others are doing or whatever distractions there may be. In the gym as with social settings, we may have our own perceptions of how we think people see us, we are not mind readers and we have no idea what people think, only our own perceptions in our own head. Forget about any preconceived ideas of how you think people look at you too. Be in the gym and focus on you, we may feel uncomfortable in these environments where there's a lot of people training hard and look fit, think of it as a big team effort than being in competition. You don't have to talk to anyone but in your mind see it all that way, *'aren't they doing great, I will be changing to meet my goals now'*

rather than 'look at them why can't I be like that'. The times I see different characters in the gyms but from my perspective I can appreciate, we are all just trying to get on with life in our own ways. For many the gym is a pattern of positive behaviour, for others it's a competition. In looking for a place to train in try and find what would suit you. The more council based facilities are more relaxed and are more family orientated. Private gyms tend to have more serious trainers, it all depends, but don't rush in and join somewhere straight away where they tie you into contracts for six months or more. Think of what times you are likely to go in there so look in there then, it might be too busy. Have a plan in mind and see how the facility fits, is it in a convenient location and how long does it take you to get there? Could it be on route home from work or just up the road from where you live. The gym I am regularly training in takes me five minutes to drive to, it's encouraging me to train more regularly as it's so convenient and a relaxed environment with a mixture of people. Does it really meet your needs, is the gym with freely available kit, pool, classes you may like to try and sports courts. I generally get guest passes or will only pay monthly commitments as I might be in another location within a month or two, as that suits me, so work out and see what really suits you. As the gym becomes regular, which will take time then it becomes a good habit and is very easy to keep a regular pattern. The same could be said for indoor or local outdoor training, we can create those new patterns of behaviour. From the success stories I see, as these things become regular and ongoing, the client sees positive results and feels good for it. Then, like a positive revolution that keeps moving forward, accomplish the session, feel good and a sense of achievement, go again. Or if you don't like exercise then let's focus on the food intake, follow all the advice on lifestyle strategies I have given and work out your daily metabolic needs then with the macronutrient breakdowns.

> **Joining a gym checklist :**
>
> - *Check what kit you are likely to use*
> - *Go at the times of day you would regularly train to see how busy the place is*
> - *With work / life can you get to the gym regularly*
> - *Is the environment to your liking*
> - *Is it at a convenient location on route to or from work, local to where you live*
> - *Are the fees peak / off peak reasonable*
> - *Can you afford monthly payments*
> - *Can you commit monthly, three or six months*
> - *Are the other facilities / classes to try*
> - *Is there good support from staff*
> - *Are you looking for a Personal Trainer*
> - *Are showering facilities satisfactory*
> - *As reiterated, if you are unsure on the exercises I have given explanations, seek guidance from an accredited trainer*

Age is just a number

I have worked within all adult ages from 16 to 79, the principles are similar throughout apart from with age comes a focus on warmup, cool down and the health-related benefits to tailored exercise. The client aged 79 I focus more on weight management, low impact, low to medium intensity exercise. If there's higher intensity added, then it's of very short duration in the session. One past client at 73 who could complete 500 meters on the rowing machine in under 2 minutes, we would both regularly have a go and became a healthy target activity for both of us. As I've highlighted, the intensity of the session is all relative to the individual's current levels.

I prefer for older clients to use more of the CV kit in gyms that are low impact and cyclical, meaning no jarring or impact on joints. Cross trainers, rowers, recumbent bikes and similar. I focus on the health benefits of exercise and mostly completed at the 60 to 70% MHR range with some short bursts of intense work added yet very manageable.

We do naturally lose a pound of muscle and gain fat each year with age yet that really is turned on its head offset to our activity levels. How much exercise we do and our lifestyle, you will discover this as the program progresses. For all the exercise I do I feel very active and ready to go, the wellbeing feeling after exercise too is a real feel - good feeling.

With age we may have different issue with cholesterol or possibly blood pressure, with the advice of a G.P. be aware and make sure the BP is in a healthy range a general rule is to check over the age of 40. Really with today's world I would suggest being mindful that you are suitable for exercise and if you feel you want to consult your G.P. there is no reason not to prior to starting.

A local client / friend I currently work with as previously mentioned, at 76 we regularly run up the steep steps near my hometown, he makes them look easy. Saying how fit & agile he feels, which is a sign of good fitness levels to complete daily tasks and general wellbeing.

Conclusion

Well done for getting to the end of the book, I hope you have taken in everything I have put forward and planning what you now need to do. My first goal for you was to read through this and understand what you need to do. I hope it all makes sense to you, I wanted to get my knowledge and experience in along with sourced information. To get you to become more aware of what's going on in the world, reflect on your own unique situation where you are then to give you all the information with complete confidence that you can create and reach the goal that you set for yourself.

I hope it's clear to you now that YOU are the magic secret.

As you take control and structure your plan, you will fulfil your weight management goals. We must change the way we are for ourselves and not to see it down to anyone else. Being overweight is a point in time and if you want it change will come. I have absolutely no doubt you will achieve your goals, given the guidance and ways to get there as you follow the information you will start to see it happen and looking back from this point being in a positive place. There was a time I left writing for months on end, I couldn't for a while bring myself to keep going through it. Sometimes ten minutes a day, even in a week. Then I went back to it and back to it, a new lease of motivation would ensue. You may experience the same on your weight loss journey, the goal is there it may take time, but don't give up. You may have some moments where focus is lost. That's ok, but your goal will always be there until you achieve it. Like any big task if never achieved before it can seem so difficult at times, but as I found overcoming those obstacles seeing things come together, and coming out the other side gives great satisfaction. It has been a mammoth task for me to write this book, over three years since I had started with many stops and starts. A sense of self belief gradually came over me as the words and pictures started to come to life, seeing what I was creating further spurred me onwards. To the final few months before completion when I was spending hours every day, it was clear what I was doing as it appeared in front of me. I hope you have the same realisations in pursuit of your goals, as you witness your own success it will encourage you forwards.

James x

REFERENCES:

University of Utah, Learn Genetics, *Evolution and Obesity*,
Available at: https://learn.genetics.utah.edu/content/metabolism/obesity 12/07/2023

[2] Diets in review, 04/29/2023, *Circus Fat Man Not So Shocking Today*,
Available at https://dietsinreview.com/diet_column/04/circus-fat-man-not-so-shocking-today 12/07/2023

[3] World population review, 2023, *Most Obese countries 2023*
Available at: https://worldpopulationreview.com/country-rankings/obesity-rates-by-country 23/04/2023

[4] Crown copyright, NHS, 28/11/2022, *what is the body mass index (BMI)?*
Available at: https://www.nhs.uk/common-health-questions/lifestyle/what-is-the-body-mass-index-bmi/ 26/06/2023

[5] Tanita,2012 - 2023, *Body Mass Index: the most well known measurement*
Available at: https://tanita.eu/understanding-your-measurements/body-mass-index 25-07-2023

[6] Jackson.A, 2009, *obesity & diabetes weight management*, certificate resource manual, Active I.Q. Trident business centre Tooting.

[7] NHS,15/12/2022 *Health survey for England, 2021 part 1, Overweight and Obesity Summary, Official statistics,*
Available at: https://digital.nhs.uk/data-and-information/publications/statistical/health-survey-for- england/2021/overweight-and-obesity-in-adults 22/04/2023

[8] NHS,15/12/2022 Health survey for England, 2021 part 1, Overweight and Obesity Summary, Official statistics,
Available at: https://digital.nhs.uk/data-and-information/publications/statistical/health-survey-for-england/2021/overweight-and-obesity-in-adults 22/04/2023

[9] Crown Copyright, 22/12/2022, *Population of England and Wales,*
Available at: Population of England and Wales - GOV.UK Ethnicity facts and figures (ethnicity-facts-figures.service.gov.uk)
22/04/2023

[10] World population review, 2023, *Obesity rates by country 2023*, Nauru
Available at: https://worldpopulationreview.com/country-rankings/obesity-rates-by-country 23/04/2023

[11] Australian Government Dept. of Foreign Affairs and trade, *Nauru country brief overview*, 22/04/2023
Available at: https://.dfat.gov.au/geo/nauru/nauru-country-brief

[12] Johnson.G , 2023,Young Pioneer Tours, *Nauru Cuisine,*
Available at: https://www.youngpioneertours.com/nauru-cuisine 23/04/2023

[13] street food guy, 09/01/2019, *Dining in Nauru,*
Available at: https://www.streetfoodguy.com/dining-in-nauru/ 23/04/2023

[14] street food guy, 09/01/2019, *Healthcare in Nauru,*
   Available at: https://www.streetfoodguy.com/dining-in-nauru/ 26/06/2023

[15] The MIT PRESS, Dauvergne.P, 22/07/2019, *A dark history of the worlds Smallest Island Nation,*
   Available at: https://thereader.mitpress.mit.edu/dark-history-nauru/ 12-08-2023

[16] The MIT PRESS reader, P. Dauvergne, A dark history of the worlds Smallest Island Nation',
   Available at: https://thereader.mitpress.mit.edu/dark-history-nauru/ 12-08-2023

[17] World population review, 2023, *Obesity rates by country 2023*, Cook Islands
   Available at: https://worldpopulationreview.com/country-rankings/obesity-rates-by-country
24/04/2023

[18] Stathis.C, 2023, *I've visited the most beautiful tropical island ive ever seen for a quick holiday from
   Australia – and its so small you cant even see it on a map,* The Daily Mail, 10/07/2023
   Available at: https://www.dailymail.co.uk/femail/travel/article-12265385/amp/Rarotonga-
Cook-Islands-stay-visiting.html 12/08/2023

[19] Explore Shaw, Shaw.E 2023, *10 facts you didn't know about the Cook Islands*
   Available at: https://www.exploreshaw.com/10-facts-you-didnt-know-about-the-
cook-islands/ 12/08/2023

[20] 6/06/2023 *Cook Islands country profile,* BBC news
   Available at: https://www.bbc.com/news/world-asia-pacific-16495238.amp 23/04/2023

[21] Worldometer, 16/07/2023, *Cook Islands Population,*
   Available at: https://www.worldometers.info/world-population/cook-islands-population/
23/04/2023

[22] Asian development bank Economic restructuring program 2002, PDF
   Available at: https://www.adb.org/sites/default/files/evaluation-document/35196/files/ppa-
coo-30346.pdf 24/04/2023

[23] Humanium, *Children of Cook Islands,*
   Available at: https://www.humanium.org/en/cook-islands/ 24/04/2023

[24] Asian Development Bank, ARIC, 2015, Cook Islands,
   Available at: https://aric.adb.org/cook-islands 24/04/2023

[25] Kidadl team, Kidadl, 26/01/2023, *45 Cook Islands facts: What its like to live On An Island,*
   Available at: https://kidadl.com/facts/cook-islands-facts-what-it-s-like-to-live-on-an-island
24/04/2023

[26] McCormack.D, 02/09/2014,'*chips before pawpaw:Cook Islanders lose taste for healthy,local food*', the
Guardian
   Available at: https://amp.theguardian.com/global-development/2014/sep/02/cook-islands-
obesity-imported-food 23/04/2023

[27] World population review, 2023, *Obesity rates by country 2023,* Palau
Available at: https://worldpopulationreview.com/country-rankings/obesity-rates-by-country 24/04/2023

[28] Britannica, 31/03/2023, *Palau,*
Available at: https://www.britannica.com/place/Palau 24/04/2023

[29] The World bank Group 2023, *Total Population, Palau*
Available at: https://data.worldbank.org/indicator/SP.POP.TOTL?locations=PW 27/04/2023

[30] Google, *Palau, Country in Oceania,*
Available at: https://www.google.co.uk/search?q=palau&ie=UTF-8&oe=UTF-8&hl=en-gb&client=safari 05/06/2023

[31] Worldtravelguide, Palau food and drink,
Available at: https://www.worldtravelguide.net/guides/oceania/pacific-islands-of-micronesia/palau/food-and-drink/
24/04/2023

[32] SIS international research, 2021, *Market Research in Palau,*
Available at: https://www.sisinternational.com/coverage/market-research-asia/market-research-palau/ 24/04/2023

[33] SIS international research, 2021, Market Research in Palau,
Available at: https://www.sisinternational.com/coverage/market-research-asia/market-research-palau/ 24/04/2023

[34] World Health Organisation, 2017, *Non-Communicable Disease & Risk Factor Surveillance,*
Available at: https://cdn.who.int/media/docs/default-source/ncds/ncd-surveillance/data-reporting/palau/palau_2016_hybrid_report.pdf 24/04/2023

[35] Britannica, Apr, 28 2023, Marshall Islands,
Available at: https://www.britannica.com/place/Marshall-Islands 05/06/2023

[36] Britannica, Mar 30 2023, *Marshall Islands,*
Available at: https://www.britannica.com/place/Marshall-Islands 24/04/2023

[37] Britannica, Robert C. Kiste, *History of the Marshall Islands,*
Available at: https://www.britannica.com/place/Marshall-Islands/History 24/04/202

[39] European Commission, 2021, *Food Consumption in the Marshall Islands: Based on the analysis of the 2019/20 Household Income and Expenditure Survey,*
Available at: https://knowledge4policy.ec.europa.eu/publication/food-consumption-marshall-islands-based-analysis-201920-household-income-expenditure_en 24/04/2023

[40] Borgen project, 29-10-2022, *Nuclear Radiation in The Marshall Islands,*
Available at: https://borgenproject.org/nuclear-radiation-in-the-marshall-islands/ 24/04/2023

[41] Country Reports, 1997 - 2023 *Marshall Islands Imports and Exports*
Available at: https://www.countryreports.org/country/MarshallIslands/imports-exports.htm 27/09/2023

[42] Moody's analytics, *Marshall Islands – Economic Indicators*
Available at: https://www.economy.com/marshall-islands/indicators 27/09/2023

[43] worldatlas.com, 2023, *'Countries with the Lowest GDP'*,
Available at: https://www.worldatlas.com/gdp/countries-with-the-lowest-gdp.html# 26/06/2023

[44] Borgenproject, Raglow.K.A, 21-05-2020, *Fighting Poverty in Tuvalu through Community,*
Available at: https://borgenproject.org/tag/tuvalu-food-futures/ 25/04/2023

[45] Journal of global health, 7-12-2022, *Does one size fit all ? Differences between islands in Tuvalu and Ecological perspectives,*
Available at: https://www.ncbi.nlm.nih.gov/pmc/articles/PMC9728012/25/04/2023

[46] worldData.info, *Tuvalu,*
Available at: https://www.worlddata.info/oceania/tuvalu/index24/04/2023

[47] Britannica, Barrie K.Macdonald*, Tuvalu: Ellice Islands,*
Available at: https://www.britannica.com/place/Tuvalu25/04/2023

[48] Country reports, 2023, Tuvalu Economy,
Available at: https://www.countryreports.org/country/Tuvalu/economy.htm24/04/2023

[49] Borgenproject, A.K.Raglow, 05-21-2020, *Fighting Poverty in Tuvalu through Community, food scarcity in Tuvalu,* para 2, 3,
Available at: https://borgenproject.org/tag/tuvalu-food-futures/25/04/2023

[50] Global nutrition report, 2023 development initiatives, *Country Nutrition Profiles,*
Available at: https://globalnutritionreport.org/resources/nutrition-profiles/oceania/polynesia/tuvalu/ 25/04/2023

[51] Borgenproject, Annie Kate Raglow, 05-21-2020, Fighting Poverty in Tuvalu through Community, para2 fact1
Available at: https://borgenproject.org/tag/tuvalu-food-futures/ 06/06/2023

[52] Federal ministry for Economic Cooperation & Development, 2023, Ethiopia, A country facing big challenges
Available at: https://www.bmz.de/en/countries/ethiopia 06/06/2023

[53] WorldData.info, Indicators of economy in South Korea, 07-06-2023
Available at: https://www.worlddata.info/asia/south-korea/economy.php

[54] Reuters, Mar 15 2023, Choonsik Yoo, Older workers pull South Korea jobless rate down to record low, unemployment levels
Available at: https://www.reuters.com/world/asia-pacific/south-korea-feb-unemployment-rate-eases-match-record-low-2023-03-14/07/06/2023

[55] 2023 world population review, South Korea Population 2023 (Live)
Available at: https://worldpopulationreview.com/countries/south-korea-population 07/06/2023

[56] Expat guide Korea, M. Kichukova Sept 18, 2020, *'Everything you need to know about fast food in Korea'*
Available at: https://expatguidekorea.com/article/everything-you-need-to-know-about-fast-food-in-korea.html   07-06-2023

[57] xReasons, May 27, 2019, 8 reasons why South Koreans Drink More than Anyone, para 1
Available at: https://medium.com/@xreasons/8-reasons-why-south-koreans-drink-more-than-anyone-7267219feaa1, 07-06-2023

[58] G.Kim & W.Wei, Business insider, *'South Korea requires all males to serve in the military here's what it's like'*
Available at: https://www.businessinsider.com/what-its-like-south-korea-mandatory-military-service-2017-5?amp   07-06-2023

[59] Today, K Kirkpatrick, *'Why the diet loved by Korean pop stars is a hit worldwide'* para 3,
Available at: https://www.today.com/today/amp/tdna162564 07-06-2023

[60] Asian inspirations, 2023, 10 basic Rules of Korean Dining Etiquette, ,
Available at: https://asianinspirations.com.au/food-knowledge/10-basic-rules-of-korean-dining-etiquette/   08-06-2023

[61] Joy Sallegue, March 16 2022, Para 6, '30 essential things to know about Korean food culture'
Available at: https://heyexplorer.com/korean-food-culture/   08-06-2023

[62] Data Commons, Japan,
Available at: https://datacommons.org/place/country/JPN/ 29-07-2023

[63] Dotash Meredith, Food & Wine, *Japanese Cooking Essentials*, para 7
Available at: https://www.foodandwine.com/how/japanese-cooking-pantry-essentials# 08-06-2023

[64] Healthline, A.Bjarnadottir, Sept 19, 2019 *What Is the Japanese Diet Plan? All You Need to Know, para 1-3*
Available at: https://www.healthline.com/nutrition/japanese-diet 08-06-2023

[65] Healthline, A.Bjarnadottir, Sept 19, 2019 What Is the Japanese Diet Plan? All You Need to Know,
Available at: https://www.healthline.com/nutrition/japanese-diet 08-06-2023

[66] Immediate media co., BBC GoodFood, N.Shubrook, 2023, *Why is the Japanese diet so healthy ?,*
Available at: https://www.bbcgoodfood.com/howto/guide/why-japanese-diet-so-healthy# 08-06-2023

[67] AtlasBig.com 2018 – 2022, Countries by McDonald's Restaurants,
Available at: https://www.atlasbig.com/en-us/countries-by-mcdonalds-restaurants 08-06-2023

[68] Britannica, Geography & Travel: Japan
Available at: https://www.britannica.com/place/Japan   19/09/2023

[69] Mamamia, Anderson S. 10/03/2014, *The Country where being overweight is illegal,*
Available at: https://www.mamamia.com.au/japans-metabo-law-where-being-overweight-is-illegal/ 21/08/2023

[70] Japan Nihon, 2023, *What is the waist limit in Japan*
Available at: https://www.japannihon.com/what-is-the-waist-limit-in-japan/
08/06/2023

[71] The Atlantic, Smith N. 6/11/2012, *What is the waist limit in Japan Diets & Dicta*
Available at: https://www.theatlantic.com/health/archive/2012/09/big-government-small-bellies-what-japan-can-teach-us-about-fighting-fat/261940/

[72] GPlusMedia, Inc. Larsen B, 2023, *Japan's Toxic Drinking Culture No One Talks About,*
Available at: https://blog.gaijinpot.com/japans-toxic-drinking-culture-no-one-talks-about/# 08-06-2023

[73] World population review, 2023, *Obesity rates by country 2023,* India
Available at: https://worldpopulationreview.com/country-rankings/obesity-rates-by-country
27/04/2023

[74] SOS childrens villages, 19-04-2018, *Poverty in India: Facts and Figures on the Daily Struggle for Survival,*
Available at: https://www.soschildrensvillages.ca/news/poverty-in-india-602 26/04/2023

[75] SOS children's villages, 19-04-2018, *Poverty in India: Facts and Figures on the Daily Struggle for Survival,*
Available at: https://www.soschildrensvillages.ac/news/poverty-in-india-602 26/04/2023

[76] BBC News, Sebastian.M, 16/01/2022, *Richest 1% own 40.5% of India's wealth says new Oxfam report*
Available at: https://www.bbc.co.uk/news/world-asia-india64286673 27/04/2023

[77] The Indian Express, 2023, *200-plus new McDonald's stores in 3-5 yrs in west and south India; 'Westlife to invest Rs 800 cr'*
Available at: https://www.financialexpress.com/industry/200-plus-new-mcdonalds-stores-in-3-5-yrs 26/07/2023

[78] Britannica, 20-04-2023, Chandler / Overton, *Cambodia,*
Available at: https://www.britannica.com/place/Cambodia 27/04/2023

[79] Worldometers info, 2023, Cambodia population (Live)
Available at: https://www.worldometers.info/world-population/cambodia-population/
27/04/2023

[80] Go guides edit team, Hotels.com, 8 best dishes in Cambodia
Available at: https://uk.hotels.com/go/cambodia/cambodia-cuisine-culture 27/04/2023

[81] Trading Economics 2023, *'Cambodia – Food Imports (% Of Merchandise Imports),*
http://tradingeconomics.com/cambodia/food-imports-percent-of-merchandise-imports-wb-data.html# 09/06/2023

[82] The Borgen project, Mar 17 2023, *Everything to know about poverty in Cambodia,*
Available at: https://borgenproject.org/about-poverty-in-cambodia/ 06-06-2023

[83] Water.org, 2023, *Cambodia's water and sanitation crisis,*
Available at: https://water.org/our-impact/where-we-work/cambodia/# 09-06-2023

[84] World population review, 2023, *Obesity rates by country 2023*, Timor Leste
   Available at: https://worldpopulationreview.com/country-rankings/obesity-rates-by-country 27/04/2023

[85] BBC travel, R Collett, 19th May 2021, *East Timor: A young nation reviving ancient laws,*
   Available at: https://www.bbc.com/travel/article/20210518-east-timor-a-young-nation-reviving-ancient-laws 27-04-2023

[86] BBC travel, R Collett, 19th May 2021, *East Timor: A young nation reviving ancient laws*,
   Available at: https://www.bbc.com/travel/article/20210518-east-timor-a-young-nation-reviving-ancient-laws 27/04/2023

[87] The World Factbook, *Explore all countries Timor Leste East & Southeast Asia*,
   Available at: https://www.cia.gov/the-world-factbook/countries/timor-leste/ 27/04/2023

[88] BBC travel, Richard Collett, 19th May 2021, *East Timor: A young nation reviving ancient laws*,
   https://www.bbc.com/travel/article/20210518-east-timor-a-young-nation-reviving-ancient-laws27/04/2023

[89] Asia development bank, Timor Leste 2016 – 2020, *Environment Assessment Summary,*
   Available at: https://www.adb.org/sites/default/files/linked-documents/cps-tim-2016-2020-ena.pdf 27/04/2023

[91] World Atlas, 2023, *What are the Major Natural Resources Of Timor-Leste*
   Available at: https://www.worldatlas.com/articles/what-are-the-major-natural-resources-of-timor-leste.html 27/04/2023

[92] 2003 World Population Review, *Obesity rates by country*,
   Available at: https://worldpopulationreview.com/country-rankings/obesity-rates-by-country 09/06/2023

[93] World Atlas, *Maps of Bangladesh*,
   Available at: https://www.worldatlas.com/maps/bangladesh 27/04/2023

[94] The World factbook, 26-04-2023, *Explore all Countries* – Bangladesh South Asia,
   Available at: https://www.cia.gov/the-world-factbook/countries/bangladesh 27/04/2023

[95] Travel Food Atlas, 12-04-2023, Traditional Bangladeshi Foods: 9 Must Try Dishes of Bangladesh
   Available at: https://travelfoodatlas.com/traditional-foods-bangladesh-top-9-must-try-bangladeshi-dishes 28/04/2023

[96] WorldAtlas, 2023, *What are the biggest Industries In Bangladesh ?*,
   Available at: https://www.worldatlas.com/articles/what-are-the-biggest-industries-in-bangladesh.html 29/04/2023

[97] Worldatlas, 'what are the biggest industries in Bangladesh'
   Available at: https://www.worldatlas.com/articles/what-are-the-biggest-industries-in-bangladesh.html 29/04/2023

[98] World Atlas, 2023, *What are the biggest industries in Bangladesh*
Available at: https://www.worldatlas.com/articles/what-are-the-biggest-industries-in-bangladesh.html 29/04/2023

[99] Nomadsunveiled,2022, *20 things Bangladesh is famous and known for,*
Available at: https://nomadsunveiled.com/what-is-bangladesh-famous-for/# 09/06/2023

[100] World population review, *Obesity rates by country 2023*, Vietnam
Available at: https://worldpopulationreview.com/country-rankings/obesity-rates-by-country 29/04/2023

[101] BBC, 08-02-2014, *Macdonalds opens first outlet in Vietnams Ho Chi Minh*
Available at: https://www.bbc.co.uk/news/world-asia-26101009 29/04/2023

[102] Mashed, Boshika Gupta, Dec 17 2021, *The real Reason Mcdonald's Flopped In Vietnam,*
Available : https://www.mashed.com/710307/the-real-reason-mcdolands-flopped-in-vietnam/ 29/04/2023

[103] Bestprice travel, July 12, 2023, 'An overall guide on fast food in Vietnam',
Available at: https://www.bestpricetravel.com/travel-guide/an-overall-guideline-on-fast-food-in-vietnam-1256.html 13/08/2023

[104] Taste atlas, Mar 13, 2023, *10 most popular Vietnamese Street Foods*
Available at: https://www.tasteatlas.com/most-popular-street-foods-in-vietnam 02/05/2023

[105] Minh-Ngoc Nguyen Aug 18, 2022, *Frequency of exercising sports in Vietnam*
Available at: https://www.statista.com/statistics/1044088/vietnam-frequency-of-exercising-sports/ 02/05/2023

[106] Macrotrends, *World Unemployment rate 1991-2023*
Available at: https://www.macrotrends.net/countries/WLD/world/unemployment-rate 02/05/2023

[107] World Atlas, 2023, *The Biggest Industries In Vietnam*, 02-05-2023
Available at: https://www.worldatlas.com/articles/top-biggest-industries-in-vietnam.html

[108] Statisica, M.N.Nguyen, 15-02-2023, Number of Employed people Vietnam 2021, by industry, para 1,
Available at: https://www.statista.com/statistics/444617/unemployment-rate-in-vietnam/ 12/06/2023

[109] Vietnam.VN, 21/03/2023, *Ha Long, Hoi An and the world's most attractive wonders printed on money*
Available at: https://www.vietnam.vn/en/ha-long-hoi-an-va-nhung-ky-quan-thu-hut-khach-nhat-the-gioi-in-tren-tien/ 28/09/2023

[110] World Population Review, *Poverty Rate by Country 2023*
Available at: https://worldpopulationreview.com/country-rankings/poverty-rate-by-country 02/05/2023

[111] World Population Review, *Average Height by Country 2023*
Available at: https://worldpopulationreview.com/country-rankings/average-height-by-country 02/05/2023

[112] World Population Review 2023, *Unemployment by country 2023,*
   Available at: https://www.worldpopulationreview.com/country-rankings/unemployment-by-country 09/05/2023

[113] Y Charts, *US Unemployment Rate, 3.50% for Jul 2023*
   Available at: https://www.ycharts.com/indicators/us_unemployment_rate 09/05/2023

[114] Nations Encyclopedia, *United States – Location, size and extent,*
   Available at: https://www.nationsencyclopedia.com/Americas/United-States-LOCATION-SIZE-AND-EXTENT.html 09/05/2023

[115] World population review 2023, Obesity Rates by country 2023,
   Available at: https://worldpopulationreview.com/country-rankings/obesity-rates-by-country 08/05/2023

[116] World population review 2023, Obesity Rates by country 2023,
   Available at: https://worldpopulationreview.com/country-rankings/obesity-rates-by-country 08/05/2023

[117] The Hill, Lynch.J, Tanner.J. 05-07-2023, 'These are the most obese states in the US, report finds'
   Available at: https://thehill.com/news/state-watch/3991207-these-are-the-most-obese-states-in-the-us-report-finds/   28/06/2023

[118] Britannica, *Economy of West Virginia,*
   Available at: https://www.britannica.com/place/West-Virginia/Economy 08/05/2023

[119] Wikipedia, *Western Pattern Diet,*
   Available at: https://en.m.wikipedia.org/wiki/Western_pattern_diet 09/05/2023

[120] CDC, May 17 2022, *Adult Obesity Facts, obesity is a common serious and costly disease,*
   Available at: https://www.cdc.gov/obesity/data/adult.html 10/05/2023

[121] CDC, May 17 2022, *Adult Obesity Facts*, obesity is a common serious and costly disease,
   Available at: https://www.cdc.gov/obesity/data/adult.html 10/05/2023

[122] Dana Joseph Jan 16th 2021, American food: The 50 greatest dishes
   Available at: https://www.edition.cnn.com/travel/article/american-food-dishes/index.html 9/05/2023

[123] CNN, Nectar Gan, Dec 25th 2020, *Over half of Chinese adults are now overweight. That's more people than the entire US population.*
   Available at: https://edition.cnn.com/2020/12/24/china/china-adult-overweight-intl-hnk/index.html#   09/05/2023

[124] BBC News, 23rd Dec 2020, *Over Half of Chinese adults overweight study finds*
   Available at: https://www.bbc.co.uk/news/world-asia-china-55428530 09/05/2023

[125] BBC News, 23rd Dec 2020, Over Half of Chinese adults overweight study finds
   Available at: https://www.bbc.co.uk/news/world-asia-china-55428530 09/05/2023

[126] WorldAtlas, *What is the Population of China ?,*
   Available at: http://www.worldatlas.com/articles/what-is-the-population-of-china.html 09/05/2023

[127] Statista, Share of he population engaged in regular physical exercising in China from 2014 to 2025,
Available at: https://www.statista.com/statistics/895987/   09/05/2023

[128] International Journal of Obesity, 19th Feb 2021, E. Hemmingsson, *The unparalleled rise of Obesity in China : A call to action'*,
Available at: https://www.nature.com/articles/s41366-021-00774-w 28-06-2023

[129] The Food Ranger, *Chinese Street Food – 200kg Street Hot Pot, Rare Street Food Tour of Kaifeng, China !*
Available at: https://youtu.be/dy59i6XMnTI 28-06-2023

[130] Dialogo Chino, Z Si, S Scott, Jan 23rd 2019, *'China's changing food habits and their global implications'*
Available at: https://dialogochino.net/en/agriculture/21163-chinas-changing-food-habits-and-their-global-implications/   28-06-2023

[131] Dialogo Chino, Z Si, S Scott, Jan 23rd 2019, 'China's changing food habits and their global implications'
Available at: https://dialogochino.net/en/agriculture/21163-chinas-changing-food-habits-and-their-global-implications/   28-06-2023

[132] Springer Link, Palgrave MacMillan, Keischnick.J, 2023, *Buddhist Vegetarianism in China*
Available at: https://link.springer.com/chapter/10.1057/9781403979278_10

[133] ContentBlvd Team, 14-05-2021, *Which Country Read The Most ? Average Books Read Per Year By Country*
Available at: https://www.contentBlvd.com/global-reading-habits/# 10/05/2023

[134] World Population Review, *GDP Capita by Country 2023*,
Available at: https://www.worldpopulationreview.com/country-rankings/gdp-per-capita-by-country 10/05/2023

[135] Golden Charter,24-01-2017, *Which countries have the longest life span and why*
Available at: https://www.goldencharter.co.uk/news-and-info/2017/which-countries-have-the-longest-life-span-and-why/   13/07/2023

[136] Worldometer, *GDP by Country*,
Available at: https://www.worldometers.info/gdp/ 10/05/2023

[137] Global Hunger Index, *Global Hunger Index Scores by 2022 GHI Rank*,
Available at: https://www.globalhungerindex.org/ranking.html 10/05/2023

[138] Jackson A. 2009, Level 4 Obesity & Diabetes Management Certificate Resource manual ,1: *'An Overview of Obesity Pandemic'* , Active IQ WMC, Trident Business Centre, 29-06-2023

[139] In Rome Cooking, 2020, *Ancient Roman Food: What did the Romans use to eat ?*
Available at: https://www.inromecooking.com/blog/recipies/ancient-roman-food-what-did-the-romans-use-to-eat/ 10/05/2023

[140] RO RD August 17th 2020, F.Lister-Fell, Malin's in Bow: the first fish and chip shop in the UK,
Available at: https://romanroadlondon.com/malin-fish-and-chip-shop-oldest/ 10/05/2023

[141] 2023, White Castle Management Co. *Our Story*,
Available at: https://www.whitecastle.com/about-us/our-history# 12/06/2023

[142] 2023, The History of Fast Food,
Available at: http://www.historyoffastfood.com/ 12/06/2023

[143] White Castle, 2023, *It began with an Idea*
Available at: https://www.whitecastle.com/about-us/our-history 29/09/2023

[144] Super Size Me, 2004 [Documentary} Morgan Spurlock,The Con

[145] The Guardian 20-08-2004, Dodd.V, *McDonalds fights back against hit film*,
Available at:
https://www.theguardian.com/media/2004/aug/20/advertising.edinburghfilmfestival2004
10/05/2023

[146] The New York Times, 12-02-2005, *McDonald's Settles Trans Fats Lawsuits*
Available at: https://nytimres.com/2005/02/12/business/mcdonalds-settles-trans-fats-lawsuits.html 10/05/2023

[147] New York Times, M. Burros, June 14 2006 KFC Is Sued Over the Use of Trans Fats in Cooking,
Available at: https://www.nytimes.com/2006/06/14/us/kfc-is-sued-over-the-use-of-trans-fats-in-its-cooking.html 10/05/2023

[148] World Population Review, *Countries without McDonald's 2023*,
Available at: https://worldpopulationreview.com/country-rankings/countries-without-mcdonalds 11/05/2023

[149] Escape writers, 10/2022, *16 things you didn't know about the Cook Islands,* 16
Available at: https://www.escape.com.au/desinations/new-zealand/17-things-you-didnt-know-about-the-cook-islands/image-gallery/83d46f93221883811db5a30aeb9a3760?page=3
11/05/2023

[150] World population review, 2023, *Countries without McDonald's*
Available at: https://worldpopulationreview.com/country-rankings/countries-without-mcdonalds 11/05/2023

[151][151] WorldAtlas, 2023, *How Many MacDonalds Locations Are There In The World ?*
Available at: https://www.worldatlas.com/articles/countries-with-the-most-mcdonald-s-restaurant.html 11/05/2023

[152] World Atlas 2023, *Countries with the Most Subway Restaurants*
Available at: https://www.worldatlas.com/amp/articles/countries-with-the-most-subway-restaurants.html 11/05/2023

[153] Wikipedia, *List of Countries with KFC franchises 2022*
Available at: https://en.m.wikipedia.org/wiki/List_of_countries_with_KFC_franchises#
11/05/2023

[154] WHO, 04/03/2022, *World Obesity Day 2022 – Accelerating action to stop obesity* Available at: https://www.who.int/news/item/04-03-2022-world-obesity-day-2022-accelerating-action-to-stop-obesity 12/05/2023

[155] Japan Truly, 2023, Novatise media, *KFC In Japan Menu 2023 Exclusive KFC Japan Menu in English* Available at: https://japantruly.com/kfc-in-japan-menu/ 30/09/2023

[156] Hearst UK, 2016, *11 Craziest Subway Sandwiches From Around The World* Available at: https://www.delish.com/food-news/g3552/subway-sandwiches-around-the-world/ 30/09/2023

[157] Hearst UK, 2023, *McDonald's Menu Items From Around The World That Will Seriously Surprise You* Available at: https://www.delish.com/uk/food-news/g34687443/mcdonalds-world-menu/ 30/09/2023

[158] Statista, *Revenue of the energy & sports drinks industry Worldwide 2014-2027 (in billion US dollars)* Available at: https://www.statista.com/statistics/691384/sales-value-energy-drinks-worldwide/ 24/08/2023

[159] Jackson A. 2009, Level 4 Obesity & Diabetes Management Cert. Resource manual, Chapter1,

[160] Jackson A. 2009, Level 4 Obesity & Diabetes Management Cert. Resource manual, Chapter1,

[161] Jackson A. 2009, Level 4 Obesity & Diabetes Management Cert. Resource manual, Chapter1,

[162] Vol.67:289-314 Jan 2016, *Wood & Runger Psychology of Habit Annual review of Psychology, Habit Automaticity,* Available at: https://www.annualreviews.org/doi/10.1146/annurev-psych-122414-033417 15/05/2023

[163] Mind 2023, Mindfulness, Available at: https://www.mind.org.uk/information-support/drugs-and-treatments/mindfulness/about-mindfulness/ 15/05/2023

[164] Jackson A. 2009, Level 4 Obesity & Diabetes Management Certificate Resource manual *Chapter 1: An overview of the obesity pandemic* Active IQ WMC, Trident Business Centre Tooting, 15/05/2023

[165] Jackson A. 2009, Level 4 Obesity & Diabetes Management Certificate Resource manual *Chapter 1: An overview of the obesity pandemic,* Active IQ WMC, Trident Business Centre Tooting, 31-07-2023

[166] WHO,2023, 05/10/2022, *Physical Activity* Available at: https://www.who.int/news-room/fact-sheets/detail/physical-activity 08/09/2023

[167] Jackson A. 2009, Level 4 Obesity & Diabetes Management Certificate Resource manual *Chapter 1: An overview of the obesity pandemic,* Active IQ WMC, Trident Business Centre Tooting, 15-05-2023

[168] MCDONALDS MENU, 2023, *Double Sausage & Egg McMuffin at McDonald's,* Available at: https://mcdonalds-menu.co.uk/double-sausage-egg-mcmuffin/ 15-05-2023

[169] Mcdonalds, 2017 – 2023, Our Menu, *Hash Browns*,
Available at: https://www.mcdonalds.com/us/en-us/product/hash-browns.html 15-05-2023

[170] McDonalds, 2017 – 2023, Our Menu, Cappuccino large,
Available at: https://www.mcdonalds.com/gb/en-gb/product/cappuccino-large.html 15-05-2023

[171] Central YMCA qualifications, 2005 *Nutrition and weight management: Food Diaries*, 1, Gt Russell St. London, 15-07-2023

[172] Crown Copyright, NHS, *What Should my Daily Intake of Calories be ?*
Available at: https://www.nhs.uk/common-health-questions/food-and-diet/what-should-my-daily-intake-of-calories-be/ 15/07/2023

[173] Crown copyright, NHS, *Portion Sizes*
https://diabetescw.co.uk/food-fitness/portion-sizes/

[174] B. Howell, Movehub 31/05/2023, *'what are the healthiest countries in the world'*?
Available at: https://www.movehub.com/blog/worlds-healthiest-countries/ 11/08/2023

[175] NHS, Crown Copyright, 15-03-2023, *'Starchy foods and carbohydrates, why do you need starchy foods?'*
Available at: https://www.nhs.uk/live-well/eat-well/food-types/starchy-foods-and-carbohydrates/ 25/08/2023

[176] Jackson A. 2009, Level 4 Obesity & Diabetes Management Certificate Resource manual, *Chapter 2: weight gain, An Explanation,* Active IQ WMC, Trident Business Centre Tooting page 147 paragraph 4. 22/05/2023

[177] Green D. Kyle books, *The PALEO diet, food your body is designed to eat, Intro: what is the paleo diet* ? 22-05-2023

[178] Green D. Kyle books, *The PALEO diet, food your body is designed to eat, Intro: what is the paleo diet ?* *'Avoid'* Introduction page 12 / 13

[179] Jackson A. 2009, Level 4 Obesity & Diabetes Management Certificate Resource manual *Chapter 2 weight Gain An Explanation,* 22-05-2023

[180] Gallop R. 2002, the G.I. DIET, The Glycemic Index, Introduction, x 1st edition 2003, Random House Canada

[181] NHS, Great Ormond Street Hospital for children, NHS Foundation Trust, *Ketogenic diet : overview.*
Available at: https://www.gosh.nhs.uk/conditions-and-treatments/procedures-and-treatments/ketogenic-diet/ 22/05/2023

[182] Muacevic A. Adler R John, PMC Pub Med Central, 2020 Advantages and Disadvantages of the Ketogenic Diet
A review article
Available at: https://www.ncbi.nlm.nih.gov/pmc/articles/PMC7480775/ 07/09/2023

[183] Jackson A. 2009, Level 4 Obesity & Diabetes Management Certificate Resource manual , *Chapter 2 Weight Gain An Explanation*, Active IQ WMC, Trident Business Centre Tooting, 22-05-2023

[184] Diabetes.co.uk 23/01/2023, *'Carnivore Diet: The All Meat Diet'*
Available at: https://www.diabetes.co.uk/diet/carnivore-diet.html 18/07/2023

[185] Everyday Health,Migala.J, 02/06/2022, *'On the carnivore Diet, Peopl Are Eating Only Meat: Here's What to Know,* Paragraph 3
Available at: https://www.everydayhealth.com/diet-nutrition/diet/carnivore-diet-benefits-risks-food-list-more/ 18/07/2023

[186] Forbes Health, L. Hochwald, 12/06/2023, *'What Is The Carnivore Diet ? Benefits, Food List And More', Risks of the Carnivore diet, Heart Disease*
Available at: https://www.forbes.com/health/body/what-is-the-carnivore-diet/ 18/07/2023

[187] Jackson A. 2009, Level 4 Obesity & Diabetes Management Certificate Resource manual,, *Chapter 2 weight gain an explanation.. 23/05/2023*

[188] Jackson A. 2009, Level 4 Obesity & Diabetes Management Certificate Resource manual, *Chapter 2 Weight Gain An Explanation,* 23-05-2023

[189] Bupa, Hennessy.N 11-01-2023, *What is intermittent fasting ?,What are the different types of Intermittent fasting?*
Available at: https://www.bupa.co.uk/newsroom/ourviews/intermittent-fasting 16/06/2023

[190] Jackson A. 2009, Level 4 Obesity & Diabetes Management Certificate Resource manual, *Chapter 2 weight gain an Explanation,* Active IQ WMC, Trident Business Centre Tooting 23/05/2023

[191] Jackson A. 2009, Level 4 Obesity & Diabetes Management Certificate Resource manual, *Chapter 2 weight gain an Explanation,* Active IQ WMC, Trident Business Centre Tooting 23/05/2023

[192] Crown copyright, NHS *Dairy and alternatives in your diet,*
Available at: https://www.nhs.uk/live-well/eat-well/food-types/milk-and-dairy-nutrition/ 23/05/2023

[193] Jackson A. 2009, Level 4 Obesity & Diabetes Management Certificate Resource manual , *Chapter 2 weight gain an Explanation,* Active IQ WMC, Trident Business Centre Tooting 28/06/2023

[194] Jackson A. 2009, Level 4 Obesity & Diabetes Management Certificate Resource manual *Chapter 2 Weight Gain an Explanation, Active IQ WMC, Trident Business Centre Tooting,* 16/05/2023

[195] NHS, Crown copyright, Oct '22, *What should my daily intake of calories be ?*
Available at: https://www.nhs.uk/common-health-questions/food-and-diet/what-should-my-daily-intake-of-calories-be/   25/05/2023

[196] Central YMCA qualifications, Level 3 nutrition and weight management *'Energy needs of the human body'*
1, Gt Russell St. London, 04/07/2023

[197] Central YMCA qualifications, Level 3 nutrition and weight management 'Energy needs of the human body'
1, Gt Russell St. London 04-07-2023

[198] Central YMCA qualifications, Level 3 nutrition and weight management *'Energy needs of the human body'* 04/07/2023

[199] Jackson A. 2009, Level 4 Obesity & Diabetes Management Certificate Resource manual Chapter 2 weight gain an Explanation, Active IQ WMC, Trident Business Centre Tooting, 16/05/2023

[200] Jackson A. 2009, Level 4 Obesity & Diabetes Management Certificate Resource manual *Chapter 2 Weight Gain an Explanation,* Active IQ WMC, Trident Business Centre Tooting, 01/07/2023

[201] Active I.Q, Lvl 4 Obesity & Diabetes Management Certificate Resource manual, *Chapter 2 Weight Gain an Explanation*, Active IQ WMC, Trident Business Centre Tooting 16/05/2023

[202] Active I.Q, Lvl 4 Obesity & Diabetes Management Certificate Resource manual, *Chapter 2 Weight Gain an Explanation*, , *Dietary Induced Thermogenesis* Active IQ WMC, Trident Business Centre, *Tooting DIT*, 17-07-2023

[203] Starbucks, Flat White, Available at: https://www.starbucks.co.uk/menu/product/743 19/07/2023

[204] Crown Copyright, 14-04-2020, NHS, 'Types: weight loss surgery', Available at: https://www.nhs.uk/conditions/weight-loss-surgery/types/ 18/07/2023

[205] Crown Copyright, 14 April 2020, NHS, Risks weight loss surgery', Available at: https://www.nhs.uk/conditions/weight-loss-surgery/risks/ 18/07/2023

[206] Jackson A. 2009, Level 4 Obesity & Diabetes Management Certificate Resource manual, Chapter 1: *An overview of the obesity pandemic, Common complications of surgery* Active IQ WMC, Trident Business Centre, Tooting 18/07/2023

[207] Jackson A. 2009, Level 4 Obesity & Diabetes Management Certificate Resource manual,, Chapter 1: *An overview of the obesity pandemic*, Active IQ WMC, Trident Business Centre Tooting 18/07/2023

[208] Jackson A. 2009, Level 4 Obesity & Diabetes Management Certificate Resource manual, Chapter 1*: An overview of the obesity pandemic,* Active IQ WMC, Trident Business Centre Tooting 18/072023

[209] Diabetes UK, *Complications of diabetes*, Available at: https://www.diabetes.org.uk/guide-to-diabetes/complications 17/05/2023

[210] Jackson A. 2009, Level 4 Obesity & Diabetes Management Certificate Resource manual, *Chapter 1: An overview of the obesity pandemic, Diabetes and the Metabolic Syndrome* Active IQ WMC, *Trident Business Centre, Tooting* 20/08/2023

[211] CYQ, 2008, Exercise & Fitness Knowledge manual: *Monitoring exercising heart rate*, 112 Great Russell Street, London, 29/08/2023

[212] Bupa 2023, Activity and calories burned calculator, Available at: https://www.bupa.co.uk/health-information/calories-calculator 19/07/2023

[213] NHS, Crown Copyright, 04-08-2021, *Benefits of Exercise*
Available at: https://www.nhs.uk/live-well/exercise/exercise-health-benefits/ 29/08/2023

[215] Jackson A. 2009, Level 4 Obesity & Diabetes Management Certificate Resource manual, *Chapter 2: Weight 4-Gain An Explanation*, Active IQ WMC, Trident Business Centre Tooting, 20-05-2023

IMAGE CREDITS:

I would like to thank the following for allowing me to use their pictures in this book, I have also included many of my travelling pictures which I hope have contributed to the book in a positive way.

Website/origin

Page	9	Wellcome Coll. 11857i	Obese man exhibiting Placard of himself looking thin	welcomecollection.org
Page	15	Tanita	Body Mass Index scale BMI	who.int/health-topics
Page	17	D.Peterson	Nauru Peace Hand	www.Pixabay.com
Page	18	J.Silver	Cook Islands Beach Palm Trees,	www.Pixabay.com
Page	20	CCPAPA	Canal Waterway Channel	www.Pixabay.com
Page	20	Pixabay	Greyscale photo of explosion	www.Pixabay.com
Page	25	M. Winkler	Seoul South Korea	www.Pexels.com
Page	26	John & Maz	Japanese temple	
Page	27	John & Maz	Bean Curd Cake	
Page	27	John & Maz	Geisha Girl	
Page	29	Steve Ward	Hyderabad, landmark India	
Page	29	Steve Ward	Hyderabad, restaurant India	
Page	33	R.King	Timor-leste	www.Pixabay.com
Page	34	Kelly	Bangladesh	www.Pexels.com
Page	48	Christels	Temple Buddhism China	www.Pixabay.com
Page	59	Ed's Doughnuts	The doughnut machine	Parkins Palladium
Page	60	EtoileOfficial	Hamburgers, cheeseburgers, Sliders	www.Pixabay.com
Page	69	J Nomias	Hamburger P French Fries	www.Pixabay.com
Page	70	Ralphs_Fotos	Squirrel, eating. Feeder	www.Pixabay.com
Page	71	YangGuangWu	China, Street, Street vendors	www.Pixabay.com
Page	76	RonRatte	Steeplechase, Cross run, Mud image.	www.Pixabay.com
Page	81	Irina_Kukuts	Cat, British, astonishment image	www.Pixabay.com
Page	86	Jeniffertn	Okinawa, Market, Japan image	www.Pixabay.com
Page	107	flutie8211	Keep calm and carry on	www.Pixabay.com
Page	126	Tim Davies	Starbucks on route from work	
Page	131	Tumisu	Success, Man, Mountain image	www.Pixabay.com
Page	144	HFC	Help For Children group image	
Page	167	ManfredRichter	Jogging, Jogger, Sports image.	www.Pixabay.com
Page	169	5477687	Winks, sleeping, snooze image	www.Pixabay.com
Page	178	geralt	Well Done	www.Pixabay.com

All images used are copyright free or authorised by the picture owner, if there is any missed accreditations attempts were made to contact relevant organisations. If there needs to be any alterations, by request this can be done in a further edition.

APPENDICES

Appendix A: Page for a Daily Diet Record, my example

TIME OF DAY	FOOD OR DRINK FULL DESCRIPTION / QUANTITY	TOTAL AMOUNT CONSUMED, WEIGHT AND NUTRITIONAL BREAKDOWN						MOOD / FEEL AT THE TIME	WHERE & DOING WHAT
		Cal Kcal	Fat	Carb	Sugars	Protein	Salt		
9.30am	1.	480	31g	30g	2g	20g	0.83g	Wasn't hungry but saw people eating & had craving	Trained a client, had no breakfast
	2.	127	7.4g	13g	0.2g	1.1g	0.64g		
	3.	86	3.1g	8.4g	8.2g	6.3g	0.19g		
11.30am	4.	50	1.8g	1.1g	4.8g	3.6g	0.11g	Relaxed, protein drink routine	After own gym session
	5.	364	5.5g	11g	5g	68g	0.13g		
12.15pm	6.	161	0.2g	37g	___	4.3g	___	Lunchtime routine, feel hungry	Home laptop work
	7.	117	0.6g	___	___	27.8g	0.34g		
	8.	162	12g	0.6g	___	11.7g	0.582g		
	9.	17 kcal							
	10.	No calories							
5.15pm	11.	1036	106g	___	___	18.68g	0.16g	Focused & now hungry routine time dinner	Finishing work, then time to cook
	12.	187	6.63g	___	___	29.81g	0.94g		
	13.	192	4.9g	33.5g	1.5g	2.7g	0.34g		
	14.	53	1g	6.8g	4.7g	2g	0.16g		
8.15pm	15.	76	1.8g	35.2g	2.6g	7.8g	0.78g	Bored, decided to make a sandwich. Wasn't hungry	TV, nothing much
	16.	108	8g	0.4g	___	7.8g	0.388g		
	17.	110	8.9g	___	___	8.2g	0.2g		
	18.	37	3.04g	0.12g	0.05g	2.29g	0.14g		
	TOTALS:	3363	202	177	29	222	5.93		

Appendix A: Description of Food Items Numbered

1.	1 Sausage Egg Mcmuffin
2.	1 Hasb Brown
3.	1 Coffee, flat white
4.	1 pint semi skimmed milk
5.	100 grams chocolate protein
6.	1 medium Jacket Potato
7.	1 Tin tuna 145g
8.	3 slices of bacon fried
9.	Coffee, flat white
10.	Water 1 pint
11.	Pork belly pieces 200g
12.	Steak pieces 100g
13.	Singapore noodles 105g
14.	Vegetable stir fry 131g
15.	2 slices wholemeal bread
16.	2 slices bacon
17.	1 large fried egg
18.	Grated cheese 1 tbsp

Appendix B: Example Page for a Daily Diet Record, ideal food / drink choices

TIME OF DAY	FOOD OR DRINK NUMBERED	TOTAL AMOUNT CONSUMED (energy) AND WEIGHT AND NUTRITIONAL BREAKDOWN						GUIDANCE POINT SUMMARY FOR THIS IDEAL DAILY DIET RECORD
			Fat	Sat. Fat	Carb	sugar	Protein	Fibre	
8am	1.	34 Kcal					7g		* All wholefoods
	2.	68 Kcal	2.8g	1.0g	0.6g		10.8g		*14 hours last meal Before breakfast
	3.	130 Kcal	2.0g	0.4g	24.2g		5.2g	3.4g	
11.30am	4.	13.5 Kcal	.05g		3.0g		0.4g	1.1g	* Low to med G.I.
	5.	27.5 Kcal	0.2g		6g		0.25g	1.75g	* Less carbs in the Evening meal
12noon	6.	157 Kcal	3.2g	1.0g			29.9g		* No processed Foods, less sugar & additives
	7.	24 Kcal	0.7g	0.2g	0.9g		2.6g	2.0g	
	8.	172 kcal	0.4g	0.2g	41.35g		2.4g	4.95g	* 3-5 fruit portions
2.30pm	9.	111 kcal	5.4g	1.5g			14.5g		* 3-5 veg portions
	10.	47 kcal	0.1g		11.8g		0.4g		* Lower calorific
	11.	66 kcal	0.1g		15.9g		1.2g		* Zero salt
5pm	12.	170 kcal	4.0g	1.5g			33.0g		* Good Fibre Content
	13.	32 Kcal	0.4g	0.1g	6.4g		1.0g	1.6g	
	14.	11 kcal	0.2g		1.8g		0.8g	1.2g	* No empty cals, Only in the apple sauce
	15.	11 kcal	0.1g			3			
	TOTALS	1074	19.02	6.4	152.4	3	106.85	14	* Use these Principles as you Create your plan

Appendix B: Description of Food Items Numbered

1.	Two large poached eggs,
2.	56g 2oz Lean ham
3.	2 slices whole grain bread
	1 pint water
4.	50g Strawberries
5.	50g Blueberries In cream
6.	Lean turkey slices, 100g
7.	Broccoli, 80g
8.	Sweet potato, 150g
	1 pint water & cranberry
9.	Left over portion 50g of Chicken curry (meat only)
10.	1 Apple
11.	3 plumbs
	Dilute orange / water 1 pint
12.	Pork chops grilled , 100g
13.	Sliced cooked peppers, 100g
14.	Cabbage 80g
15.	Apple sauce 1 tsp
	Half pint water

Comparing Appendix A to Appendix B daily diet records shows a huge calorie difference. My examples was at 3363 and this ideal example is 1074. Well below the daily required amount, and look at the amount of food. Amounts in grams has been checked and is accurate and meets daily needs. Choose healthy wholefoods, they're comparatively low calorific, and we are unlikely to feel hungry after. Another meal can be added and still within the daily calorie range. Food selection is so important without the need to restrict intake.

Appendix C: Daily Food Diary sheet analysis

Times

Starting at 9.30am and then the last meal is at 8.15pm, the last meal is too late to then sleep a couple of hours later. We need the times to be smaller and start earlier ideally around 7.30 / 8am and then last meal is at 5 - 6pm latest. Burning calories throughout the day more so and then the break for 14 to 15 hours until breakfast. Ideally, I should remove the sandwich I ate late, and the contents wasn't the best choices with the bacon too.

Calorie matching

I am over on the calorie amount by quite a bit that day, with a maintenance total of 2141kcal and what I had eaten totalled 3363kcal to gain weight is anything plus 250 calories here totalling 2391. After the weight gain threshold, I have an extra 972 calories. Way over what I needed for the day, but then the exercise I took part in will impact on that surplus. Do you do this regularly, looking at your daily amounts, become aware of what's going on with this in relation to you.

Percentage of Macronutrients of Appendix 1 Page for a Daily Diet Record, My Example

FATS	32%
CARBOHYDRATES	28%
Carbs (of which sugars)	4.6%
PROTEIN	35%
SALT	0.9%

As per the calorie calculations and ideal percentages on page 122 under 'How much food and Drink Do We Need Per Day', that is good percentages to follow.

Total Kcal: 3363	**3514**		The total calories of 3363 is the totals of the label's kcals. In red the total 3514 is the label macronutrient breakdown numbers actually added up. Showing there can be discrepancy in their information. We will go with the kcal original totals of 3363. Just an example of how far can we trust the accuracy of product labelling. Another reason for all natural food options.
Protein	**808**	**23%**	
Carbs	**708**	**20%**	
Fats	**1998**	**57%**	

Appendix C: Thermogenesis (Dietary Induced) DIT

DIT Calories needed to breakdown: Protein 30%   Carbohydrates 8%   Fats 3%

Referring to the energy we use to digest the food we eat. It's hard to accurately work out the different factors of the other thermogenesis points, consider the impact and take into consideration. Do you sit about or on the go sometimes / most of the time, it does all makes an impact.

D.I.T	Gram changes	Calorie changes		
PROTEIN	202g = 142g	808	to	568
CARBOHYDRATES	177g = 163g	708	to	680
FATS	222g = 215g	1998	to	1935
NEW TOTAL		**3363**	to	**3183**

We can see the biggest amounts of calories before and after DIT which means before and from the actual digestion is in fats intake, at 57% of the day's intake and the least amount of energy used to store the macronutrient. Fats really do need looking at, we can see in the daily record that the main culprit is the pork belly which does have a lot of fat, then the sausage & egg Mc muffin, then with the total of five slices of bacon. This must be changed, if it was a daily occurrence then the weight would pile on over a relatively short space of time. Not to mention how unhealthy that is.

The Day's activity

The first morning session was recorded at 3.98 km, at a duration of 56.16 minutes an average of 286 calories burnt, so let's take that off that overall intake then the gym training session after at using an online calculator:

Bupa, 2023, *Activity and calories burned calculator*, 24-07-2023
https://www.bupa.co.uk/health-information/calories-calculator

40 minutes weight training at 90kg weight the calories burnt are 360kcals.

From these two activities the total burn is 546kcals, yet considering the afterburn principle where the metabolism works faster after exercise is finished, the total here will be more, but for the purposes of the analysis we'll go with just the activity total.

Food choice changes

Primarily lean white meats to replace the pork, breakfast muffin and bacon.

Labelling issue between total Kcal and the macronutrient breakdown

There seems to be a discrepancy between the total Kcals in the day record and the sum of the macronutrients as we work out from the fats, carbs and protein. It's a discrepancy of 151 calories which could be the result of a number of factors but as it's a small amount we will go with the breakdown total at 3514 kcal.

The total now after the days activities is (at 3514) now is 2968, still 827kcal over the maintenance calorie amount and that's a quarter of a pound of fat added right there, we need to be aware !

The new example sheet from the diet plan significantly increases the portions of fruit and vegetables, also better quality in far less fat meat choices. Also the minimal amount ' of which sugars' as the good example sheet is all of wholefoods. As we should really be eating being our regular staple diet.

No caffeine and mostly water during the day.

Appendix A analysis

Macronutrients	Portions	My suggested portions	Difference
Good carbohydrates	3	2 - 3	In range
Vegetables	1	2 – 4	-1
Fruit	0	2 – 4	-2
Dairy	2	2 – 3	In range
Meat, fish, poultry	7	2 - 3	+4
Good fats	1 – 2	1 – 2	In range
Bad carbs / sweets/ sugar	2	0 / 0.5	+1.5
Bad snacks / drink / other	0	0	In range
Alcohol	0	0	In range
Hydration / good drinks	2.5 pints	1.5 – 2.5 litres	In range

Example sheet

The example to revise this daily record shows just how much the total Kcal difference really is quite significant with the amount of food shown with it's breakdown.

Appendix B Analysis

Macronutrients	Portions	Suggested portions	Difference
Good Carbohydrates	2	2 – 3	In range
Vegetables	3	2 – 4	In range
Fruit	4	2 – 4	In range
Dairy	2	2 – 3	In range
Meat, fish, poultry	4	2 – 3	In range
Good Fats,	1	0 / 1	In range
Bad carbs/sweets/ sugar	0.5	0 / 0.5	In range
Bad snack / drinks /other	0	0	In range
Alcohol	0	0	In range
Hydration / good drinks	4 3.5 pints, 2 litres	1.5 / 2.5 litres	In range

The USDA in 2011 brought out a revised way to analyse what's on your plate, known as 'myplate'

USDA, 'what is my plate', 25-07-2023
https://www.myplate.gov/eat-healthy/what-is-myplate

It is a revised update from the previous food pyramid of the 90's which just seemed to focus to heavily on carbohydrates but with no real distinctions between good & bad. We know the issue is the energy dense foods, added sugars and high in fats. We need to distinguish the good from bad fats. How much salt / sodium we are consuming. I have a revised table which addresses this somewhat, but it's important to be aware and to follow these guidelines on creating a sound diet plan. So you are aware of everything you need to be then you can create your own weekly food plans knowing with confidence you will reach your goals.

Are you hydrated

NHS guidelines suggest *'Most of us need between 1.5 and 2.5 litres of fluid a day which is the same as six to eight cups a day'*

NHS, Kent community Health, 16, 12, 2022, *Healthy Hydration,* 24-07-2022

This can see quite a lot at first but spread out throughout the day and as it becomes routine it does get much easier. A combination of all the good food choices, extra fruit, and vegetables then the good regular hydration will then help us feel more alert and ready to take on the daily tasks more readily.

The self-analysis grid is there for you to be aware of what you are doing. It certainly showed me what I was doing on a bad day and has made me become more aware of these sneaky habits that I was unaware of. I hope it will do the same for you too, I have included headers which highlight any wrongdoings in your diet with the 'bad' examples. I would urge you complete the 7-day diet for yourself to include the weekends, you need to see what is going on in a full week. Write it all down and then really look at it, it will show you what's going on and help you to change.

Appendix C: Breakdown of analysis terms

Following the modern-day diet guidance, each term needs to follow the healthy mid-week guidelines given on macronutrients.

Good carbohydrates

Wholegrain, porridge large flake oatmeal, Buckwheat, Barley, rice, (Basmati wild brown long grain) Pasta, spaghetti, vermicelli, Linguini, Macaroni, Capellini

Vegetables

To reiterate, Apples, plums, pears, cherries, blueberries, raspberries, strawberries, peaches, oranges,

Dairy

Low fat / sugar yoghurt, ice cream, cottage cheese, small portion regular cheese

Meat, fish, poultry

Lean ham, all lean white meat, pork, turkey, chicken, eggs

Good Fats

Those liquid at room temperature,

Bad carbs / sweets / sugar

Chocolate, high G.I. snacks, full fat & sugar ice cream, in high quantity

Bad snacks / drinks / other

Crisps, processed snack meats, high fat low volume processed foods, in high quantity

Hydration / good drinks

Water, cordial, no sugar, no caffeine,

Alcohol

Beer, wine, vodka, Whiskey, Brandy and so on

As with the guidance in the modern-day diet, I am giving examples which can get you a structured weekly diet plan. You can build on this using the principles I have put forward to develop your knowledge and build on your ongoing weight management and self-development. Rather than just saying 'do this, don't do that' to understand the guidelines and work on it for yourself will give far more impact than just following.

Appendix D : Calorie Equivalence

One big factor we need to understand about food and drink is the calorie equivalence of a fast food quick choice compared to a good choice, homemade from scratch. Here are four examples of a breakfast, lunch, dinner, and snack comparison :

1.   Breakfast, McDonalds porridge & one portion 40g home prepared

	Mcdonalds	**Scott's old Fashioned porridge Oats**
Energy Kcal	154	150
Fat	3.0g	3.2g
Saturated	1.3g	0.6g
Carbohydrates	23g	24g
Of which sugars	6.4g	0.4g
Fibre	1.9g	3.6g
Protein	7.8g	4.4g
Salt	0.17g	0g

This is without the fruit or added yoghurt, notice the differences in 'of which sugars'. The fat content is very similar the fast food option does have more saturated fat, less fibre and added salt.

2.   Off the examples, comparing a good lunch #2 which includes 2 slices granary bread   2 slices chicken breast, sliced tomatoes, lettuce and light mayo . Compared to a Subway   roast chicken breast Sub.

	Subway roast chicken foot sub	**Good lunch #2**
Energy Kcal	615	343
Fat	7.52g	12.28g
Saturated	2.35g	2.29g
Carbohydrates	79.9g	40.67g
Of which sugars	14.57g	5.65g
Fibre	9.87g	4.1g
Protein	51.7g	16.07g
Salt	2.9g	2.19g

3.   Comparison of a main dinner one example from the Turkey, cooked rice and mixed vegetables offset to a KFC three piece meal with three pieces of chicken, chips, beans and a tropicana drink.

	KFC three piece meal	**Good dinner #5**
Energy Kcal	1205	483.2
Fat	53.8g	3.48g
Saturated	22g	0.6g
Carbohydrates	99.7g	48.18g
Of which sugars	32.2g	5.52g
Fibre	0g	4.76g
Protein	72.9g	57.82g
Salt	5.64g	1.60g

A Daily Kcal total of Fast Food to the Modern-Day Diet Examples :			As we discussed in the fast food factors of obesity, as we breakdown components of the daily comparable intakes, look at the differences and just where the weight is gained. As seen throughout the top obese nations, staying on this stuff is a big reason they are in the tops spots.
Energy Kcal	1974	976	
Fat	64g	19g	
Saturated	26g	3g	
Carbohydrates	203g	113g	
Of which Sugars	53g	12g	If they are regular choices for you, take a look at the nutritional information. You need to see the realisation of what's going on in regard to obesity.
Fibre	12g	12g	
Salt	9g	4g	

We need to understand the calorie equivalence of the choices we make, (with the good choices it's clear we can eat double the equivalence in calories is similar to the left side calorie dense examples) and if we make those more fast food and convenience choices more often then we really are taking on more of the poorer calories in 'saturated fat' and 'of which sugars' and more often at mealtimes. Reason being that as the higher Glycaemic Index carb choices, processed containing more sugar and fat will mean there is less equivalent food content for our digestive system to break down and could leave us feeling hungry. Then with more chance to go snacking. Regarding the above fast food to modern day diet example, were excluding the snacking and daily drink choices, if we compared sugary drinks and crisps / chocolate snacks offset to more healthy options, the results would be even more shocking.

I want you to really take in the relevance of the daily food selections that we make and just how they do impact on us. In a day these meal examples of the fast food shows us just how much fat we would be taking on, in a day ! Also the amount of which sugars, likely refined sugar added which is so easily converted to fat. I hope the severity of this is sinking in and just how much we do need the modern day diet to get things under control yet still live our lives and increase our health and relationship with food and drink.

SPECIAL THANKS:

To those that have helped in contribution to this book, it has been a tough ride getting it to completion. All I can say is you only know what it's like to write a book when you have done it. Hats off to everyone that has, I can now say I have too and what a ride it has been.

Mum,
For being so supportive.

Lee McGeorge,
Helping with getting the text from what I thought was completed to what needed to happen to get it to the final book.

Steve Ward,
For the supportive chats, messages, proofread and pictures from your adventure.

Lewis Macleod,
For wanting to sort the proofreader and support on days out in the West End

Steve Hills,
For advice in writing and how to navigate Amazon, whilst we had a beer in Jazz.

Alan Perrin,
For our training and offering me to give my first group talk on health and for the book, seeing how I would be in front of people. I haven't done this since my teaching days.

Dan Swerty,
For the early help when I needed direction and advice.

Helen Harris,
For our training chats and encouragement

Tim Davies,
With the photos and business curries

Thanks to everyone else who offered support, and positive words, including John, team HFC, Stuart, Ged and friends at the London Club, Fi for the help & advice, and Maria for the calls. Locally Juliette many thanks, Wendy, Brenton, and Joel. To Mick, Andy and Ed, Martin & Paul. Barbara in Thailand, where the initial idea of writing began. All helping, assisting, or pushing me to get there and get it done. It has been a very tough time since early 2020 and then the lockdowns, I hope I have gone some way to help getting across the experience and information as it is intended.

They say there is a book in all of us, so now get out there and write your book !

Printed in Great Britain
by Amazon

40929813R00126